Welcome to the World of Computers, 4th Edition

RUSSEL STOLINS
Institute of American Indian Arts

GREG P. MARSHALL II
Whatcom Community College

DAN MARSHALL-CAMPBELL
Whatcom Community College

JILL MURPHY
ExecuTrain of San Francisco

LABYRINTH
LEARNING™

Berkeley, CA

President:
Brian Favro

Product Development Manager:
Jason Favro

Managing Editor:
Laura A. Popelka

Production Manager:
Rad Proctor

eLearning Production Manager:
Arl S. Nadel

Editorial/Production Team:
Everett Cowan, Alona Harris, Sandy Jones,
Margaret Young

Indexing:
Afterwords Editorial Services

Cover Concept:
Huckdesign

LABYRINTH
LEARNING™

Welcome to the World of Computers, 4th Edition
by Russel Stolins, Greg P. Marhsall II, Dan Marshall-Cambell, and Jill Murphy

Labyrinth Learning
2560 9th Street, Suite 320
Berkeley, California 94710
800.522.9746
On the web at lablearning.com

ITEM: 1-59136-525-2
ISBN-13: 978-1-59136-525-9

Manufactured in the United States of America.

GLOBUS 0 9 8 7 6 5 4 3 2 1

Welcome to the World of Computers, 4th Edition

Table of Contents

UNIT 1
Windows Basics

LESSON 1
Getting Your First Look 3

LESSON 2
Starting Programs 31

Quick Reference Table Summary

Behind the Screen Summary

Preface

What Is Covered: *Welcome to the World of Computers, 4th Edition* introduces students to basic computer tasks using Windows 7, typing with a word processor, navigating the web, and working with email. In Unit 1, students get an overview of computer concepts and the basics of using Microsoft® Windows 7 and the Documents library. Next, students work with Word as they type letters and use AutoCorrect, Copy and Paste, and other features. They also learn basic techniques to browse for, open, move and copy, and delete and restore files. In Unit 2, students move on to browsing the web with Internet Explorer. They perform searches, interpret a list of keyword search hits, narrow their searches, and open multiple browser windows. They also create and manage favorites. The book ends with a discussion of webmail. Students send and receive email messages, work with attachments, create folders to store their messages, and more.

What Is Different: For more than a decade, Labyrinth has been working to perfect our *unique instructional design*. The benefit of our approach is that learning is faster and easier for students. Instructors have found that our approach works well in self-paced, instructor-led, and "blended" learning environments. The Labyrinth approach has many key features, including the following:

- *Concise concept discussions* followed by Hands-On exercises that give students experience with those concepts right away.

- *Figures* are always in close context with the text so no figure numbers are necessary.

- *Quick Reference* sections summarize key tasks with generic steps that will work without repeating an exercise. These can be particularly useful during open-book tests.

- *Hands-On exercises* are carefully written and repeatedly tested to be absolutely reliable. Many exercise steps are illustrated with figures to make them easier to follow.

- *Skill Builder exercises* provide additional practice on key skills using less detailed exercise steps as the student progresses through the lesson.

We are now expanding our book list by adapting this approach to teaching other application programs in addition to Microsoft® Office, including Intuit® QuickBooks®, Adobe Photoshop Elements®, Macromedia® Dreamweaver®, digital photography, and more.

Comprehensive Support: This course is also supported on the Labyrinth website with a comprehensive instructor support package that includes detailed lesson plans, PowerPoint presentations, a course syllabus, extensive test banks, and more. Our unique WebSims allow students to perform realistic exercises with the web, email, and application program tasks that would be difficult to set up in a computer lab.

We are grateful to the many instructors who have used Labyrinth titles and suggested improvements to us during the many years we have been writing and publishing books. *Welcome to the World of Computers, 4th Edition* has benefited greatly from the reviewing and suggestions of Anita Jones, West Central Technical College (Waco, GA); Gordon Pike, Haywood Community College (Clyde, NC); Susan Swanson, Nicolet Area Technical College (Rhinelander, WI); Clay Teague, Central Georgia Technical College (Macon, GA); Jacob Walker, Grant Adult Education (North Highlands, CA); and Kathy Yeomans, Ventura Adult & Continuing Education (Ventura, CA).

How This Book Is Organized

The information in this book is presented so that you master the fundamental skills first, and then build on those skills as you work with the more comprehensive topics.

Visual Conventions

This book uses many visual and typographical cues to guide you through the lessons. This page provides examples and described the functions of each cue.

`Type this text`	Anything you should type at the keyboard is printed in this typeface.
	Tips, Notes, and Warnings are used throughout the text to draw attention to certain topics.
Command→ Command→ Command, etc.	This convention indicated how to give a command from the Ribbon. The commands are written: Ribbon Tab→Command Group→ Command→Subcommand.
QUICK REFERENCE	Quick Reference tables provide generic instructions for key tasks. Only perform these tasks if you are instructed to in an exercise.
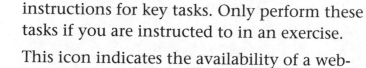	This icon indicates the availability of a web-based simulation for an exercise. You may need to use a WebSim if your computer lab is not set up to support particular exercises.
	Supplementary information available on the web page for this book is highlighted with this icon. Visit the web page periodically for helpful tips and content.
	Hands-On exercises are introduced immediately after concept discussions. They provide detailed, step-by-step tutorials so you can master the skills presented.
	The Concepts Review section includes both true/false and multiple choice questions designed to gauge your understanding of concepts.
	Skill Builder exercises provide additional hands-on practice with moderate assistance.

Windows Basics

In this unit, you will work with Windows and Word. In Lesson 1, you will log on to the computer and explore the Windows Desktop. You also will use the mouse to start programs and execute tasks. Other topics in this lesson include using pop-up menus; adding, moving, and removing Gadgets; exiting Windows; and turning off the computer properly. In Lesson 2, you will navigate and arrange programs on the start menu; minimize, maximize, size, and move program windows; and use the taskbar. Other topics in this lesson include opening programs from the Start menu, working with drop-down menus, using the mouse effectively, and typing and editing text. In Lesson 3, you will explore the Word window and learn about the Ribbon, the Quick Access toolbar, and the Mini toolbar. Other topics in this lesson include creating and saving documents, saving modified documents, scrolling, printing, closing documents, using Cut, Copy, and Paste, and working with proofreading tools. In Lesson 4, you will use the Control Panel to set mouse properties. You will also learn about file organization and the Documents library. Other topics in this lesson include creating and opening folders, using Cut, Copy, and Paste with files, and deleting and restoring files.

Windows Basics

Getting Your First Look

Windows 7 is the newest version of Microsoft's Windows operating system. With this release, Microsoft continues with its goal of making access to the functionality of the computer easier and less frustrating for the new computer user. As you work through this lesson, you will have the opportunity to learn and practice starting a computer using Windows 7, navigating basic features of the opening screen known as the Desktop, using mouse skills necessary to navigate in Windows 7, and properly shutting down the computer.

LESSON OBJECTIVES

After studying this lesson, you will be able to:

- Log on to the computer using a user-name and a password
- Describe the basic layout of the Windows 7 Desktop screen
- Use the right-click and dragging mouse motions
- Shut down the computer correctly
- Add, move, and remove Gadgets

Additional learning resources are available at labpub.com/learn/silver/wtwc4/

Case Study: Starting Something New

Alberta moved into her son's home. Her son, Ted, wanted Alberta to have access to the family computer. He thought she could play games such as Solitaire, learn to use email, and search the Internet. To give Alberta privacy, her son set up a separate username and password.

Alberta was scared the first time she sat down at the computer, but Ted said, "Push the power button and start using it. And don't worry; you won't break anything." Her son explained the logon screen and showed her how to enter her password.

When another colorful screen appeared, Ted said, "That's the Desktop. Here is an icon for Solitaire. It's like a light switch to start the game. Put your mouse pointer over the top of the icon and double-click; just click the left mouse button twice; click, click." Alberta double-clicked, and the game started. It looked just like the real game.

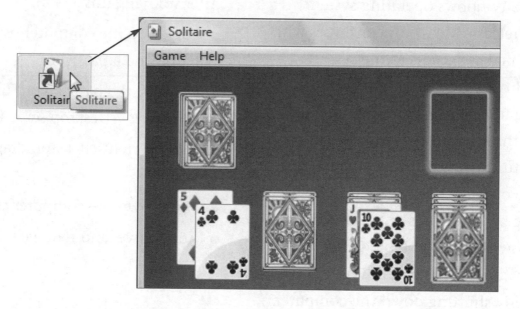

"Practice using your mouse by holding down the left button on a card, dragging it to the right place, and then releasing the button to drop it. And remember, don't worry about breaking anything!"

At first it was difficult, but after awhile, Alberta became more comfortable with the mouse and rarely had to look at it before she clicked. She began to think, "This computer is going to be fun."

Logging On to Windows

Most computer systems used in schools and businesses are networked together. An important part of network security is making sure everyone using computers on the network is authorized to do so. Logging on to the computer is the process of entering your username and password into the computer so that access can be granted.

Passwords

A critical piece of the login process is the password. Your password allows you into the computer. Passwords can contain upper- and lowercase letters as well as numbers and symbols. You must enter the password exactly as it was given to you.

 WARNING! None of your passwords should ever be shared. Sharing passwords is one of the top reasons people have computer and financial information stolen.

Creating Your Own Passwords

When you create your own passwords on a home or office computer, make sure they cannot be easily guessed. Don't use familiar names, birthdays, or common words. Following are some examples of good and poor passwords.

Good Passwords	Poor Passwords
!GreeN2	Fido
8ate8	Johndoe
Fun2Dr1v	12345678
AcEsn8s	Password

What Happens During the Startup Process?

From the moment you turn on the computer and throughout the login process, the computer and Windows 7 are working together to get ready for you. Windows 7 is not one giant program but a collection of hundreds of little programs. As the computer starts, various parts and pieces of Windows 7 are starting as well. Together they form the *operating system* that we see and work with on the screen.

 NOTE! Throughout the rest of this book, Windows 7 will be referred to as simply Win 7.

HANDS-ON 1.1 **Log on to Win 7**

In this exercise, you will log on to your computer using the login name and password provided by the instructor.

1. If necessary, turn on the computer and monitor. (The computer may already be switched on in a computer lab.) Ask the instructor for help if you cannot locate the power buttons.

   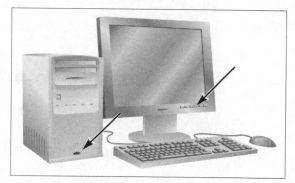

   After a pause, the computer begins starting up. This will usually take about a minute. When the startup process is complete, a login screen appears. If you are performing this exercise at home, a different screen will appear.

2. Follow the steps for your location to log on:

Computer Lab

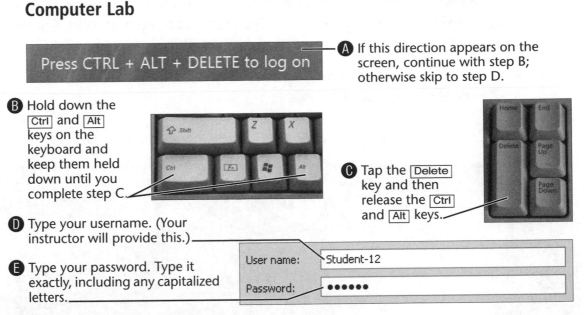

Press CTRL + ALT + DELETE to log on

A If this direction appears on the screen, continue with step B; otherwise skip to step D.

B Hold down the [Ctrl] and [Alt] keys on the keyboard and keep them held down until you complete step C.

C Tap the [Delete] key and then release the [Ctrl] and [Alt] keys.

D Type your username. (Your instructor will provide this.)

E Type your password. Type it exactly, including any capitalized letters.

User name: Student-12

Password: ●●●●●●

F Tap the [Enter] key or click the Enter button with your mouse.

The Win 7 Desktop appears. If your login name or password was not correct, you will be asked to reenter both again. Simply do so, paying close attention to typing the username and password correctly.

Home Computer

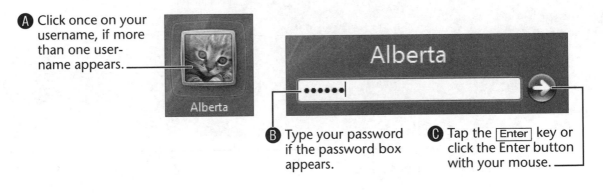

A Click once on your username, if more than one user-name appears.

Alberta

Alberta

●●●●●●

B Type your password if the password box appears.

C Tap the [Enter] key or click the Enter button with your mouse.

The Win 7 Desktop appears. If your login password was not correct, you will be asked to reenter it again. Simply do so, paying close attention to typing the username and password correctly.

The Win 7 Desktop

Once you have logged on to the computer, you will be looking at the Win 7 Desktop. The Desktop is the primary work area in Win 7, and like your desk at school, everything you work on is placed in this area.

The Desktop has many unique features that help you be more efficient in using the computer.

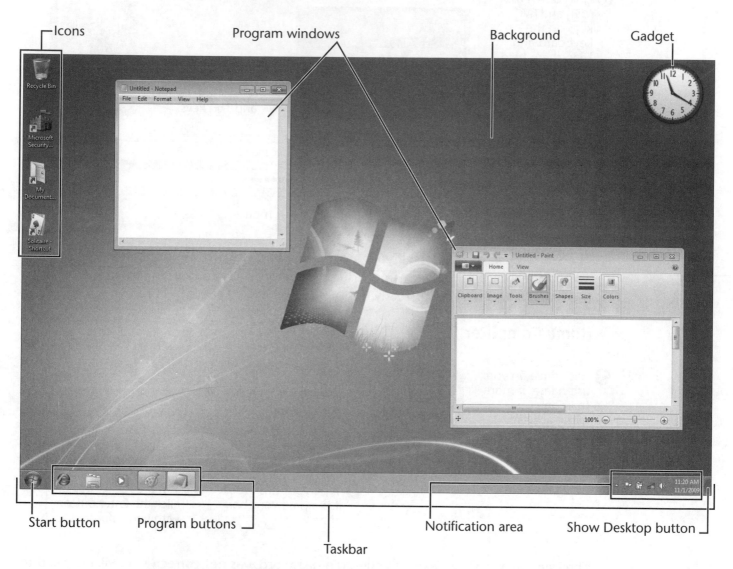

This is what the Win 7 Desktop looks like with some common features displayed.

Start Button 🟦 The round button in the bottom-left corner of the screen displaying the Windows logo is called the Start button. Access to most of Win 7's features, your software, and your documents starts from this button. Microsoft wants you to remember that everything "starts" with this little round button.

Icons   Icons are small pictures on the screen that represent programs or other features. You can launch these programs and features by double-clicking on their icons. In the previous illustration, you will notice an icon in the upper-left corner labeled Recycle Bin. This represents the Recycle Bin folder, where files are moved when deleted (as discussed later in this book).

Typical Win 7 icons

Notification Area   The Notification Area is located on the taskbar in the bottom-right corner of the computer screen (see the previous  illustration). The Notification Area contains icons for programs that are currently running but don't necessarily need a lot of user interaction. Programs listed here can include antivirus programs, Internet connection software, Microsoft Outlook email, and possibly the software that runs your printer.

 TIP! If you point your mouse pointer over an icon in the Notification Area, a small dialog box called a ScreenTip will appear, telling you what that program does or is doing. ScreenTips are helpful if you're curious about what's going on in your computer.

Basic Computer Components

Your computer is a collection of hardware parts working together with Windows and other software applications. Knowing the name and function of various components can give you a better understanding of the computing process.

Processor The processor is the "brain" of the computer. It processes instructions to run programs to help you get work done, or play. The speed of your computer depends a great deal on the design of the processor. Most processors these days are designed to contain multiple computers (called "cores") on a single chip. Most basic computers now have two (dual) cores. This means the computer can work on two tasks simultaneously. This is enough to

Intel's Core i7 processor contains the circuitry of four computers on a single chip.

efficiently browse the web, access email, word process, and perform other basic tasks. Most business and gaming computers have four or more cores, giving them even greater processing power to display high-resolution game screens and run multiple programs at once.

Random Access Memory If the processor does the work, the computer's random access memory (RAM) is where the work actually gets done. Think of RAM as the computer's "workbench." Everything you see on the screen is taking place in RAM. More RAM allows your computer to run more programs efficiently (multitask), or to run

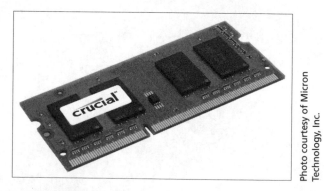

RAM comes with snap-in modules of varying capacities.

very complex programs or games. Most computers allow you to add more RAM, which is easily installed via snap-in modules. Tablets and smartphones have a fixed amount of RAM.

Storage Hardware   Your computer can use a variety of storage devices and services. See Behind the Screen: Storage Basics section on page 94 for details.

Network Hardware   Virtually all computers have hardware to access a network, particularly the Internet. For example, every notebook computer has wireless receiver built-in. This can detect and connect to wireless access in the home or in public places such as libraries, cafes, and schools. Many computers also have a port into which you can plug a network cable for wired access.

Universal Serial Bus (USB) Port   A USB port is the small rectangular port or connector now common on all computers. USB ports allow you to connect various pieces of equipment to your computer using a single standardized cord and plug. Once a device is connected via the USB port, Windows recognizes the equipment and helps with its configuration. USB ports come in two primary versions: USB 2 and USB 3. New computers have USB 3 ports, which are also compatible with USB 2 devices. The main difference is speed. In real-world usage, USB 3 ports communicate about three to four times faster than USB 2s.

Thunderbolt Port   Thunderbolt is a relatively new high-speed connection that works like a USB. Thunderbolt ports allow you to connect multiple devices, such as an external hard drive, optical drive, or even a second monitor. Thunderbolt is approximately six times faster than USB 2.

Using a Mouse

The mouse is your main tool for controlling programs on the Win 7 Desktop. Moving the mouse controls the movements of a mouse pointer on the screen. The mouse should be held in your hand with your index finger resting lightly on or above the left mouse button. You may find that dragging your thumb on the mouse pad or your desktop as you move and click can help control the movement of the mouse.

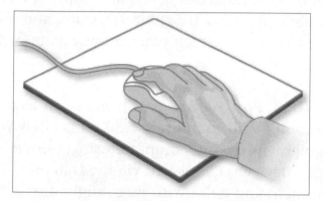

Make sure you are holding the mouse with your hand. Your index finger should be resting lightly on the left mouse button.

 NOTE! Make sure you keep your wrist straight when using the mouse. The top of the mouse should always point toward the top of the mouse pad. Don't steer the mouse like a car. Twisting or turning the mouse disorients the mouse pointer.

Mouse Motions

There are five basic actions that you can take with the mouse: point, click, drag, double-click, and right-click. With an understanding of these basic actions, you can control most features of Win 7 with the mouse.

Point   Pointing is holding the tip of the mouse pointer over an object on the screen. When pointing with the mouse, it is very important to keep your mouse steady so that your mouse pointer stays pointed on the correct screen item.

 TIP! Only the tip of the mouse cursor is active. The remainder of the mouse cursor is there to make the cursor easier to see.

Incorrect; tip
of pointer is
too low.

Incorrect; tip
of pointer is
too high.

Correct; tip of pointer
is over icon. Notice
how the icon is "lit up."

Click   A click or single-click is used when pushing on-screen buttons. This entails pushing the left mouse button one time. It is important when clicking that you hold the mouse still and click gently. If you wiggle the mouse while clicking, the computer may think you want to drag the object.

Drag   Dragging is used to move items around the screen. A drag works like a click except that you do not let go of the mouse button. Once you position your mouse pointer over the item you want to move, click and hold down the left mouse button until the Desktop item is in the new location, and then you can lift your finger off the button. This action is often referred to as *drag and drop*.

Double-Click   Double-clicking involves positioning the mouse over a Desktop item and clicking twice with the left mouse button. Double-clicking usually is used to start a program or to open a file or folder. As with clicking, it is important to hold the mouse still. If you wiggle the mouse when double-clicking, the computer might not open the item you clicked but instead might interpret the mouse movement as an attempt to drag the item.

 NOTE!   Be patient if you are having trouble double-clicking. A double click does not have to be lightning fast. You have about a second to complete the two clicks. Slowing down your clicking speed will help keep you from wiggling the mouse.

Right-Click   Right-clicking is done with the right mouse button. Clicking with this button displays a pop-up menu. The choices on the menu will change depending on which Desktop object you have clicked. You will learn more about right-clicking later in this lesson.

 TIP!   If you accidentally click on the right mouse button, a pop-up menu may appear on the screen. You can make the accidental menu disappear by clicking another place on the Desktop with the left mouse button or by tapping the ESC key in the upper-left corner of your keyboard.

 **HANDS-ON 1.2** **Practice Using the Mouse**

In this exercise, you will use the mouse to point, click, and drag the Recycle Bin on the Desktop.

1. Make sure the mouse is positioned on the desk so you can place your entire hand on the mouse as shown in the following illustration. Hold the mouse loosely so your hand is comfortable while you rest your fingers over the two mouse buttons.

2. Follow these steps to start using the mouse:

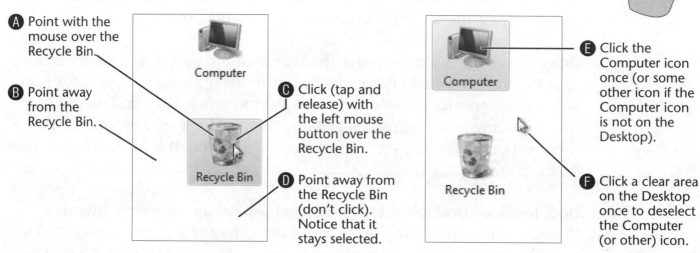

A Point with the mouse over the Recycle Bin.

B Point away from the Recycle Bin.

C Click (tap and release) with the left mouse button over the Recycle Bin.

D Point away from the Recycle Bin (don't click). Notice that it stays selected.

E Click the Computer icon once (or some other icon if the Computer icon is not on the Desktop).

F Click a clear area on the Desktop once to deselect the Computer (or other) icon.

3. Locate the Recycle Bin on your Desktop then hold your mouse pointer over the Recycle Bin and read the ScreenTip that appears.

4. Point at the Recycle Bin and single-click to select the icon. Notice the change in appearance when the icon is selected.

Practice Dragging

Dragging is a basic technique to move objects on the screen, select text, and perform many other tasks and commands.

5. Follow these steps to drag the Recycle Bin to a new location on the Desktop:

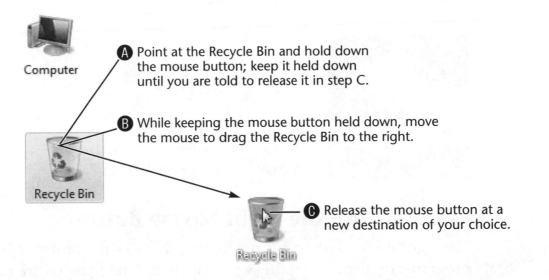

Computer

Ⓐ Point at the Recycle Bin and hold down the mouse button; keep it held down until you are told to release it in step C.

Ⓑ While keeping the mouse button held down, move the mouse to drag the Recycle Bin to the right.

Recycle Bin

Ⓒ Release the mouse button at a new destination of your choice.

Recycle Bin

6. Carefully drag the Recycle Bin back to its original location on the Desktop.

Using Gadgets

Gadgets are small productivity programs that can help put useful information at your fingertips. Gadgets can be a simple Desktop clock or more complicated programs that provide a picture slide show, the day's weather, or current news headlines.

The Clock is an example of a Gadget that comes installed with Win 7.

Clicking with the Right Mouse Button

The right mouse button is used frequently in Win 7 and within many programs to display helpful pop-up menus. These menus are context-sensitive. This means that the menu that appears will contain tasks related to the object on which you have clicked.

To display a pop-up menu, place the tip of the mouse pointer over an object (for example, a command in the Start menu) and click the right button on the mouse. When the pop-up menu appears, choose items from the menu with the left mouse button.

View	▶
Sort by	▶
Refresh	
Paste	
Paste shortcut	
Undo Delete	Ctrl+Z
NVIDIA Control Panel	
New	▶
Screen resolution	
Gadgets	
Personalize	

Right-clicking on the Desktop brings up a menu of commands related specifically to the Desktop. The Gadgets item on the menu will bring up a selection of Gadgets.

Standard Gadgets

- **Clock**—This Gadget is a standard clock used to tell time.

- **Slide Show (a picture viewer)**—This Gadget randomly scrolls through the sample pictures that are provided with Windows. It can be set to show your own pictures instead of samples.

- **Feed Headlines (an RSS reader)**—This Gadget is used by intermediate and advanced users to gather news stories from various sources on the Internet and compile them into one list for easy reading.

Adding, Removing, and Changing Gadgets

Gadgets are not permanently attached to the Desktop. They can be added or moved anywhere on the Desktop. If you no longer need a particular Gadget, it can be removed at any time.

Another Gadget feature is a small toolbar that appears when the mouse pointer hovers over a Gadget. It provides quick commands to close or change the Gadget's options and a handle to drag the Gadget.

X—The Close button lets you remove the Gadget.

The Options button lets you change the Gadget.

The Drag Gadget handle lets you move the Gadget.

A small toolbar with quick commands appears when you point at a Gadget.

QUICK REFERENCE: Using Gadgets

Task	Procedure
Add a new Gadget	• Right-click on the background of the Desktop and choose Gadgets from the pop-up menu. This will bring up the Gadget menu with a complete list of optional Gadgets.
Move a Gadget	• Position your mouse over the Gadget and then drop the Gadget anywhere on the Desktop.

Task	Procedure
Remove a Gadget	• Right-click on the Gadget and choose Close Gadget from the menu.
	• Point at the Gadget and click the Close **X** button on the toolbar that appears.
Change Gadget options	• Right-click on the Gadget and choose Options from the menu.
	• Point at the Gadget and click the Options 🔧 button on the toolbar that appears.

HANDS-ON 1.3 Add, Move, and Remove Gadgets on the Desktop

In this exercise, you will add the Clock and Slide Show Gadgets to the Desktop. Then you will move the Gadgets before removing both from the Desktop.

Add Gadgets

1. Follow these steps to add the Clock and Slide Show Gadgets to the Desktop:

Ⓐ Point with the mouse over the background of the Desktop and click with the right (not the left) mouse button.

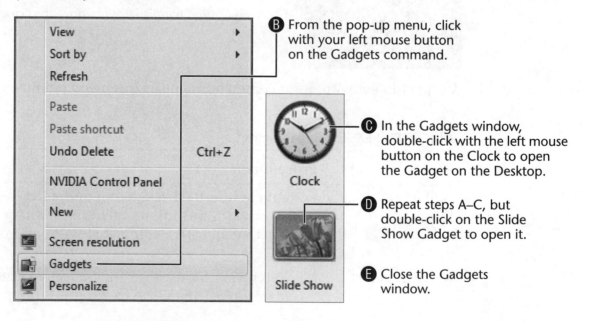

Ⓑ From the pop-up menu, click with your left mouse button on the Gadgets command.

Ⓒ In the Gadgets window, double-click with the left mouse button on the Clock to open the Gadget on the Desktop.

Ⓓ Repeat steps A–C, but double-click on the Slide Show Gadget to open it.

Ⓔ Close the Gadgets window.

Win 7 opens the Clock and Slide Show Gadgets on the Desktop.

Move Gadgets

2. Point over the clock, hold down the left mouse button and drag the clock anywhere on the Desktop, and then release the mouse button to drop it into position.

3. Point over the slide show and then drag and drop it anywhere on the Desktop.

   The clock and slide show remain where you drop them until moved again or removed from the Desktop.

Remove Gadgets

4. Point with the mouse over the clock and click with the right (not the left) mouse button.

5. From the pop-up menu, choose Close Gadget to remove it from the Desktop.

6. Point over the slide show and click the Close button on the toolbar that appears.

Logging Off and Switching Users

Logging off the computer is different from turning the computer off. When you log off, the programs you are using are closed, your documents are saved to the hard drive, personal login information is removed from memory, and the computer is made ready for the next user to log on.

!NOTE! Logging off does not shut off power to the computer. The computer is left running, but it is prepared for another user to log on.

Switch User

Multiple users can be logged on to a single computer at the same time. Each user can customize the environment of the computer to meet his or her needs. When you switch users, the previous user's information, screen settings, and programs are set aside in the computer's memory, and the new user's information is made active.

Benefits of Using Switch User This is most useful at home when more than one person shares a computer. When each user logs on, it takes time for Win 7 to load programs and personal settings into RAM. Switching between users who have already logged on is much faster, because programs and settings already are in RAM.

QUICK REFERENCE: Logging Off and Switching Users

Task	Procedure
Log off Windows	• From the Shut Down menu ▶ button (located at the bottom of the Start menu next to the Shut Down button) choose Log Off.
Switch users	• From the Shut Down menu ▶ button, choose Switch Users. • After a pause, the screen displays available login names.
Lock and unlock Win 7	• Click the Shut Down menu ▶ button and choose Lock. This will lock the computer. • To unlock the computer, choose the icon representing the user you would like to log in as.

HANDS-ON 1.4 Practice Switch User

In this exercise, you will give the Switch User command and then log back in using your own username.

1. Follow these steps to switch users:

Ⓐ Click the Start button.

Ⓑ Click the Shut Down menu ▶ button next to the Shut Down button.

Ⓒ Choose Switch User from the menu.

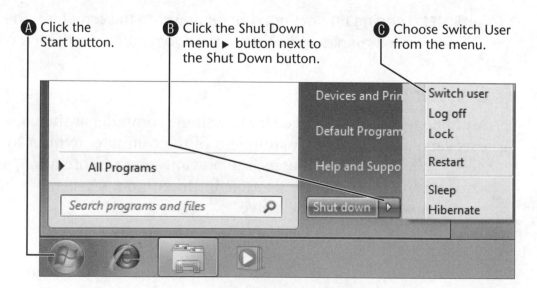

There will be a pause as Win 7 prepares to display the login screen. Wait for this screen to appear before continuing with the next step.

2. Click your username or type it in the appropriate box.

3. Type your password in the Password box and then tap the $\boxed{\text{Enter}}$ key on the keyboard.

   After a pause, Win 7 returns you to the Desktop. You could just as easily have logged in as someone else in step 2.

Shutting Down

Win 7 is a very large collection of programs. If it is not shut down properly, you may discover upon restarting your computer that error messages appear—or worse, Win 7 doesn't start at all. Win 7 needs time to properly shut down all of its software parts and pieces correctly. Just turning off the power doesn't give Win 7 this needed time.

Shut Down Methods

There are four ways to shut down Win 7, depending on what you want to do next. Available options are displayed via the Start button using the Shut down button and the Shut down menu:

- Shut Down

- Restart

- Hibernate

- Sleep

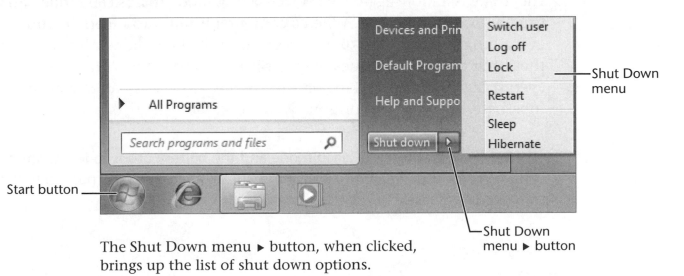

The Shut Down menu ▶ button, when clicked, brings up the list of shut down options.

Restart

The restart mode closes all open program windows, logs you out, and powers down the computer. The computer then restarts and Win 7 reloads. Sometimes Win 7 will ask you to restart the computer after a new program has been installed. The new program can't be used until the system restarts and the new software is integrated into Win 7.

Sleep

In sleep mode, the computer uses a lot less energy because the computer slows down. Any documents you are working on are saved, the processor works more slowly, the monitor is turned off, and other settings are triggered that allow the computer to save power. Most Win 7 computers also feature a sleep button on they keyboard for easy access to this command.

 Most new computer keyboards feature a sleep button as a convenient means to activate the computer's sleep mode.

 TIP! On most laptops, closing the lid will immediately cause the laptop to go into sleep mode and start conserving battery power.

Hibernate

Hibernate is a more aggressive power-saving mode than sleep mode and is usually found on laptops. When a computer is put into hibernate mode, everything you were working on is saved to the hard drive. All equipment is then shut down. When the computer is turned back on, Win 7 loads everything you were working on exactly the way it was before you activated hibernate, and you can continue your work.

TIP! If your laptop is in sleep mode and the battery drops to less than 10 percent power, Win 7 will automatically switch to hibernate so that no data is lost.

Shut Down

This command closes all programs, logs you out of the computer, and turns off the power to the computer. When you are done with the computer for the day, it is important to turn off the computer using the Shut Down command.

⚠ WARNING! Never hold down the power button to turn a computer off unless you have no other choice. Win 7 needs time to close its various parts and pieces down properly. Turning the power off abruptly can corrupt parts of the Win 7 software and can even cause the computer to not restart.

QUICK REFERENCE: Shutting Down Win 7

Task	Procedure
Shut down Win 7 and the computer	• Close all open programs. • Click the Shut Down button (located at the bottom of the Start menu). `Shut down`
Go into sleep mode	• Choose Sleep from the Shut Down menu ▸ button.
Exit sleep mode	• Move the mouse or tap the `Spacebar` on your keyboard.

HANDS-ON 1.5 Practice Using Sleep Mode

In this exercise, you will practice putting the computer into sleep mode and then back into working mode.

1. Make sure all programs are closed.

2. Follow these steps to go into sleep mode:

Ⓐ Click the Start button.   Ⓑ Click the Shut Down menu ▶ button.   Ⓒ Choose Sleep from the menu.

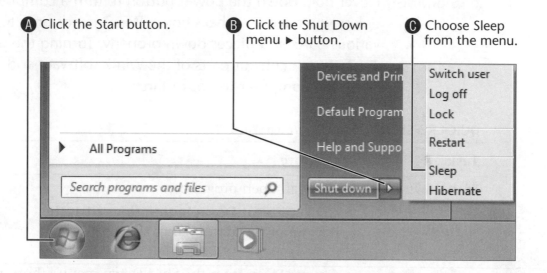

3. Move the mouse or press the ⸢Spacebar⸥ on the keyboard to bring the computer out of sleep mode.

4. If the Welcome screen appears, choose your screen name and enter your password if requested. (You may also have to use the ⸢Ctrl⸥+⸢Alt⸥+⸢Delete⸥ keys if you are in a computer lab.)

   The computer is now ready to work again.

Shut Down Win 7

Now you will end your Win 7 session by logging off.

5. Make sure any open programs are closed.

6. Click the Start 🪟 button.

7. Click the Shut Down button at the bottom of the Start menu.

   It may take the computer 15 seconds or more to completely shut down.

Concepts Review

All of the Concepts Review quizzes for this book are available on the student web page. Your instructor will let you know how to complete the quizzes (in the book or online).

True/False Questions

Page number

1. Access to most features in Win 7 is through the Start button located in the bottom-left corner of the screen.   **true**   **false**   _____

2. Icons are small pictures that represent programs or other features in Win 7.   **true**   **false**   _____

3. Sleep mode is used to save energy when the computer is not going to be operated for a while.   **true**   **false**   _____

4. Drag and drop is used to move icons on the screen.   **true**   **false**   _____

5. It's okay to simply switch the power off when you're done using the computer.   **true**   **false**   _____

6. Gadgets are productivity tools designed to put information at your fingertips.   **true**   **false**   _____

Multiple Choice Questions

7. Which of these is the best password?
   Page number: _____
   a. Fido
   b. G476rty
   c. JohnSmith
   d. Password

8. Which of these is *not* a mouse action?
   Page number: _____
   a. Single-click
   b. Double-click
   c. Roll
   d. Point

9. Which item is *not* on the Shut Down menu?
   Page number: _____
   a. Switch User
   b. Restart
   c. Hibernate
   d. Pause System

10. Icons _____.
   Page number: _____
   a. are small images that can represent documents, photos, and programs
   b. can be found in many areas of Win 7, including the Desktop and the taskbar
   c. act as the start buttons for programs
   d. All of the above

 # Skill Builders

SKILL BUILDER 1.1 **Practice Mousing with Solitaire**

In this exercise, you will open and play Solitaire to enhance your mousing skills.

1. Click the Start  button and choose Games from the right pane.

   A new window appears to display the games that come installed with Win 7.

2. From the Games menu, double-click on the Solitaire icon. Or click once on Solitaire and tap the [Enter] key on the keyboard.

   A new window appears and deals the cards for a new game automatically.

3. Follow these basic mousing moves for playing Solitaire:

   ┌Click Help on the menu bar and then click View Help to learn more about Solitaire. (It's probably easiest to have a classmate show you if you don't know this game already.)

   To move cards from one pile to another, drag and drop the card on its new location. (You need an ace to start placing cards in the four empty squares.)

To turn cards from the card pile over, simply click on the pile.

 TIP! If the card jumps back to its original location, it was placed in an illegal location.

4. When you are finished, click Game on the menu bar and then choose New Game to start a new game of Solitaire. To close the Solitaire program, click Game on the menu bar and choose Exit. Choose Don't Save to exit the game.

Practice Mousing with Mousercise

In this exercise, you will practice using the mouse with the online software Mousercise.

Before You Begin: This exercise runs on the Internet, so you need to know how to navigate with a web browser. (The Internet is introduced in Lesson 5, Browsing Web Pages.) A friend or family member should be able to help you get the exercise started in step 1 if you don't yet use the Internet.

1. Launch Internet Explorer and navigate to the web page for this book:
   `labpub.com/learn/silver/wtwc4`

2. Click the Mouse Practice link for Lesson 1.

3. Follow the on-screen instructions.

4. Close [X] the Internet Explorer window when you are finished.

Try This at Home

Practice Switch User

In this exercise, you will practice switching from one user login to another.

Before You Begin: Skip this exercise if there is only one user listed on the Win 7 Welcome screen. You need at least two user accounts to switch between users.

1. Click the Start ⊕ button.

2. Follow these steps to switch users:

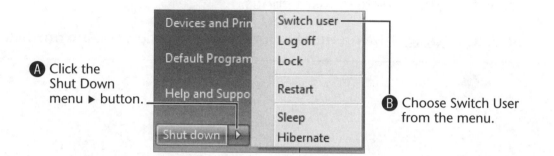

Ⓐ Click the Shut Down menu ▸ button.

Ⓑ Choose Switch User from the menu.

After a pause, Win 7 displays a screen with the available usernames.

3. Choose a different username that you would like to switch to, type the password, and tap the ⸢Enter⸣ key on the keyboard.

   Win 7 starts the switch. This can take 15 seconds or more to accomplish, depending on the speed of your computer and the amount of RAM available for the operation.

4. Click the Start button, click the Shut Down menu ▸ button, and choose Switch User again.

5. Log in with your own username and password.

   There is another pause as Win 7 switches you back to your Desktop. Notice that everything is just how you left it before switching to the other username.

6. Click the Start button, click the Shut Down menu ▸ button, and choose Log Off.

   There is a pause as Win 7 logs you off.

7. Log in to the other username.

8. Log off the other username.

Change a Gadget's Options

In this exercise, you will open the Clock Gadget from the list of available Gadgets and change its options.

1. Right-click on the Desktop background and choose Gadgets from the pop-up menu.

2. Double-click on the Clock Gadget from the Gadget choices presented.

3. Close ✖ the Gadget window.

4. Follow these steps to change the options for the clock:

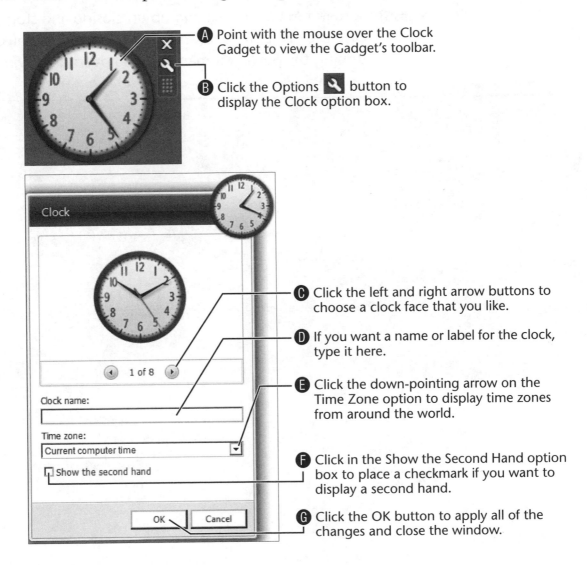

Ⓐ Point with the mouse over the Clock Gadget to view the Gadget's toolbar.

Ⓑ Click the Options 🔧 button to display the Clock option box.

Ⓒ Click the left and right arrow buttons to choose a clock face that you like.

Ⓓ If you want a name or label for the clock, type it here.

Ⓔ Click the down-pointing arrow on the Time Zone option to display time zones from around the world.

Ⓕ Click in the Show the Second Hand option box to place a checkmark if you want to display a second hand.

Ⓖ Click the OK button to apply all of the changes and close the window.

You can have more than one clock on the Desktop. You might have a different look and a different label on a second clock displaying a different time zone.

TRY THIS AT HOME 1.3 **Practice Shutting Down**

In this exercise, you will practice shutting down the computer properly.

1. Make sure that all of your open programs are closed.

2. From the Start menu choose Shut Down.

   The computer will take a minute or two to complete its shutdown tasks. Be patient and wait for the computer to finish.

3. If the computer doesn't turn off the power automatically, you will need to power off the computer and the monitor.

    WARNING! Sometimes Win 7 will hang up on closing and stop responding. Give the computer a few minutes to correct the problem before turning the power off manually and overriding Win 7.

Starting Programs

In this lesson, you will become familiar with various components of the Start menu, launch a program and learn the features used to control a program window. You also will explore two programs that come with Win 7: a picture-editing program called Paint and a word-processing program called WordPad. As you use these programs that have very different purposes, you will learn similarities and differences between their program controls, including menus, toolbars, ribbons, mouse pointers, and scroll bars. Although applications from many different software companies are installed on your computer, the Win 7 operating system provides standardized tools for launching and controlling application programs.

LESSON OBJECTIVES

After studying this lesson, you will be able to:

- Navigate and arrange program commands on the Start menu
- Open programs from the Start menu
- Minimize, maximize, size, and move program windows
- Describe basic features of the Win 7 taskbar
- Use common features found in drop-down menus, on toolbars and ribbons, and on the scroll bars
- Use the mouse effectively as the appearance and function of the mouse pointer changes
- Type and edit text in a computer program

Additional learning resources are available at labpub.com/learn/silver/wtwc4/

Case Study: Starting at the Beginning

William is going back to school and has bought a new computer to help him complete his homework. He has very little experience using a computer and feels a bit confused by all of the programs. He has tried clicking on the Desktop icons and has clicked on the Start menu, but the programs have so many different purposes: Several play music, one is like a checkbook, one is for drawing pictures, another is a notepad, and there also are card games. Before learning the different applications he will be using to do his homework, he decides to first learn what the programs have in common. If he can learn the standardized Win 7 features used in most programs, it will be much easier to learn new applications. William starts with the Start menu.

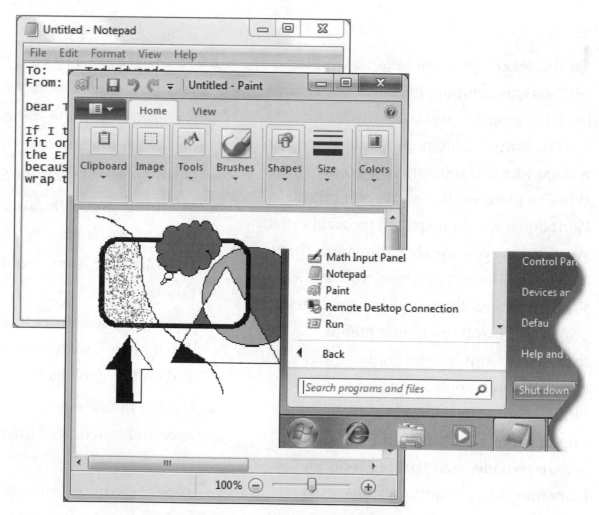

Notepad and Paint are small programs found in the Start menu's Accessories folder.

Working with the Start Menu

The Start menu is the one place you can go to launch most of the programs installed on your computer. Like all menus, the Start menu is a collection of commands. The Start button gives access to commands to launch all of the programs that come with Win 7. When you install a new program, Win 7 adds a command for it to the Start menu. Commands on a menu often have a descriptive label and an icon.

About Commands

A command is a link that can launch (start or open) a document, folder, or program, or execute a variety of other tasks. You might compare a command to a light switch on the wall used to turn on a ceiling light. Clicking (or double-clicking) on a command launches the object to which it is linked. More than one command can be linked to the same object. Commands can be located on the Desktop, in a menu, on a toolbar, or on a ribbon.

HANDS-ON 2.1 **Display and Dismiss the Start Menu**

In this exercise, you will display and dismiss the Start menu using both the mouse and the keyboard.

1. Click the Start 🪟 button to display the Start menu.

The Start menu is displayed. Observe the left and right panes of the Start menu.

2. Click the Start 🪟 button again to dismiss the Start menu.

3. Press the WIN ⊞ key on the keyboard to display the Start menu.

4. Press the WIN ⊞ key again to dismiss the Start menu.

It's easy to dismiss the Start menu if you pull it up by mistake.

Start Menu Panes

The Start menu is divided into left and right panes:

- The left pane has a list of commands to various programs, including the All Programs folder. There is also a Start Search text box at the bottom.

- The right pane usually displays commands to display various parts of the computer system. At the bottom, there is also a Shut Down button with a Shut Down menu ▸ button attached.

> **TIP!** The appearance of the Start menu may vary depending on the version of Win 7 being used on the computer. Although the appearance may vary, all Start menus function in the same manner.

Pinned program area, to keep frequently used programs immediately available

List of recently used programs

Menu that displays a complete list of programs on the computer

Start button

Commands to display various parts of the computer system

Shut Down and Shut Down menu ▸ buttons

Getting Started

Windows Media Center

Sticky Notes

Snipping Tool

Remote Desktop Connection

Magnifier

All Programs

Search programs and files

Student

Documents

Pictures

Music

Games

Computer

Control Panel

Devices and Printers

Default Programs

Help and Support

Shut down ▸

Major features of the Start menu

Jump Lists in the Start Menu

A new feature in Win 7 is the use of Jump Lists in Start menu. Jump Lists are attached to Start menu commands and provide additional commands that link to files recently created with that program or that link to other related tasks. When a Jump List is attached to a command in the Start menu, a right-pointing arrow ▶ can be seen on the right side of the command. The list will "fly out" to the right for viewing when the mouse pointer is placed over the command.

A right-pointing arrow on the Start menu command indicates that there is an attached Jump List.

Launching Programs

Commands in the left pane of the Start menu are divided into three sections with gray menu separators:

- The top section has commands that are "pinned" in placed until removed by you.

- The center section has a list of recently used programs. Win 7 adds commands to this list as you launch new programs.

- The All Programs command near the bottom of the Start menu displays a list of most programs installed on the computer. Win 7 adds a command to this list automatically when a program is first installed.

 TIP! Check the recently used programs section of the Start menu first when you want to launch a frequently used program.

HANDS-ON 2.2 Launch a Program from the Start Menu

In this exercise, you will launch the Paint program from the Start menu.

1. Use your mouse or the keyboard to display the Start menu.

   Run your mouse pointer over the commands in the left pane and notice the selection bar that appears when your mouse pointer is above a command. You can click anywhere along the selection bar to launch a command.

2. Click the All Programs command.

3. Follow these steps to start the Paint program:

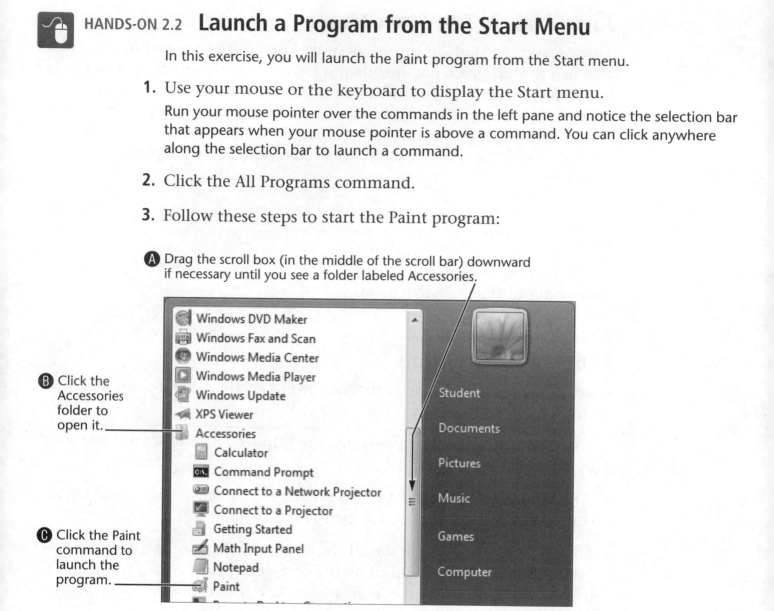

Ⓐ Drag the scroll box (in the middle of the scroll bar) downward if necessary until you see a folder labeled Accessories.

Ⓑ Click the Accessories folder to open it.

Ⓒ Click the Paint command to launch the program.

The Start menu will be dismissed, and after a short pause, the Paint program will open on the Desktop.

TIP! In the rest of this book, Start menu commands will be written like this: Choose Start→All Programs→Accessories→Paint.

4. Close the Paint program by clicking the red Close ☒ button in the upper-right corner of the window.

Recently Used Programs List

Win 7 automatically adds commands for programs to the recently used programs list of the Start menu. Sometimes a program is added to the list the first time you launch it. Other times you may need to use a program twice to have it added to the list. When the recently used programs list becomes full, the command of the program that has been unused the longest is hidden. You can also remove a command from the recently used program list.

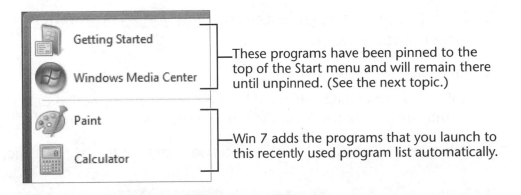

These programs have been pinned to the top of the Start menu and will remain there until unpinned. (See the next topic.)

Win 7 adds the programs that you launch to this recently used program list automatically.

Pinning Programs to the Start Menu

Commands can be pinned to the top section of the left pane and stay there until unpinned. Unlike the recently used program list, pinned commands are not added or hidden by Win 7; *you* choose which programs get pinned or unpinned.

 TIP! Go ahead and pin programs you use a lot. This leaves more room on the frequently used programs list for programs you use less often.

QUICK REFERENCE: Pinning Commands to the Start Menu

Task	Procedure
Remove a program from the recently used programs list	*Right*-click (not left-click) any program command in the Start menu and choose Remove from This List from the pop-up menu.
Pin a command to the Start menu	*Right*-click any program command in the Start menu and choose Pin to Start Menu from the pop-up menu, or drag the command from the recently used programs list and drop it in the pinned section.
Unpin a Start menu command	*Right*-click on the pinned command and choose Unpin from Start Menu from the pop-up menu.

HANDS-ON 2.3 Pin Commands to the Start Menu

In this exercise, you will open and close a program from the All Programs folder. A command will be added to the recently used programs list. You will then pin commands to the top section of the Start menu and, finally, unpin the commands from the top of the Start menu.

1. Choose Start →All Programs→Accessories→Notepad.

   Win 7 launches the Notepad program, a very basic text-typing program.

2. Close Notepad by clicking the red Close 　X　 button in the upper-right corner of the window.

3. Click the Start button.

   Notice that a Notepad command has been automatically added to the recently used programs list in the center section of the left pane.

4. Follow these steps to pin the Notepad program to the Start menu:

Ⓐ Point at the Notepad command in the recently used programs list.

Ⓑ Hold down your left mouse button and drag the Notepad command up toward the top of the left pane.

Ⓒ Release the mouse button when the Pin to Start Menu ScreenTip appears.

Getting Started

Windows Media Center

Paint

Notepad

📌 Pin to Start menu

Student

Documents

Pictures

Win 7 places the Notepad command into the pinned list.

5. Click a clear area of the Desktop to close the Start menu.

6. Click the Start button.

   The Notepad program appears right where you pinned it.

Pin Another Program

7. Follow these steps to pin another program to the Start menu:

Ⓐ Click All Programs to display the program list.

Ⓑ Click the Accessories folder.

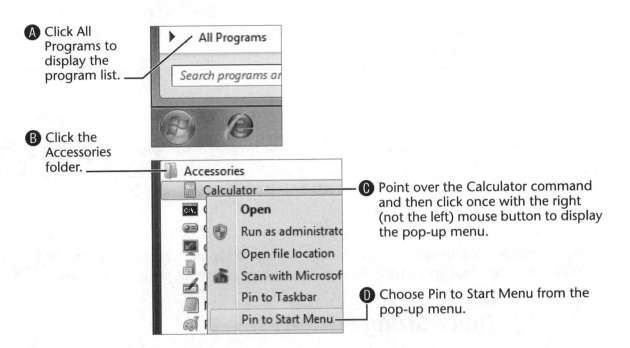

Ⓒ Point over the Calculator command and then click once with the right (not the left) mouse button to display the pop-up menu.

Ⓓ Choose Pin to Start Menu from the pop-up menu.

Win 7 pins the program command to the bottom of the pinned program list.

8. Click a clear area of the Desktop to close the Start menu and then click the Start ⊞ button again.

Unpin the Programs

To clear the pinned programs for the next student, you will unpin the two programs.

9. Follow these steps to unpin the Calculator command:

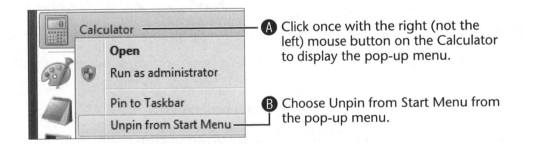

Ⓐ Click once with the right (not the left) mouse button on the Calculator to display the pop-up menu.

Ⓑ Choose Unpin from Start Menu from the pop-up menu.

Win 7 removes the command from the pinned area.

10. Right-click the Notepad command in the pinned area and then choose Unpin from Start Menu from the pop-up menu.

11. Click a clear area of the Desktop to close the Start menu.

Controlling Program Windows

Every program you open in Win 7 is displayed within its own window. This window, known as the program window, has controls and features that are similar in most programs. These basic controls are Win 7 standards; learn to use them in one program, and you will be able to work with similar controls in most new programs you use.

┌Title bar   Window quick sizing buttons ──┐

| Untitled - Notepad   □ □ X |
| File   Edit   Format   View   Help |

Here is an example of a program window for Notepad, a program that comes with Win 7. The quick sizing buttons and title bar are standard controls in all program windows.

Quick Sizing Buttons

The quick sizing buttons consist of the Minimize, Maximize, Restore Down, and Close buttons located in the upper-right corner of most program windows. These buttons, along with the program button on the taskbar, are used to reconfigure or to close a program window.

QUICK REFERENCE: Using Window Quick Sizing Buttons

Button	Name	How It Works
▬	Minimize	Removes the program window from the screen but continues to run it and leaves its program button on the taskbar
▢	Maximize	Enlarges a program window to fill the screen
❏	Restore Down	Resizes a program window to the smaller size it was before it was last maximized
X	Close	Exits a program
◿	Program button (on taskbar)	Minimizes an open window or reopens a window that has been minimized

The Minimize and Maximize Buttons The Minimize button shrinks the program window from the Desktop, leaving only its program button on the taskbar. The program continues to run. To open the program window again, click the program's button on the taskbar. The program will open again to the size it was before it was minimized.

TIP! If a program window is open, you also can click its program button on the taskbar to minimize the window.

Maximize ⬜ is just the opposite of minimize. Maximize enlarges a program to fill the entire Desktop so that other programs become hidden behind it.

Why minimize or maximize programs? Having multiple programs open on your Desktop can be like having a messy desk. Minimizing windows will hide the distracting clutter of open windows, while maximizing a window will simply cover other opened windows.

Minimize Compared to Close The Minimize button makes a program window shrink from the screen, but it does not close the program. If you are in the middle of a Spider Solitaire game and minimize, the Spider Solitaire program button is still on the taskbar. When you click the program's taskbar button, the game will return to its previous size, and your card game is ready for you to continue.

When you click the Close ❌ button, you end the card game and exit the program, and the program button is removed from the taskbar.

FROM THE KEYBOARD

Alt + F4 to close (exit) a program

TIP! A quick way to close a minimized program is to *right*-click the program button on the taskbar. This displays the control menu (shown in the figure to the right) that includes a Close Window command at the bottom.

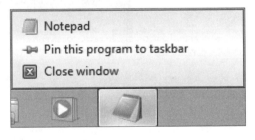

The Maximize and Restore Down Buttons The center quick sizing button toggles between the Maximize and Restore Down buttons; they are never shown at the same time. If you click Maximize, the center button changes to Restore Down. Conversely, if you click Restore Down, the center button changes to Maximize, as shown here:

Maximize button

Restore Down button

When you click the Maximize button...

... the center button changes to Restore Down.

When you click the Restore Down button...

... the center button changes to Maximize.

The Program Button on the Taskbar When a program is opened, its program button appears on the taskbar. The button displays the program's icon without a label. If you position the mouse cursor over the program button (without clicking), additional information about the program will be displayed on a ScreenTip. Clicking on the program button can minimize an open program window, restore a minimized window to its former size, or make an inactive program active.

Quick Sizing Button Exceptions Occasionally a program will not use all of the standard controls. Certain control buttons may be missing or *grayed out*. This is discussed later in the Nonstandard Program Windows section of this lesson, but in the following example, the Minimize and Maximize buttons are missing:

Taskbar and Start Menu Properties

| Taskbar | Start Menu | Toolbars |

The Aero theme was used for images in this book. The appearance of quick sizing buttons may change with other themes or in different programs, but their functions remain the same. Following are some variations.

Buttons in
WordPad with
Aero theme

Buttons in
WordPad with
Basic theme

Buttons in
Adobe Photoshop
Elements 8

HANDS-ON 2.4 Practice Using Quick Sizing Buttons

In this exercise, you will open the Paint program and practice using the quick sizing buttons to minimize, maximize, and restore down the program window.

1. Choose Start ⊞→All Programs→Accessories→Paint to launch the program. (If necessary, review steps 1–3 in Hands-On 2.2.)

   The Paint program will open either maximized or in a restored-down size.

2. If the program window does not fill the screen, click the Maximize ▣ button.

   The program window enlarges to fill the entire Desktop (except for the taskbar). Also notice that the center quick sizing button has changed to a Restore Down button.

   It is usually a good idea to maximize ▣ any program window when it first opens to take full advantage of the entire screen.

3. Click the Restore Down ▣ button.

   Notice how the program window is restored back to its original smaller size.

4. Click the Minimize ▬ button.

   Now you can see the Desktop. The program window shrinks off of the Desktop, leaving only a program button on the taskbar. Locate the button for the Paint program on the taskbar at the bottom of the screen.

5. Click the Paint program button on the taskbar to restore the Paint program onto your Desktop.

Program button on the taskbar

Each program button on the taskbar has an icon that helps you to identify the program. Paint uses a paint palette and a brush as its icon.

6. Click the Close ▣ button to exit Paint.

Moving and Resizing Program Windows

Program windows can be moved around on the Desktop the way you move papers and objects around your desk at home. Unlike your desk at home, program windows can be resized to fill the Desktop or reduced to a smaller size.

Title bar _____   Border _____   Resizing handle _____

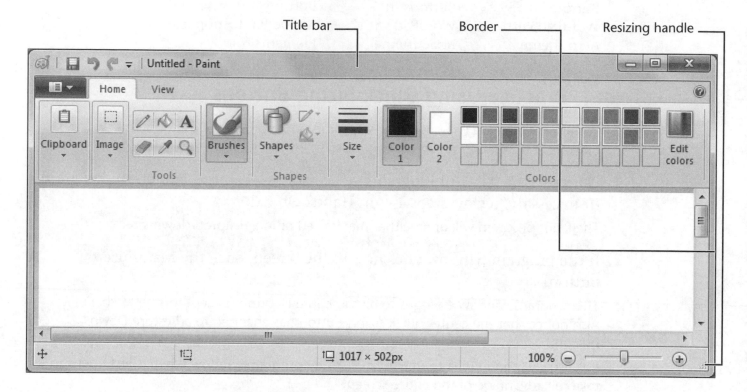

Title Bar   The title bar on top of every program window serves several purposes. It displays the name of the program, and it also may display the name of the document or other object being edited by that program. Control buttons are located at the right and left ends of the bar.

Finally, the title bar provides a *handle* to move the program window. If you position the tip of your mouse pointer over any empty space on its title bar (not its border), you can hold down your left mouse button and drag a program window around the Desktop.

Resizing a Window   To resize a restored-down program window, position the mouse pointer over the resizing handle, located in the bottom-right corner. When the mouse pointer changes into a double-headed arrow, you can hold down your left mouse button and drag to resize.

A program window has a narrow border surrounding it. You can also resize a window by dragging the border from any side or any corner. Dragging any side border will resize only that side of the window. Dragging any corner will resize both sides attached to the corner.

If your mouse pointer will not change to a double-headed arrow when you point at a border, then the program window cannot be resized.

Resizable

Not resizable

The double-headed mouse pointer indicates that the Paint window can be resized.

This window cannot be resized because the mouse pointer did not change when pointed at a border.

!TIP! New users will find the resizing handle in the lower-right corner easier to use than the narrow border because the handle has a larger "hot spot."

The Snap Feature Another new feature in Win 7 is called Snap. Snap is a new way to maximize, restore down, or view two windows side-by-side on the Desktop. Snap is accomplished by simply dragging windows to the top or sides of the Desktop.

QUICK REFERENCE: Using Snap to Resize Windows

Task	Procedure
Maximize a window	• Use the title bar to drag a restored-down window to the top edge of the Desktop until the mouse pointer touches.
Restore down a window	• Use the title bar to drag a maximized window away from the top edge of the Desktop.
Display two windows side-by-side	• Use the title bar to drag one window to the left edge of the Desktop until the mouse pointer touches. The window fills the left half of the Desktop. • Use the title bar to drag another window to the right edge of the Desktop until the mouse pointer touches. The window fills the right half of the Desktop.

In this exercise, you will move, resize, and snap the Paint program window.

1. Choose Start ⊞→All Programs→Accessories→Paint to launch the program. (If necessary, review steps 1–3 in Hands-On 2.1.)

2. If necessary, restore down the program window.

3. Use the title bar to move the program window around the Desktop.

   ⚠ **TIP!** A program window cannot be resized if it is maximized.

4. Practice resizing the program window using the resizing handle and border sides or corners.

5. Initiate the Snap feature by using the title bar to drag the window to the left edge of the Desktop until the mouse pointer touches the edge.

6. Repeat step 5 by dragging the window to the right edge, bottom edge, and top edge, and finally by dragging the window away from all edges.

7. Close the Paint program.

Nonstandard Program Windows

Although Win 7 establishes *standards* used by most programs, there are times when the standards are ignored or modified for appearance reasons or because certain functions are not necessary to use a program. In some programs the features are simply missing, while in other programs the features are modified in appearance or grayed out and do not work.

HANDS-ON 2.6 **Open Sticky Notes and the Calculator**

In this exercise, you will open Sticky Notes and the Calculator to discover some of their nonstandard features.

Open Sticky Notes

1. Choose Start ⊞→Sticky Notes. Or, if necessary, choose Start→All Programs→Accessories→Sticky Notes.

2. Follow these steps to explore the few features available on a Sticky Note:

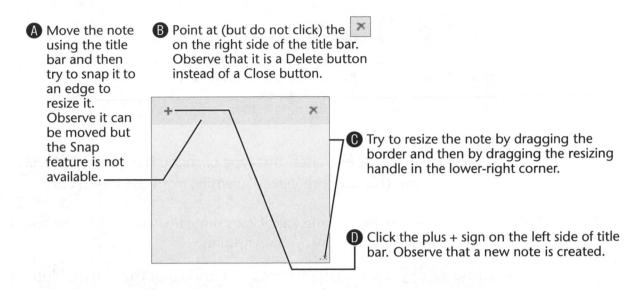

A Move the note using the title bar and then try to snap it to an edge to resize it. Observe it can be moved but the Snap feature is not available.

B Point at (but do not click) the ⊠ on the right side of the title bar. Observe that it is a Delete button instead of a Close button.

C Try to resize the note by dragging the border and then by dragging the resizing handle in the lower-right corner.

D Click the plus + sign on the left side of title bar. Observe that a new note is created.

Open Calculator

3. Choose Start ⊞ →All Programs→Accessories→Calculator to launch the program.

4. Follow these steps to try out some features of the program:

A Click the Maximize ◻ button. Notice that the Maximize button will not select (turn blue) when you point at the button and will not activate when you click the button. Although the button is displayed, it does not function. In fact, it is slightly grayed out to let you know that it is not active.

B Try to resize the window by dragging the border and by dragging the resizing handle in the lower-right corner. Observe that there is no actual border or resizing handle. They have not been included. This program doesn't allow you to resize its window.

Calculator's Standard View

5. Follow these steps to change the look of the Calculator window:

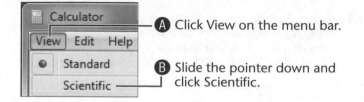

Ⓐ Click View on the menu bar.

Ⓑ Slide the pointer down and click Scientific.

!NOTE! In future exercises, this type of menu bar command will be written like this: Choose View→Scientific from the menu bar.

This is the way to expand the Calculator's program window and change its function to a scientific calculator, with many more features.

6. Close [X] the Calculator program and click the Delete Note [×] button to remove any Sticky Notes.

Working with the Win 7 Taskbar

The taskbar runs the width of the Desktop at the bottom of the screen. The center section of the taskbar displays the programs you have opened. When a program is opened, its program button is placed on the taskbar.

Only one program window can be *active,* and it will be displayed in front of other inactive programs open on your Desktop. The active program button will be brighter than other program buttons on the taskbar. Clicking on an inactive program button will make that program active and move its window in front of others on the Desktop.

Pinned programs ——

Inactive program button

The notification area ——

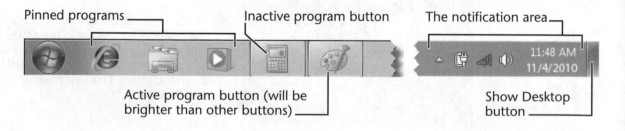

Active program button (will be brighter than other buttons) ——

Show Desktop button ——

Notification Area

The Notification Area on the right end of the taskbar has four primary functions in Win 7:

- Display the system clock and current date

- Display icons for tasks and functions that are running in the background, such as antivirus software

- Display notifications of system events, such as program updates

- Provide access to some programs whose icons display there

Icon ScreenTips   Your computer can have many icons in the Notification Area. It can be difficult to determine their purpose or even to which program they are linked. When you point with the mouse over an icon, a ScreenTip appears to describe the name of the program linked to the icon and other information about it.

ScreenTips can tell you about each icon in the Notification Area.

HANDS-ON 2.7   Change Taskbar Settings

In this exercise, you will open the taskbar and Start Menu Properties dialog box to observe setting options and to make changes to the taskbar settings.

1. Follow these steps to display the taskbar properties window:

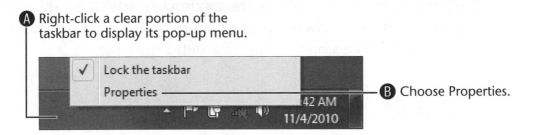

Ⓐ Right-click a clear portion of the taskbar to display its pop-up menu.

Ⓑ Choose Properties.

2. When the Taskbar and Start Menu Properties dialog box appears, follow these steps to change taskbar appearance:

Ⓐ Click the Taskbar tab.

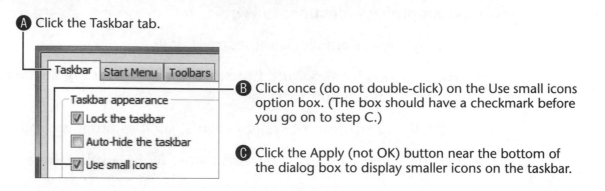

Ⓑ Click once (do not double-click) on the Use small icons option box. (The box should have a checkmark before you go on to step C.)

Ⓒ Click the Apply (not OK) button near the bottom of the dialog box to display smaller icons on the taskbar.

The icons are smaller, which enables more program buttons to be displayed on the taskbar. However, notice that the current date is no longer displayed in the Notification Area.

 TIP! The Apply button makes the changes but leaves the dialog box open. The OK button applies the changes but also closes the box.

3. Remove the checkmark in the Use Small Icons option box and click Apply again.

Notice that larger icons have been restored on the taskbar.

4. Click OK to close the dialog box.

Pinning and Unpinning Programs

Win 7 enables users to pin program buttons to the taskbar in much the same way they pin programs to the Start menu. Typically, the taskbar is set to be displayed even when windows are maximized, which means that the pinned program buttons are always available. A pinned program that is not currently open will not have a button border around the icon.

Pinned program buttons do not have
borders when the program is closed.

QUICK REFERENCE: Pinning and Unpinning Programs

Task	Procedure
Pin a program	• *Right*-click on the program button to display pop-up menu.
	• Choose Pin This Program to Taskbar.
	• The program button will remain on the taskbar even when the program is closed until it is unpinned.
Unpin a program	• *Right*-click on the program button to display pop-up menu.
	• Choose Unpin This Program from Taskbar.

HANDS-ON 2.8 **Pin and Unpin a Program**

In this exercise, you will open Notepad, pin the program button to the taskbar, and then unpin the program from the taskbar.

1. Choose Start ⊕→All Programs→Accessories→Notepad to launch the program.

2. Follow these step to pin the program to the taskbar:

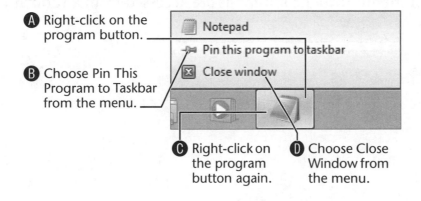

Ⓐ Right-click on the program button.

Ⓑ Choose Pin This Program to Taskbar from the menu.

Ⓒ Right-click on the program button again.

Ⓓ Choose Close Window from the menu.

The Notepad icon remains on the taskbar. Once the program is closed, it no longer has a button border around it.

3. Follow these steps to unpin the Notepad program:

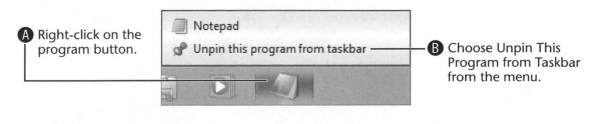

Ⓐ Right-click on the program button.

Ⓑ Choose Unpin This Program from Taskbar from the menu.

The Notepad icon is removed from the taskbar.

Using Program Commands

Within programs, commands have traditionally been accessed from a series of drop-down menus on a menu bar or command buttons on a toolbar. In 2007, Microsoft introduced the "Windows Ribbon framework" in some of its programs as a new way to display commands. Win 7's versions of WordPad and Paint found in this book both use the newer ribbon feature.

Menu Commands

Drop-down menus are featured in most Windows-based programs. Menus are lists of commands traditionally organized in a series along a menu bar under the title bar. The first menu on most menu bars is the File menu, the second is the Edit menu, and the last is the Help menu. This is part of the traditional standardization found in Windows-based programs, such as the Notepad program used in this book.

Programs that use the newer ribbon system to display commands do not have a menu bar. There is a single menu button in the upper-left corner of the ribbon that replaces the File menu. The button is usually named for the program, for example Paint menu or WordPad menu. Rather than using a series of menus, other commands are accessed from a toolbar or the ribbon.

The following illustration shows some of the similarities and differences in the File menu in Notepad and the Paint menu in Paint.

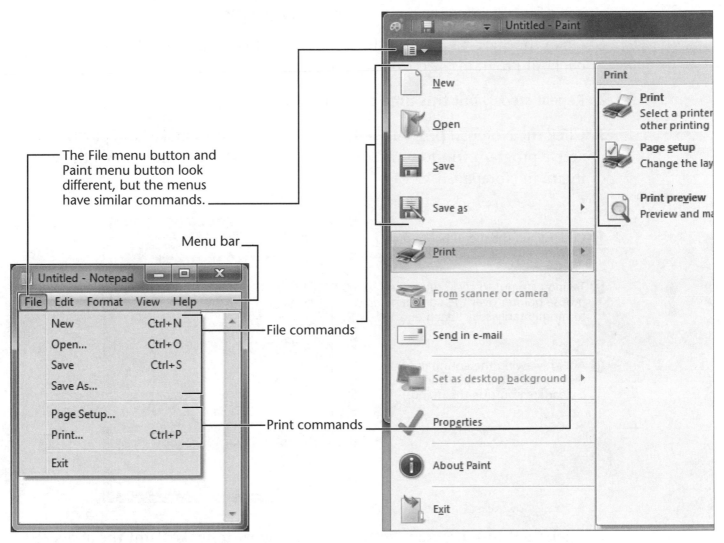

The File menu button and Paint menu button look different, but the menus have similar commands.

Menu bar

File commands

Print commands

Notepad's File menu

Paint's Paint menu

Many of the commands in Notepad's File menu are standard to most programs, including Paint. On the other hand, Paint (a picture-editing program) has commands related to drawing or picture tasks, such as From Scanner or Camera or Set as Background, that do not appear in the File menu of Notepad (a word-processing program).

 TIP! Menu commands do not always appear in the same order in different programs, and the text labels can vary.

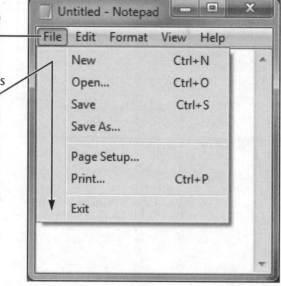

HANDS-ON 2.9 Compare Drop-Down Menus

In this exercise, you will launch Notepad and Paint. You will compare common features in the File and Paint drop-down menus in these programs.

1. Open the Start 🪟 menu. Click Notepad if it is available in the left pane or click All Programs→Accessories→Notepad.

2. Repeat step 1, but this time to launch Paint.

3. Click the Notepad program button on the taskbar to make Notepad the active program window and then follow these steps to drop down the File menu in Notepad:

Ⓐ Click File on the menu bar to drop down the menu.

Ⓑ Taking care not to click, run your mouse pointer over the commands to momentarily select each one.

Ⓒ After reviewing the commands, dismiss the menu by clicking in a clear area outside the menu.

4. Click the Paint program button on the taskbar to make Paint the active program and then repeat step 3 with the Paint menu to compare its similarities and differences to Notepad's File menu.

Notice that the menus have common features, including New, Open, Save, Save As, Page Setup, Print, and Exit.

5. Compare the Notepad's traditional Edit menu with the Home tab on Paint's new ribbon where the commands Cut, Copy, and Paste have been relocated.

6. Close [X] Notepad, but leave Paint open.

Commands in Programs with Ribbons

Two of the programs used in this book, Paint and WordPad, have incorporated ribbons. In addition to commands in the program menu discussed above, these programs have commands on a Quick Access toolbar located on the title bar and commands on the ribbon arranged with a number of tabs.

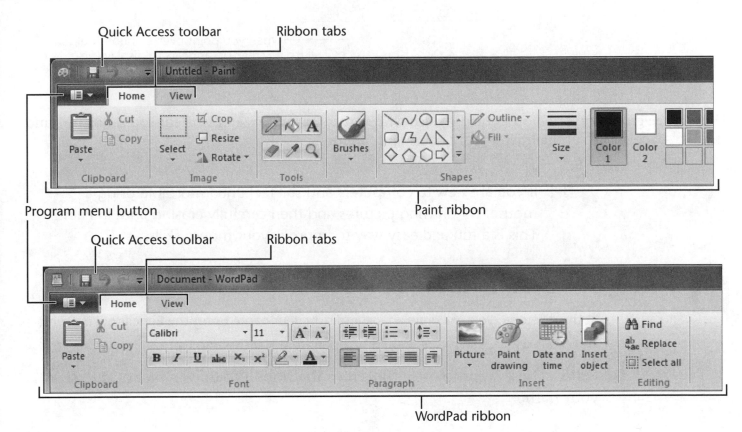

Both of these ribbons have features and some tools in common, but many tools are specific to each program's function—Paint to create and edit pictures and WordPad to create and edit text.

Quick Access Toolbar   A toolbar is used to display series of commands as small buttons or drop-down lists. Commands on a toolbar or ribbon are often referred to as "tools." The Quick Access toolbar typically has three tools displayed: Save, Undo, and Redo. These commands will be discussed later.

Ribbon Tabs   Paint and WordPad have only two ribbon tabs: Home and View. Other programs may have many more tabs.

A ribbon has many tools. Tabs on the ribbon are used to arrange tools by task. On each tab, related tools are assembled into command groups. Each command group has vertical separators and a label. Within each group tools can be displayed as buttons, drop-down lists, or galleries.

The icon for each tool attempts to indicate its purpose, but you can point over a tool to display its name and function on a ScreenTip.

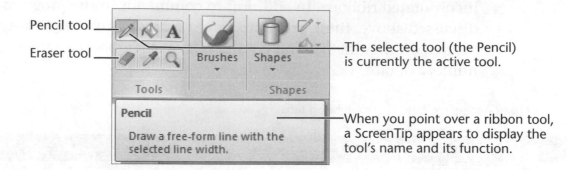

Pencil tool

Eraser tool

The selected tool (the Pencil) is currently the active tool.

Pencil

Draw a free-form line with the selected line width.

When you point over a ribbon tool, a ScreenTip appears to display the tool's name and its function.

These three groups on a ribbon tab are divided with vertical separators and labeled: Tools, Brushes, and Shapes. A ScreenTip can identify a tool's name and function.

 TIP! If you are new to computers and still feel uncomfortable using a mouse, try drawing pictures and then carefully erasing lines in Paint. This is a fun and easy way to improve your mouse skills.

HANDS-ON 2.10 Draw in the Paint Program

In this exercise, you will draw a face and sign your name using the Pencil tool in Paint.

Before You Begin: Paint should be open from Hands-On 2.9.

1. Follow these steps to use a tool from the ribbon to draw a face and to sign your name:

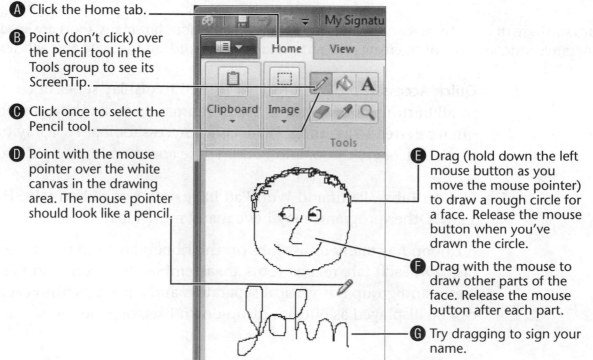

Ⓐ Click the Home tab.

Ⓑ Point (don't click) over the Pencil tool in the Tools group to see its ScreenTip.

Ⓒ Click once to select the Pencil tool.

Ⓓ Point with the mouse pointer over the white canvas in the drawing area. The mouse pointer should look like a pencil.

Ⓔ Drag (hold down the left mouse button as you move the mouse pointer) to draw a rough circle for a face. Release the mouse button when you've drawn the circle.

Ⓕ Drag with the mouse to draw other parts of the face. Release the mouse button after each part.

Ⓖ Try dragging to sign your name.

You will save your work in the next exercise.

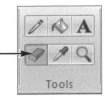

Tools

NOTE! If you don't like what you've drawn, choose the Eraser tool from the Tools group, drag to erase, and then choose the Pencil to try again.

Saving Your Work

When you type a letter or create a drawing as you did in the previous exercise, you might want to save it so you can look at it later. The computer does not save your work unless you command it to do so. This section looks at two commands used to save your work: Save and Save As.

Where Your Work Is Located

In Lesson 1, Getting Your First Look, you learned that all of the things displayed on your screen are temporarily stored on the RAM chips of the computer. The work you have done so far in Paint is only temporarily stored in RAM. If the power goes out or the computer is shut down, the information in RAM will be erased, and your work will be lost.

You must save your work on a permanent storage device such as a hard drive or a USB flash drive to keep it from being erased. See the Behind the Screen: Storage Basics section on page 94 for descriptions of storage devices.

Win 7 needs to know two things the first time you save your work:

- What do you want to call it?

- Where do you want to store it?

Files and Folders

These two basic terms, files and folders, will be covered in more detail in the next lesson but need to be defined here.

- **File**—A file is collection of data stored with a name. Examples of files are a letter you've typed and saved, a drawing in Paint that you've saved, or a picture copied from the Internet.

- **Folder**—A folder is an electronic location in which you store related groups of files. For example, My Pictures and the Pictures library are folders already created for your username in Win 7 where you can store photos and other pictures.

Choosing a Storage Location

Today's computers provide a variety of storage choices, including internal and external hard drives, CDs, DVDs, and USB flash drives. When you are ready to save, you have an opportunity to choose which storage device you want to use. And remember, if you don't choose, the computer will choose for you (using what is called a *default* setting).

On the Internal Hard Drive   When saving your work (file) for the first time, most Win 7 programs will direct you to a predetermined location (folder) on the internal hard drive. On your home computer:

• WordPad directs you to a folder named Documents library.

• Paint directs you to a folder named Pictures library.

In most computer lab settings, students save their work on USB flash drives. This makes it easy to access files on your home computer as well.

Using the predetermined location is usually appropriate for new users until they learn more about Win 7's storage system.

On a Portable USB Flash Drive   You can choose a different location from the one chosen by a program. Storing files on a USB flash drive (also called a thumb, pen, or keychain drive) has become a popular way to save files that need to be carried from one computer to another. A flash drive is a device with a USB plug attached to a storage card. The flash drive can be plugged into any USB port on a computer.

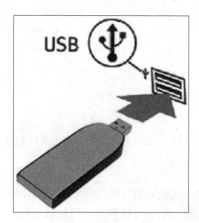

Connecting a flash drive to a computer

Storing Your Exercise Files

You can store your exercise files on various media, such as the hard drive inside your computer, a USB flash drive, or a network drive at a school or company. This lesson will show files being stored in the Documents folder on the hard drive. The Documents folder is the default storage location for Windows 7.

If you use a storage location other than the default folder, you will substitute your own location for those shown in the figures. See Storing Your Exercise Files for additional information on alternative file storage media. Storing Your Exercise Files is available on the student web page for this book at labpub.com/learn/silver/wtwc4.

Creating a Filename

Data that is stored on a storage device is called a file. It might be a text document, a picture, a song, a movie, or any other kind of data. The first time you store data, it must be given a filename. The filename must follow Win 7's naming conventions (rules).

> **!TIP!** Choose a filename that will help you recognize the file's contents months from now. A filename like Letter to Ted Edwards is more useful than Ted Letter. If possible, keep the length less than 20 characters or so to make it easier to read in various windows and dialog boxes.

 HANDS-ON 2.11 **Save a New Document**

In this exercise, you will save your Paint picture to your hard drive or USB flash drive for the first time. This will protect your work from a power failure.

Before You Begin: Paint should be open from Hands-On 2.10.

Name Your Picture

1. If necessary, click the Paint program button on the taskbar to make Paint the active program window.

2. Click the Paint menu ▦▾ button and choose Save.

   Paint opens a Save As dialog box the first time a document is saved.

Notice that Paint directs you to a Libraries folder (in this example Pictures) and has provided the temporary filename Untitled.

Pictures is the default folder chosen by Paint.

Paint also proposes an initial filename for the unsaved picture.

3. Follow the steps for your storage location to give your picture a filename:

The Pictures Folder on the Hard Drive

Ⓐ If the temporary filename is not already selected, double-click on the name to select it, and then type **My Signature**.

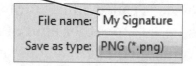

Ⓑ Click the Save button.

Paint saves your file to the hard drive. The new filename, My Signature, is displayed on the title bar.

My Signature - Paint

Skip the rest of this exercise and continue reading the Save Versus Save As section on page 62.

Your USB Flash Drive

Ⓐ Carefully place your USB flash drive into a USB port. This may be a port on the front or back of the computer, or there may be a cable you can plug the drive into. Your instructor or a classmate can help if necessary.

File name:	My Signature
Save as type:	PNG (*.png)

Ⓑ If the temporary filename is not already selected, double-click on the name to select it and then type **My Signature**.

Ⓒ Click the first drop-down list ▶ button on the Address bar. A list of storage locations drops down. Drop-down list buttons are often identified with a right-pointing arrow ▶ that, when clicked, becomes a down-pointing arrow ▼.

Ⓓ Choose Computer from the list.

Ⓔ Click the second drop-down list ▶ button.

Ⓕ Choose your USB flash drive (the drive name and drive letter probably will be different from what you see here).

Ⓖ Click the Save button or tap ⏎ Enter on the keyboard.

A copy of My Signature is saved on your flash drive. The new filename, My Signature, is displayed on the title bar.

My Signature - Paint

Save Versus Save As

The first time you save a document with the Save command, Win 7 opens a Save As dialog box to gather a filename and a storage location. After a file has been saved, choosing the Save command will save the changes without opening a dialog box because Win 7 already knows the filename and location.

The Save As command also is used to make a copy of a file in two ways:

- It lets you save an existing file with a different name (leaving the original file intact).

- It lets you save an existing file to another location (the filename can be the same or different).

 HANDS-ON 2.12 **Use Save As to Create a Copy**

In this exercise, you will create a copy of a file with a new filename using the Save As command.

Before You Begin: My Signature should be open in Paint from Hands-On 2.11.

1. Click the Paint menu ![menu button] button and choose Save As.

   > **!TIP!** In the rest of this book, program menu commands will be written like this:
   > Choose Paint menu ![menu button] →Save As.

   A Save As dialog box appears. The folder location shows where My Signature is saved, and the filename is selected and ready to be replaced.

2. Type the new filename **My Signature Copy**.

3. Click the Save button or tap ⟨Enter⟩ on the keyboard.
   A copy of My Signature is saved on the drive, and the new version is now displayed in the Paint window. The new filename, My Signature Copy, is displayed on the title bar.   `My Signature Copy - Paint`

4. Close ![X button] the Paint window. Choose Yes or Save if you are prompted to save any changes.

Using the Work Area

Up to this point, you have concentrated on features on the perimeter of program windows, such as borders, menus, and control buttons. These are the tools that help when you are working in a program. Now you will look more closely at the work area, the place where you use the tools and do the work.

Mouse Pointers

In the previous exercise, you saw that the mouse pointer looked like a pencil when the Pencil tool was active. This Win 7 feature changes the appearance of the mouse pointer when the function of the mouse pointer has changed.

QUICK REFERENCE: Using Win 7 Mouse Pointers

Mouse Pointer	Function
⏳	Normal selection pointer
I	Text selection pointer
+	Precision selection pointer
O	System busy pointer
✥	Move pointer
↕	Vertical resize pointer

Tool Galleries

Many tool groups in Paint include galleries. A gallery is a collection of tools or options. Tools in a gallery may be shown in full view or partial view or may be hidden from view as a button on the ribbon. If part of the gallery is in view, a scroll bar is provided to view other tools. If a gallery has been hidden, its gallery button will display a downward-pointing arrow. The button must be selected for its drop-down gallery to be displayed.

 TIP! Users new to a program with a ribbon will find it easier to use the ribbon if the window is maximized. Some tool groups and galleries compress to become only buttons as a window is made smaller.

Paint will remember the most recently selected choice the next time you use that tool. Also, be aware that options such as line thickness in the Size gallery can change when different tools are selected.

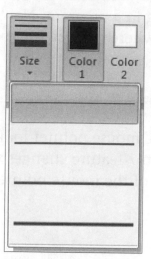

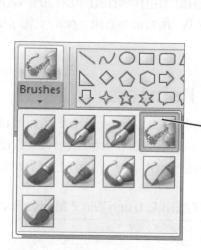

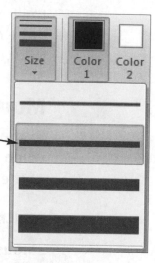

The line thickness options in the Size gallery available when Pencil is the active tool.

Airbrush is the selected tool in this drop-down Brushes gallery.

Size options are different when Airbrush has been made the active tool.

 HANDS-ON 2.13 **Change Mouse Pointers in Paint**

In this exercise, you will select different tools from the Paint program ribbon and observe appearance changes to the mouse pointer as you create a drawing.

1. Open Paint again with Start ⊞→All Programs→Accessories→Paint.

2. Maximize ▣ the window and then click the Home tab.

3. Click the buttons in the Tools group one at a time and move your mouse over the white canvas to see the mouse pointer.

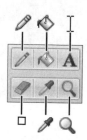

Notice the changing appearance of the mouse pointer.

4. Follow these steps to step up options for the Rectangle tool:

Ⓐ Choose the Rectangle tool from the Shapes gallery.

Ⓑ Click the Outline tool and choose the Solid Color option.

Ⓒ Click the Fill tool and choose Solid Color.

Ⓓ Click the Color 2 tool and choose Gray-25% from the color palette.

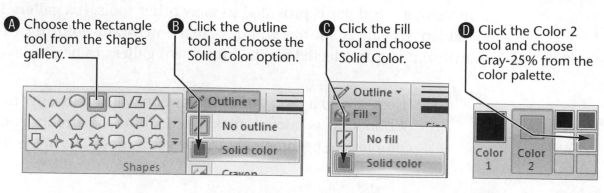

5. Point near the top of the drawing area and then drag down and to the right to make a box, as shown below.

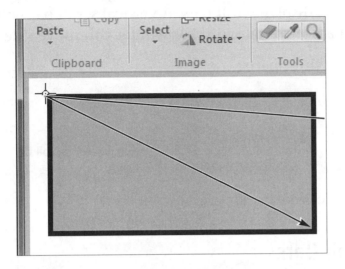

The line color is determined by the Color 1 choice; the fill color is determined by the Color 2 choice.

6. Follow these steps to set up and use the Eraser tool:

Ⓐ Choose the Eraser tool. Ⓑ Pick any size for the eraser from Size gallery.

Ⓒ Click Color 2 and choose white as the background color.

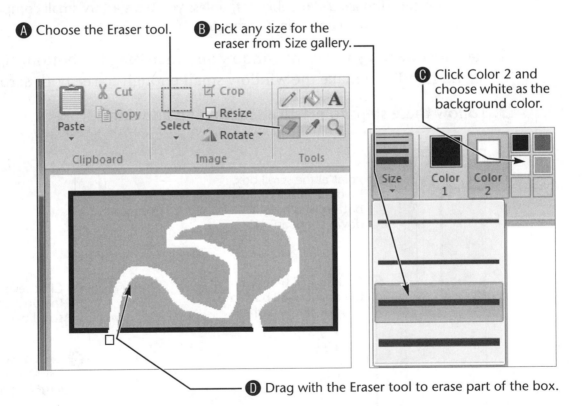

Ⓓ Drag with the Eraser tool to erase part of the box.

Notice that the mouse pointer changes to reflect the size and color of the Eraser. The Eraser tool does not actually erase; rather, it paints the Color 2 choice.

Scroll Bars

When part of your picture or content is too large be seen in the program window, Win 7 will display scroll bars. A vertical scroll bar will let you move up or down, and a horizontal scroll bar will let you move side to side.

Each scroll bar has three parts:

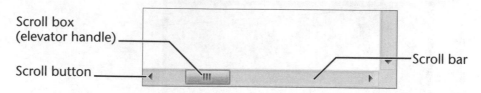

Scroll box
(elevator handle)

Scroll button

Scroll bar

Horizontal and vertical scroll bars

HANDS-ON 2.14 Use Scroll Bars

In this exercise, you will resize the Paint window and use the vertical and horizontal scroll bars.

1. If necessary, maximize 🔲 the Paint window.

   Are scroll bars displayed? Probably not, unless you have a very small computer screen (which isn't likely on a new Win 7 computer).

2. Restore down 🔲 the Paint window and then drag the bottom-right corner sizing handle to make the window small enough to see both scroll bars.

3. Follow these steps to practice scrolling up and down:

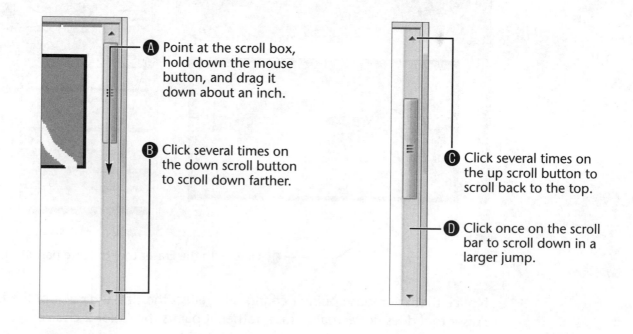

A Point at the scroll box, hold down the mouse button, and drag it down about an inch.

B Click several times on the down scroll button to scroll down farther.

C Click several times on the up scroll button to scroll back to the top.

D Click once on the scroll bar to scroll down in a larger jump.

4. Try using parts of the horizontal scroll bar to scroll from side to side.

5. Close ▬X▬ the Paint program. Choose Don't Save if you are prompted to save any changes.

Typing with WordPad

WordPad is a basic word processing program included with Win 7 that is used to type letters and other simple documents. Although it is a basic program, it makes an excellent learning program because it has many features common to other applications.

WordPad Ribbon

Like the Paint program, the Win 7 version of WordPad now uses a ribbon instead of the traditional system of a menu bar and toolbars. Many of the features used in WordPad ribbon are like those found in Microsoft Word 2007 and 2010.

Tabs The WordPad ribbon has two tabs: Home and View. On each tab, tools with a related function are assembled into command groups, which are further divided with vertical separators and labeled.

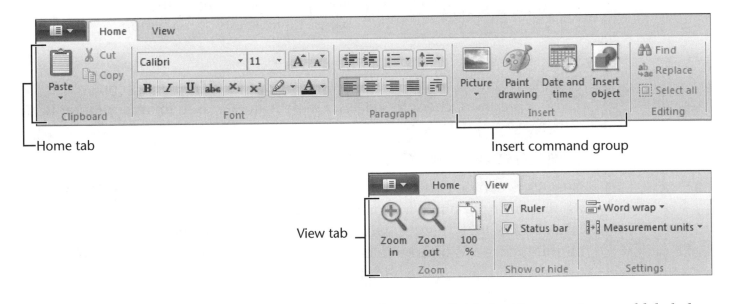

Related tools on each tab are assembled into command groups, divided with separators, and labeled.

Drop-Down Lists WordPad has several drop-down lists on the Home tab. Three frequently used drop-down lists are located in the Font group: Font family, Font size, and Font color. The purpose of a drop-down list is to offer other choices. A button with a down-pointing arrow is provided to view the choices. Some drop-down lists (such as Font family) are quite long and include a scroll bar.

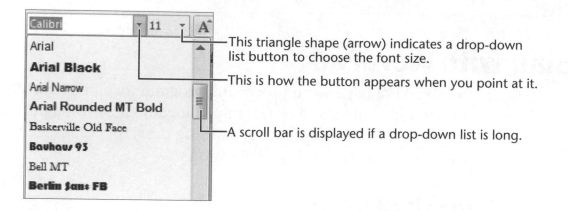

This triangle shape (arrow) indicates a drop-down list button to choose the font size.

This is how the button appears when you point at it.

A scroll bar is displayed if a drop-down list is long.

ScreenTips   Just as you saw with Paint, WordPad's ScreenTips help you determine the function of tools or drop-down lists on the ribbon. When you rest your mouse pointer over a tool or drop-down list, a ScreenTip will appear with its name and a brief description.

A ScreenTip with a name and brief description appears when the mouse pointer rests over a button.

!TIP!   When you discover a useful feature such as ScreenTips in one program, check to see if the same feature is used in other programs.

The Cursor and the Mouse Pointer

New users can be confused in word-processing programs such as WordPad by what appear to be two cursors: One is the blinking *cursor* in the text and the other is the *mouse pointer* (which can be most anywhere you point). The blinking cursor is often also called the *insertion point*. When you type, the text goes in front of the blinking cursor.

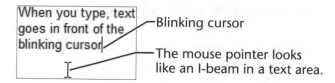

Blinking cursor

The mouse pointer looks like an I-beam in a text area.

The blinking cursor is located at the top of the white writing area when WordPad is first opened. This white writing area is equivalent to a sheet of paper.

 TIP! Most of the word-processing skills learned in this lesson can be used to type email and in most other word-processing programs.

Special Keys on the Keyboard

Computer keyboards are more complex than those of typewriters. Some keys on the keyboard of a computer have special functions and are not found on any typewriter.

Backspace and Delete Keys On a typewriter, backspace is used to move backward through the text. The ⌱Backspace⌱ key on a computer keyboard erases text to the left of the cursor. The ⌱Delete⌱ key erases text to the right of the cursor.

The ⌱Backspace⌱ key erases text to the left of the cursor.

The ⌱Delete⌱ key erases text to the right of the cursor.

Tab Key The ⌱Tab⌱ key is similar to the tab key on a typewriter. It moves the cursor right to the next half-inch mark on the ruler. This is a useful key for creating accurately aligned columns.

Enter Key The ⌱Enter⌱ key has two functions: It ends a paragraph and moves any text below or to the right of the cursor down one line.

HANDS-ON 2.15 Practice Basic Typing in WordPad

In this exercise, you will do basic typing using the [Tab], [Spacebar], and [Enter] keys; correct mistakes using the [Backspace] and [Delete] keys; and move around using the [Home], [End], and arrow keys.

1. Open WordPad with Start ⊞ →All Programs→Accessories→WordPad.

2. Type the following:

    To: [Tab] Ted [Spacebar] Edwards [Enter]
    From: [Tab] Margo [Spacebar] Collie [Enter]
    [Enter]
    Dear [Spacebar] Ted,

    Notice that using the [Tab] key aligns the both first names to the half-inch mark on the ruler. The [Spacebar] puts a space between words. When [Enter] is typed once, it ends a paragraph and moves the cursor down to a new line. When the [Enter] key is typed twice in succession, the second [Enter] creates a blank line and moves the cursor down to a second new line.

3. Tap [Enter] twice.

    This creates two new lines.

4. Type the following:

    If I type a sentence that is too long to fit on
    one line, I do not have to tap the Enter key when
    I get near the margin because the words will
    automatically wrap to a new line. [Enter]
    [Enter]
    Typing is fun.

    Most email and word-processing programs will automatically wrap text.
    It is necessary to tap [Enter] only when you want to end a paragraph and force text to start on a new line.

Save Your Work

When you finish a significant piece of work on a document, it's always a good idea to save it.

5. Choose WordPad menu→Save to save the document.

WordPad displays the Save As dialog box. The temporary name, *Document,* is selected and ready to be replaced.

6. Type a new filename: **Memo to Ted Edwards**

7. Follow the appropriate steps to store the file on the USB flash drive:

Ⓐ Click the drop-down list button and choose Computer.

Ⓑ Click the second drop-down list button and choose your USB flash drive.

Ⓒ Click the Save button or tap Enter on the keyboard.

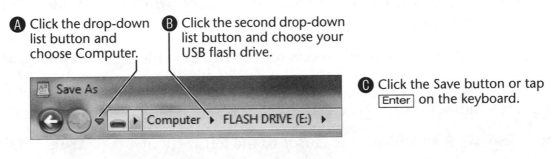

WordPad saves your letter to the USB flash drive. You may see a small light flash on the drive, indicating that Win 7 is working on a file there. Notice that the name of the file now appears in the top-left corner of the title bar.

Memo to Ted Edwards - WordPad

8. Close ▮ x ▮ WordPad.

Concepts Review

All of the Concepts Review quizzes for this book are available on the student web page. Your instructor will let you know how to complete the quizzes (in the book or online).

True/False Questions

Page number

1. Program commands are automatically added to the Start menu when programs are installed on the computer. **true   false** _____

2. Program commands in the Start menu are like light switches to launch programs. **true   false** _____

3. A Jump List can provide quick access to recently used files. **true   false** _____

4. If you open three programs, you will have three active program windows. **true   false** _____

5. The `Backspace` key moves the cursor to the left without erasing text. **true   false** _____

6. When typing text, new text goes in front of the I-beam mouse pointer and not in front of the blinking cursor. **true   false** _____

Multiple Choice Questions

7. Which is not a quick sizing button?
   Page number: _____
   a. ▣
   b. ▣
   c. ▶
   d. ✕

8. The feature on the side and bottom of a program window that lets you navigate through the document is called a(n) _____.
   Page number: _____.
   a. elevator bar
   b. scroll bar
   c. zoom bar
   d. view bar

9. How can you tell if a program is active?
   Page number: _____
   a. The window will be the biggest.
   b. Its name is grayed out in the title bar.
   c. Its program button will look brighter on the Win 7 taskbar.
   d. All of the above

10. What happens if a program command is in the pinned program area of the Start menu?
    Page number: _____
    a. It stays until the computer is shut down.
    b. The program command is locked until it is unpinned.
    c. The program launches when the computer is started.
    d. It stays there until it is unpinned.

Skill Builders

SKILL BUILDER 2.1 Pin and Unpin Programs

In this exercise, you will pin two commands to the Start menu and use the commands to launch both programs. Finally, you will unpin the commands from the Start menu.

Add Two Programs to the Pinned List

1. Choose Start 🪟 →All Programs→Accessories.

2. Right-click the WordPad and Paint items to pin these commands to the pinned programs area of the Start menu.

3. Click the Back command to close All Programs as shown at right.

   The Back command closes the All Programs folder, so you can view the recently used and pinned programs lists. Notice that the newly pinned programs are on the pinned list.

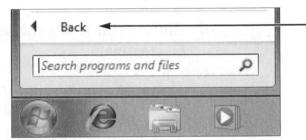

Launch Pinned Programs

4. Click WordPad to launch the program.

5. Launch Paint using Start 🪟 →Paint.

   Leave the programs open on the Desktop for the next exercise.

Remove the New Commands

6. Open the Start 🪟 menu.

7. Right-click WordPad and Paint and unpin them from the pinned list.

8. Close [X] the Paint and WordPad programs.

Try This At Home

Create a Map

In this exercise, you will create a map in Paint and save it to your hard drive.

1. Open Paint (Start→All Programs→Accessories→Paint).

2. Maximize 🔲 the Paint window.

3. Choose View tab→Rulers if rulers are not displayed.

   Rulers in Paint are marked in pixels (px) because digital pictures are made up of pixels.

Make a Map

4. Choose Home tab and use the following steps to create a small map (you can be creative):

   ⚠️**TIP!** As you try these tools, *you will make mistakes*. Remember to immediately use Undo on the Quick Access toolbar to undo the mistake. You may want to use ⌨Ctrl + ⌨Z from the keyboard to undo (hold down ⌨Ctrl and tap ⌨Z). 🔄 Undo

A Choose Shapes→Rectangle. Set options: Outline→Solid, Fill→No Fill, Size→Thinnest.

C Choose Brushes→Brush. Set option: Size→Thickest.

 E Choose Shapes→Line. Set option: Size→Thinnest.

 G Choose Tools→Pencil. Set option: Size→Thinnest.

I Choose Shapes→Rectangle. Set options: Outline→Solid, Fill→Solid, Color 2→ Gray 25%.

B Drag a small map area about 300px by 300px from the upper-left corner of the canvas.

D Draw the highway.

F Draw three lines for roads and train track.

H Draw rail ties.

J Draw the house.

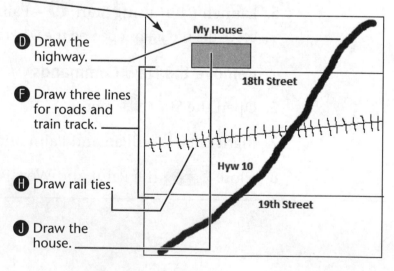

5. Follow these steps to add text to the map:

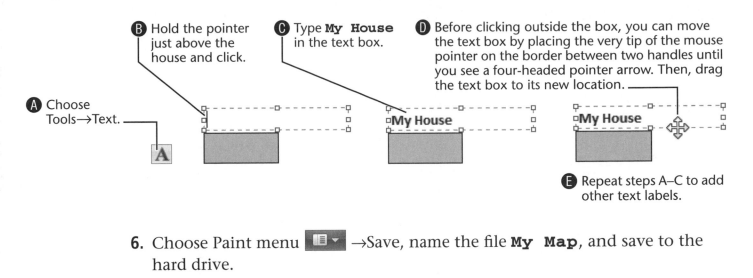

B Hold the pointer just above the house and click.

C Type **My House** in the text box.

D Before clicking outside the box, you can move the text box by placing the very tip of the mouse pointer on the border between two handles until you see a four-headed pointer arrow. Then, drag the text box to its new location.

A Choose Tools→Text.

E Repeat steps A–C to add other text labels.

6. Choose Paint menu 〈menu icon〉 →Save, name the file **My Map**, and save to the hard drive.

7. Close 〈X button〉 the Paint window.

Using a Word Processor

In this lesson, you will learn the basics of Word 2007 and Word 2010. First, you will work with Word's dramatically new Ribbon interface. Then you will type letters and learn to save your documents. You will edit text you've typed and use the Copy and Paste commands to create a second letter without retyping. You will work with printing features including Print Preview, which allows you to see how a printed document will look before you actually print it. You will use AutoCorrect, which corrects many commonly misspelled words and typographical errors automatically as you type, and Word's user-friendly Spell Check feature.

LESSON OBJECTIVES

After studying this lesson, you will be able to:

- Create a new document using Word
- Edit a document by inserting and deleting text
- Use the Copy and Paste commands
- Identify key parts of the Word Ribbon interface
- Print documents
- Work with Word's Spell Check and AutoCorrect features

Additional learning resources are available at labpub.com/learn/silver/wtwc4/

Case Study: Researching a Family History

Suzanne is writing a family history and decides to begin by sending letters to family members to gather information. The task provides a perfect opportunity to use some of Word's tools that make writing easier. Using AutoComplete to insert the date in her letters is a perfect example of one of those tools.

July 20, 2010 (Press ENTER to Insert)

July

July 20, 2010

Dear Uncle Charlie and Aunt Dorothy,

I am writing our family history, and I would like to ask you some questions about your part of the family. Would you please provide the following information for each family member?

- Date of birth
- Place born
- When and where married
- Children's names
- Names of children's spouses

Using the Spell Check feature helps Suzanne ensure that her letters are error-free.

Calibri (Bo 11

B I ≡ aby A

Dogg

Dog
Doggy
Dug
Dogs
Ignore
Ignore All
Add to Dictionary

Defining Word Processors

Microsoft Office Word 2007 and Word 2010 are word processing application programs. (From this point forward, both versions will be referred to simply as "Word" unless there is a need to refer to a specific version.) As in all word processing programs, you use Word to electronically create and edit text. After creating a document, you can easily make editing changes. You can also make big changes, such as adding or deleting a couple of paragraphs in the middle of a page. When you do, the existing text moves out of the way to make room for new text or collapses to close the gap when you delete text.

Word is great for formatting text, and it also provides special features such as Spell Check and even an AutoCorrect feature that corrects many of your mistakes for you.

Starting Word

You start Word from the Start ![start button] button as you would any other Windows program. The following figure shows various locations from which you can start the Word program. You can also "pin" Word to the Start menu or Win7 taskbar, making access even easier.

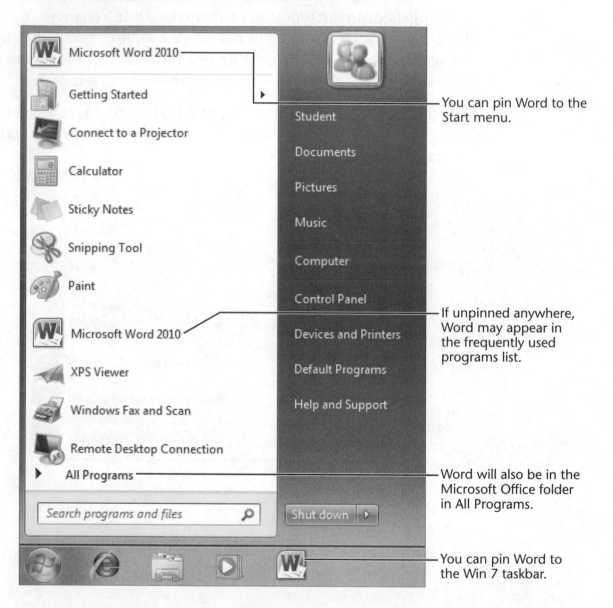

You can pin Word to the Start menu.

If unpinned anywhere, Word may appear in the frequently used programs list.

Word will also be in the Microsoft Office folder in All Programs.

You can pin Word to the Win 7 taskbar.

HANDS-ON 3.1 **Start Word**

In this exercise, you will use the Start button on the taskbar to start Word.

1. If necessary, start your computer.

   The Windows Desktop appears.

2. Follow these steps to start Word 2007 or Word 2010:

   > **⚠ NOTE!** The location of items on the menus will likely vary from one computer to another so the following figures may not match the menus on your computer.

   Substitute Word 2007 for Word 2010 in the figures if you are using that version.

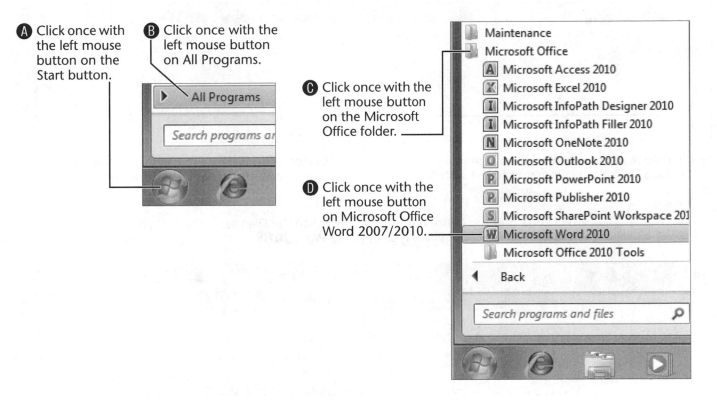

Ⓐ Click once with the left mouse button on the Start button.

Ⓑ Click once with the left mouse button on All Programs.

Ⓒ Click once with the left mouse button on the Microsoft Office folder.

Ⓓ Click once with the left mouse button on Microsoft Office Word 2007/2010.

There is a pause as the Word program starts. The Word window may or may not fill the screen, so with your next command you will maximize the Word window.

3. If necessary, click the Maximize 🔲 button in the upper-right corner of the Word window.

   Word's Ribbon at the top of the window looks like a very large toolbar. The next topic will describe how the Ribbon works to help you issue commands.

Introducing the Word Window

The document window is where you type information into Word. It allows you to access Word commands via the Ribbon and the Quick Access toolbar.

File menu—This button leads to file management tasks, including opening, printing, and saving your work.

Quick Access toolbar— Frequently used commands appear here, and you can add your own favorites.

Title bar—The name of your document appears here. You see a generic Documentx name until you save and name your document.

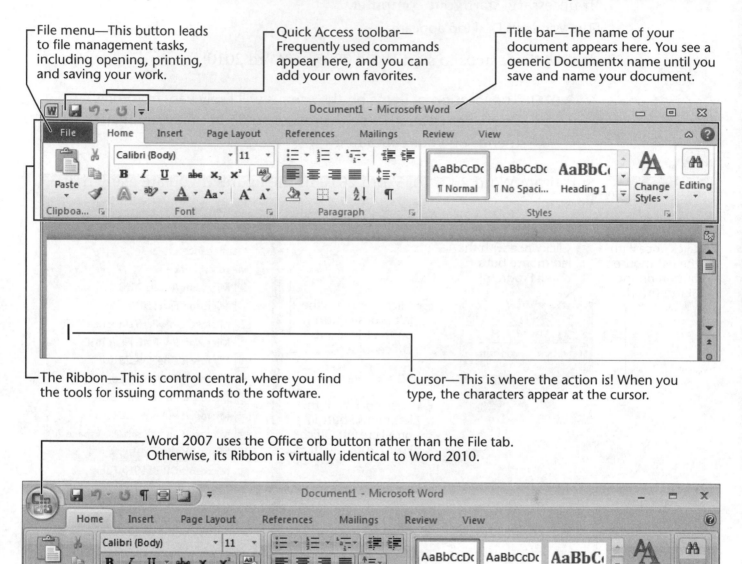

The Ribbon—This is control central, where you find the tools for issuing commands to the software.

Cursor—This is where the action is! When you type, the characters appear at the cursor.

Word 2007 uses the Office orb button rather than the File tab. Otherwise, its Ribbon is virtually identical to Word 2010.

About Application Programs

Computer program software can be broken down into two primary types that are useful for beginners to understand:

- **Operating System**—This is software that controls your computer. Windows 7 and 8 are examples of operating systems. Examples of other operating systems used with desktop and notebook computers include Linux and Macintosh System X.

- **Application Programs**—This is software you use to get work done and is described in more detail below.

Application Programs   An application program is software designed to help you get something done. Word and WordPad are examples of programs for writing. PowerPoint is an example of a presentation program that allows you to create lively multimedia presentations. Spreadsheet programs, such as Excel, help you work with lists and numbers.

Help for the Homeless
2014 Budget Summary

	Q1	Q2	Q3	Q4	Totals
Mortgage & Insurance	11,337	11,337	11,337	11,337	45,348
Utilities	2,021	1,464	1,504	1,809	6,798
Food	5,480	4,512	3,452	5,437	18,881
Staff Salaries	17,685	17,685	17,685	17,685	70,740
Maintenance & Repairs	2,188	3,113	3,928	3,392	12,621
Outreach & Fundraising	820	2,006	576	712	4,114
Grand Totals	39,531	40,117	38,482	40,372	158,502

Excel is an example of an application program that helps you work with numbers and perform calculations.

Application Program Suites   Office 2010/2013 are suites of application programs that perform a variety of tasks well. A suite consists of several programs usually sold together as one package, which is less expensive than buying them individually. Word, Excel, and PowerPoint are part of the Office 2010/2013 suites.

More About the Ribbon

As you learned in Lesson 2, Starting Programs, the band running across the top of the screen is the Ribbon. This is where you will find the commands you need to build, format, and edit your documents. The Ribbon is essentially equivalent to the menu bar you may have used with other programs. The Ribbon functions like a visual menu bar.

The Ribbon consists of three primary areas: tabs, command groups, and commands. The tabs include Home, Insert, Page Layout, and so on. A group contains related commands within a tab. Groups on the Home tab, for instance, include Clipboard, Font, Paragraph, Styles, and Editing. An example of a command in the Font group is Bold.

NOTE! Unless there is a difference in the way the two versions of Word work, this book uses figures from Word 2010. Whenever there is a significant difference between the two programs, you will see figures from both Word 2007 and Word 2010.

Be aware that the arrangement of the buttons on the Ribbon can vary, depending on your screen resolution and how the Word window is sized. Following are two examples of how the Paragraph group might appear on the Ribbon.

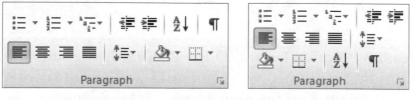

The width of the Word window can alter the display of buttons on the Ribbon.

The Quick Access Toolbar

The Quick Access toolbar in the upper-left corner of the screen contains frequently used commands. It operates independently from the Ribbon. Word lets you add new commands to the Quick Access Toolbar.

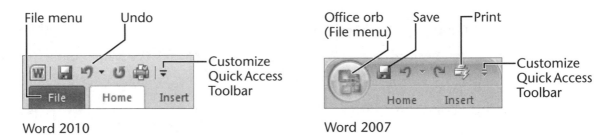

Word 2010   Word 2007

The Mini Toolbar

There's another toolbar in Word, and it contains frequently used formatting commands. When you select (highlight) text, the Mini toolbar fades in. After a pause, it fades away. If you choose to go on and learn more about formatting in Word, you will likely use the Mini toolbar then.

In the following example, the Mini toolbar appears when you select text.

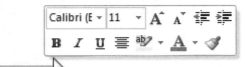

 HANDS-ON 3.2 **Use the Ribbon and Observe the Mini Toolbar**

In this exercise, you will explore the various tabs and groups on the Ribbon.

Display the Ribbon Tabs

1. Click once with the left mouse button on the Insert tab on the Ribbon (to the right of the Home tab), as shown.

   The commands available on the Insert tab are now visible.

Notice the Pages, Tables, and Illustrations groups on the Insert tab.

2. Click once with the left mouse button on the Page Layout tab.

This tab on the Ribbon displays commands for arranging text on the page.

3. Feel free to examine other tabs on the Ribbon.

4. Click once with the left mouse button on the Home tab.

Observe the Mini Toolbar

You need to select text in order to be able to see the Mini toolbar. Next you will type your name and then select it.

5. Type your name.

6. Follow these steps to select your name:

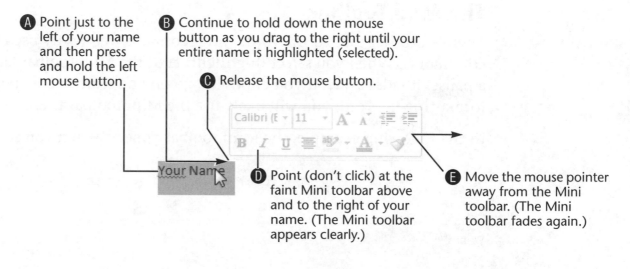

Ⓐ Point just to the left of your name and then press and hold the left mouse button.

Ⓑ Continue to hold down the mouse button as you drag to the right until your entire name is highlighted (selected).

Ⓒ Release the mouse button.

Ⓓ Point (don't click) at the faint Mini toolbar above and to the right of your name. (The Mini toolbar appears clearly.)

Ⓔ Move the mouse pointer away from the Mini toolbar. (The Mini toolbar fades again.)

7. Keep your name selected and tap the Delete key to delete your name.

Typing Text in Word

Just as you saw with WordPad, Word inserts whatever you type at the flashing cursor. As you type, the cursor moves along in front of the text.

AutoComplete

AutoComplete can do some of your typing for you. It recognizes certain words and phrases, such as names of months and days of the week, and offers to complete them for you. You accept a phrase that AutoComplete proposes by tapping Enter.

September (Press ENTER to Insert)
Sept

Word is offering to finish typing the word September.

Using AutoComplete to Insert the Current Date   If you are typing a month with a long name, type until you complete the name of the month, and Word will offer to enter the entire current date.

> July 20, 2010 (Press ENTER to Insert)
> July|

If you are typing a month with a short name, such as June, Word won't offer to complete the month, but when you finish typing the month, Word will offer to enter the complete current date.

You will use AutoComplete to enter the month into a letter.

HANDS-ON 3.3 Use AutoComplete

In this exercise, you will allow AutoComplete to help you type the current date.

!NOTE!   When typing the names of months, AutoComplete does not prompt for months with short names, such as May, June, and July. If you want to insert the current date, type the *complete* month name and AutoComplete will prompt for the complete current date.

1. Type the current month's complete name followed by a space.
   The AutoComplete tip appears suggesting the complete current date.

2. Tap Enter to accept the date.

!TIP!   If you make a typographical error (typo), use the Backspace key (deletes characters to the left of the cursor) or the Delete key (deletes characters to the right of the cursor) to delete it and then continue typing.

Leave the document open as you will continue to use it throughout the lesson.

The Enter Key and Word Wrap

As you learned with WordPad, you tap the Enter key when you have a short line that must remain short. The greeting line in a letter is a good example. It consists of a short line.

Dear Uncle Charlie and Aunt Dorothy, Enter

You can also use the Enter key whenever you need to create blank lines, such as between paragraphs.

When Not to Use the Enter Key   When you type along a line and reach the right-hand margin, Word automatically wraps down to the next line. You *should not* tap the Enter key at the end of lines *within* a paragraph. If you do, it can make your life very difficult when it is time to make editing changes. Just let it wrap!

 TIP! As you complete the exercises in this lesson, the text on your screen may not begin a new line at the same location the pictures show. Don't be concerned; just let the text wrap at the end of the lines and use Enter at the locations indicated.

Line Spacing

Word 2007and 2010 introduce new default line spacing. Rather than a default of single spacing, which has been the standard for word processors from the beginning, Word now uses 1.15 line spacing. This additional space can make your documents easier to read. The new spacing also includes some extra space at the end of paragraphs. This makes it easy to see the start of new paragraphs without having to indent the first line.

Removing the Additional Spacing ‡≡ Word 2007 and 2010 introduce a Line Spacing command to the Ribbon. It allows you to change the line spacing within a paragraph and to remove or restore additional spacing above/below the paragraph.

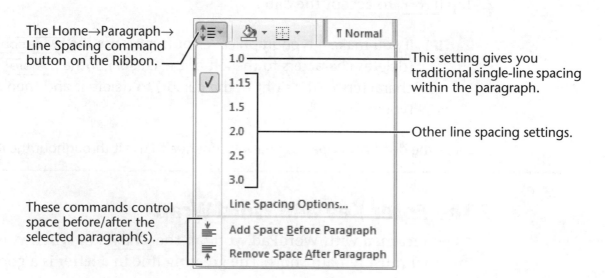

The Home→Paragraph→ Line Spacing command button on the Ribbon.

This setting gives you traditional single-line spacing within the paragraph.

Other line spacing settings.

These commands control space before/after the selected paragraph(s).

Use the Enter Key and Word Wrap

In this exercise, you will use the Enter key to force the greeting line to remain a short line. Then you will let Word Wrap take care of the line endings in the first paragraph of the letter.

1. Tap Enter twice, following the date, to add space before the greeting line.

    Word inserts a fresh line each time you tap the Enter key.

2. Type the following greeting line: **Dear Uncle Charlie and Aunt Dorothy,**

3. Now tap Enter to keep the salutation line short and to add white space before the body of the letter.

4. Type the first paragraph as shown, but don't tap Enter when you reach the right margin.

    Don't be concerned if your line width is not the same as that shown here. Word Wrap will take care of the line endings.

    I am writing our family history, and I would like to ask you some questions about your part of the family. Would you please provide the following information for each family member?

Nonprinting Characters

The Show/Hide ¶ button on the Ribbon displays nonprinting characters. Word has a number of nonprinting characters that are not visible unless you turn on the feature. They do not appear on the printed page even when the characters appear on the screen.

The Enter, Spacebar, Tab, and Shift+Enter keys create nonprinting characters. Being able to see these characters can help you make sure the spacing is correct in your document.

Dear·Uncle·Charlie·and·Aunt·Dorothy,¶ ——— Paragraph symbols are the nonprinting characters that appear when you tap Enter.

I·am·writing·our·family·history,·and·I·would·like·to·a

Would·you·please·provide·the·following·informatio ——— Small dots between words represent spaces.

•→ Date·of·birth¶

•↳ Place·born¶ ——— The Tab key generates these arrow symbols. Here, they separate bullets from the list (see the next topic).

•→ When·and·where·married¶

An example of nonprinting characters displayed by the Show/Hide button

Bullets

Word processors make it easy to create a bulleted list. Bullets automatically indent each line and place a small dot at the beginning. Bullets are a great way to visually convey that the lines are part of a list. When you use bullets, Word automatically eliminates the extra space between the lines. (You can switch off this setting if you wish, but it usually works better to keep it on.)

- Date of birth
- Place born
- When and where married
- Children's names
- Names of children's spouses

Bullets visually indicate a list.

QUICK REFERENCE: Using Bullets and Line Space Settings

Task	Procedure
Make a bulleted list	• Tap $\boxed{\text{Enter}}$ to start the first line of the bulleted list. • Choose Home→Paragraph→Bullets ⊞ from the Ribbon. • Type to the end of the list, tapping $\boxed{\text{Enter}}$ at the end of each item. • At the end of the list, tap $\boxed{\text{Enter}}$ to add a new line. • Choose Home→Paragraph→Bullets ⊞ from the Ribbon again to switch off bullets.
Adjust the line spacing	• Click inside the paragraph you wish to adjust the spacing for. • Choose Home→Paragraph→Line Spacing ⬍≣ from the Ribbon and make the desired setting.

HANDS-ON 3.5 Finish the Letter

In this exercise, you will complete the letter and practice using the [Enter] key while allowing the Word Wrap feature to do its job. You will use the bullets command to create a list, and you will also display nonprinting characters.

1. Follow these steps to turn on the display of nonprinting characters:

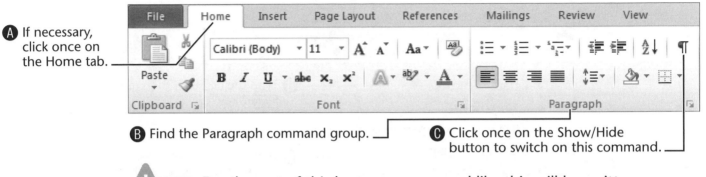

Ⓐ If necessary, click once on the Home tab.

Ⓑ Find the Paragraph command group.

Ⓒ Click once on the Show/Hide button to switch on this command.

NOTE! For the rest of this lesson, a command like this will be written as: Choose Home→Paragraph→Show/Hide ¶ from the Ribbon.

Word displays the hidden, nonprinting space and paragraph characters. You will see new nonprinting characters appear as you continue to type.

2. Click once at the end of the paragraph you typed in the previous exercise and tap the [Enter] key.

I·am·writing·our·family·history,·and·I·would·like·to·ask·you·some·questions· about·your·part·of·the·family.·Would·you·please·provide·the·following· information·for·each·family·member?¶ ←

Word starts a new line below the paragraph.

Create a Bulleted List

3. Follow these steps to create a bulleted list:

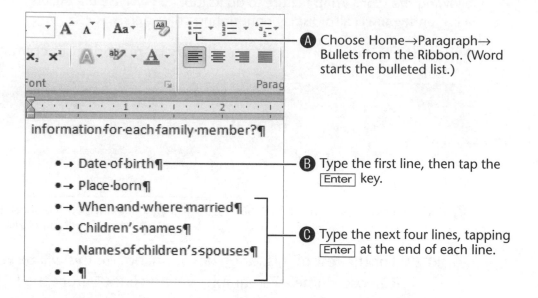

A Choose Home→Paragraph→ Bullets from the Ribbon. (Word starts the bulleted list.)

B Type the first line, then tap the [Enter] key.

C Type the next four lines, tapping [Enter] at the end of each line.

Word creates the neatly formatted list. There is an empty bullet at the bottom of the list, but this will disappear when you switch off bullets in the next step.

4. Choose Home→Paragraph→Bullets :≡ from the Ribbon.

The bullet on the last line disappears. Word also automatically adds spacing between the end of the list and the new paragraph.

Finish Typing the Letter

5. Taking care only to tap the [Enter] key at the end of a paragraph or short line, type the end of the letter.

> Would·you·also·let·me·know·if·you·are·aware·of·any·extraordinary·
> accomplishments·or·events·in·the·lives·of·any·of·your·family·members?¶
>
> Sincerely,·¶
>
> ¶
>
> Your·niece·Suzanne¶

6. Choose Home→Paragraph→Show/Hide ¶ from the Ribbon.

Word switches off display of the nonprinting characters.

Feel free to turn the nonprinting characters feature on and off as you wish during this lesson.

Saving a Document for the First Time

As you use an application program, your work is placed in the computer's RAM (which you learned about in the previous lesson) and reflected on the screen. However, RAM is erased when the power is switched off or the system is restarted. This is why you must save your work as a file to a storage device (such as a hard drive or a USB flash drive) if you wish to permanently record it. See the Behind the Screen: Storage Basics section on page 94 for a description of these devices.

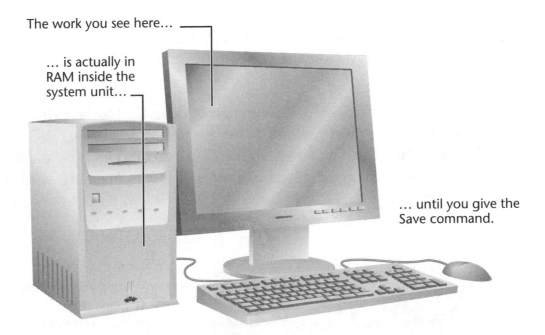

The work you see here...

... is actually in RAM inside the system unit...

... until you give the Save command.

File Defined

A file contains data that has been saved and given a name. In a moment, you will save your letter, and it will become a user data file on the hard drive of your computer. Files on your computer can contain word processing documents, digital photographs, music, checking account data, and many other types of information.

Storage Basics

Your computer stores files in a variety of locations. This topic describes the most common storage locations and technologies.

Disk Drive   The primary storage of your computer is a drive, which holds the programs and files you work with. Increasingly, these drives are *solid state drives* (SSDs), which use flash drive technology to store files without any moving parts. SSDs process data very quickly, and are also very expensive considering they have the same amount of storage space as a traditional hard drive.

Vendors are starting to develop *fusion,* or hybrid, drives that store some files on an SSD and the rest on a traditional hard drive. These combine the speed of an SSD with the higher storage capacity of a hard drive. With a fusion drive, your programs run off of the very fast SSD, while your documents, photos, music and videos reside on the less expensive, traditional hard-drive space.

Photo courtesy of Micron Technology, Inc.

A solid state drive (SSD) has no moving parts. It's small and requires much less power compared to a traditional mechanical hard drive.

Cloud Drive   A *cloud drive* stores your files somewhere on the Internet. The files are available whenever you have an Internet connection. The physical location of the files doesn't really matter. In reality, cloud drives exist in huge warehouse-sized facilities in various locations around the world. Examples of cloud drives include Dropbox, Google Drive, and Microsoft SkyDrive. One benefit of a cloud drive is that you can access your files from any computer, not just your personal computer, notebook, smartphone, or tablet. Some cloud drive services synchronize your files among your various devices.

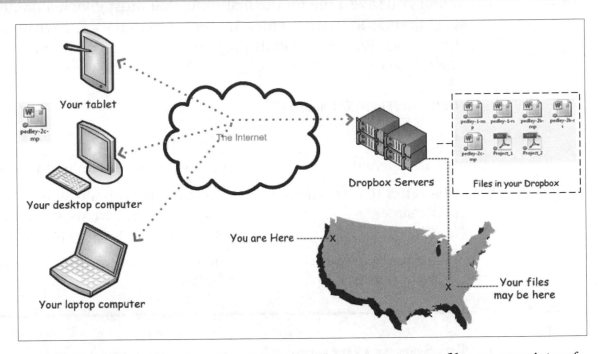

A cloud drive service such as Dropbox can offer access to your files on a variety of devices from any location with an Internet connection.

USB Flash Drive   A flash drive (also called a thumb or pen drive) stores your files on chips inside a small housing. Flash drives are a very handy way to transport files. They are also quite easy to lose. So make a habit of backing up your flash drive regularly.

Optical Drive   Fewer and fewer computers include an optical drive that can read Blu-ray Discs, DVDs, and CDs. These drives use a laser to read data (such as movies or photos) stored on a plastic disc. If your computer doesn't include an optical drive, it's easy to add an external one, connected via a USB or Thunderbolt port.

Naming Files

When you save a file for the first time, you must give it a name. Windows has specific rules for naming files. If you try to name a file without following these rules, Windows will display an error message and ask you to try again. The following Quick Reference table lists the rules for naming files.

QUICK REFERENCE: Naming Files

Rule	Description
Filename length	A file name can contain up to 255 characters.
Characters that are allowed in filenames	A filename may contain alphabetic characters, numbers, spaces, periods, commas, semicolons, dashes, apostrophes, and parentheses.
Characters that are not allowed in filenames	A filename *cannot* contain the following characters: \ / : * ? " < >	

Saving a Document

In Word, you can save a document to a file by issuing one of two commands: Save or Save As. The first time you save a document, Word automatically starts the Save As command and allows you to give the document a name. After that, when you make modifications to a document, you use the Save command to update the file. In the next exercise, you will see how easy it is to store your work for future use.

The Save As Command

In addition to using the Save As command the first time you save a document, the Save As command is also used:

- When you want to save an existing document under a different name (this makes a copy of the document).

- When you want to save an existing document in a different location (the same name or a different name).

![mouse icon] **HANDS-ON 3.6 Save the Letter**

In this exercise, you will save the letter you just typed. This way, if there is a power failure your letter will be saved.

1. Follow the steps for your version of Word to open the Save As dialog box:

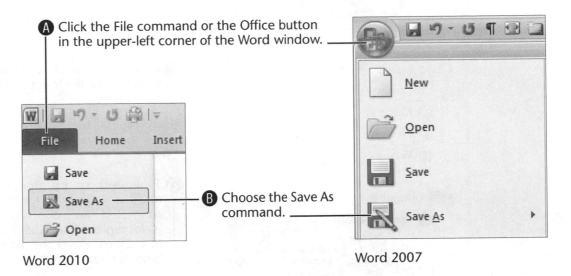

Ⓐ Click the File command or the Office button in the upper-left corner of the Word window.

Ⓑ Choose the Save As command.

Word 2010   Word 2007

For the rest of this lesson, these commands this will be written like this:

Word 2010: Choose File→Save As to display the Save As dialog box.
Word 2007: Choose Office→Save As to display the Save As dialog box.

Notice that Word uses the first line of your letter to suggest a filename, as shown at right. In this case, the first part of today's date. This name will be replaced as you start typing the new name.

File name: June 4

2. Follow these steps to store your document on the hard drive:

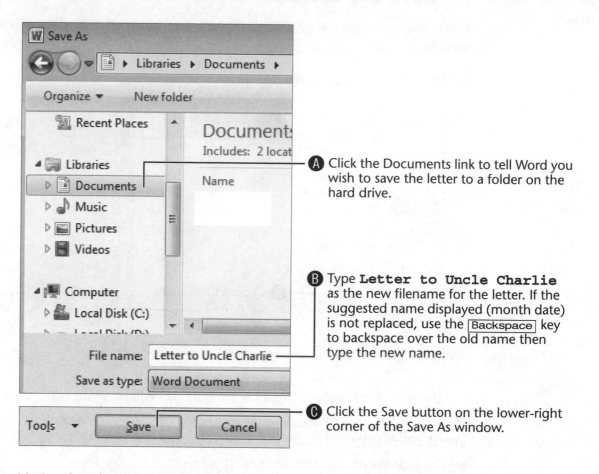

Ⓐ Click the Documents link to tell Word you wish to save the letter to a folder on the hard drive.

Ⓑ Type **Letter to Uncle Charlie** as the new filename for the letter. If the suggested name displayed (month date) is not replaced, use the Backspace key to backspace over the old name then type the new name.

Ⓒ Click the Save button on the lower-right corner of the Save As window.

Notice that the title bar at the top of your Word screen contains your document's new name. Your document is saved on the computer's hard drive.

Leave the file open.

Saving a Modified Document

As you know, the first time you save a document you give it a name. If you make changes to the document after that, you must save it again so the changes are not lost. There are two methods for doing this, which are shown in the following table.

QUICK REFERENCE: Saving a Modified Document

Task	Procedure
Save using File/Office button	**Word 2010:** Choose File→Save. **Word 2007:** Choose Office →Save.
Save using the Quick Access toolbar	Click the Save button on the Quick Access toolbar.

TIP! When you perform a Save rather than a Save As, no dialog box appears. The Save happens in the background.

Scrolling the Word Window

When you create longer documents, the computer screen won't be large enough to display the entire contents. In this case, you must scroll your view of the document. Like most Windows programs, Word displays scroll bars on the right and bottom sides of the window when the contents are too large to display. The following figure shows the main features of scroll bars, and the next exercise gives you the opportunity to try them out.

Scroll arrows   Scroll box

I am writing our family history, and I would like to ask you some questions about your part of th
Would you please provide the following information for each family member?

- Date of birth
- Place born
- When and where married
- Children's names
- Names of children's spouses

Would you also let me know if you are aware of any extraordinary accomplishments or events ir
lives of any of your family members?

Sincerely,

This horizontal scroll bar performs similar scrolling functions as the vertical scroll bar.

Page: 1 of 1   Words: 85   100%

Dragging on this corner changes the size of the Word window when it is not maximized.

 HANDS-ON 3.7 Save the Changes to Your Letter

In this exercise, you will add postscript text to your letter and resave the document. You will also adjust the size of the Word window and practice using the scroll bars.

Before You Begin: Your Letter to Uncle Charlie should still be on the screen.

1. The flashing cursor should be at the bottom of the letter. If it is not, click at the bottom of the letter to place the cursor there.

2. If necessary, tap the [Enter] key to place the cursor on the line below the signature.

3. Type the following postscript:

   P.S. Let me know if you have any interesting family photographs I can copy.

4. Click the Save  button on the Quick Access toolbar (shown at right) in the upper-left corner of the Word window to save the modification to the letter.

There is a brief pause as Word replaces the old version of the file with a new version containing your changes.

Adjust the Size of the Word Window

Now you will adjust the size of the window so you can practice using the scroll bars.

5. Click the Restore window sizing button if the Word window is maximized.

Notice that the middle sizing button turns into Maximize 🔲 after the window is restored. You restored the window so you can change its size and shape manually.

⚠️**TIP!** You cannot change the size or shape of a maximized window.

6. Follow these steps to adjust the size of the Word window:

Ⓐ Point at the bottom-right corner of the window until you see the mouse pointer change to a double-arrow shape, as shown here.

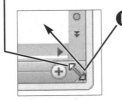

Ⓑ Hold down the left mouse button and keep it held down as you move the mouse to make the window smaller. Make it narrow enough so that the vertical scroll bar appears. You may have to drag to the left to make this happen.

Ⓒ Release the left mouse button when both scroll bars are visible.

The mouse motion you just performed is called dragging. You can also drag on the side and top/bottom borders of a window, but it is usually easiest to drag from a corner.

Now you can no longer see the entire document. The scroll bar gives you the ability to view a specific section of a document.

7. Follow these steps to use the scroll bar to change your view of the document:

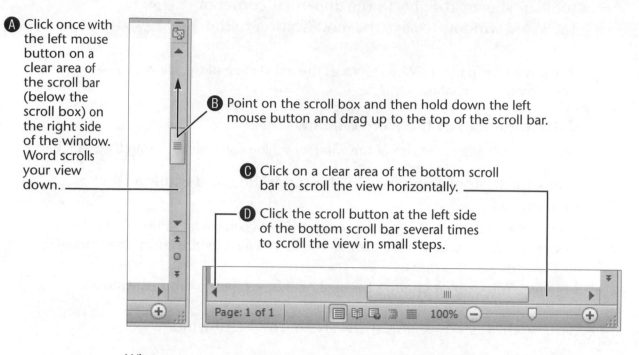

A Click once with the left mouse button on a clear area of the scroll bar (below the scroll box) on the right side of the window. Word scrolls your view down.

B Point on the scroll box and then hold down the left mouse button and drag up to the top of the scroll bar.

C Click on a clear area of the bottom scroll bar to scroll the view horizontally.

D Click the scroll button at the left side of the bottom scroll bar several times to scroll the view in small steps.

Whenever you cannot see an entire document in the Word window, these scroll bars allow you to bring the part you want to see into view.

8. Maximize 🔲 the Word window.

Printing and Closing a Document

Once you've typed a document, you will likely want to print it. Then when you are finished working with the document, you will close it. Both the Print and Close commands are conveniently located on the Office menu.

The Print Dialog Box

You use the Print dialog box to select specific options about your print job.

If your computer can use more than one printer, all printers will be listed here.

You can tell Word to print only a specific part of a document.

You can tell Word to print more than one copy of the document.

Print		?	X

Printer

Name: \\STUDIO\HP psc 2500 Series ▼ [Properties]

Status: Idle
Type: HP psc 2500 Series
Where: USB001
Comment:

[Find Printer...]
☐ Print to file
☐ Manual duplex

Page range
- ● All
- ○ Current page   ○ Selection
- ○ Pages: _____

Type page numbers and/or page ranges separated by commas counting from the start of the document or the section. For example, type 1, 3, 5–12 or p1s1, p1s2, p1s3–p8s3

Copies

Number of copies: 1 ▲▼

☑ Collate

The Word 2007 Print dialog box

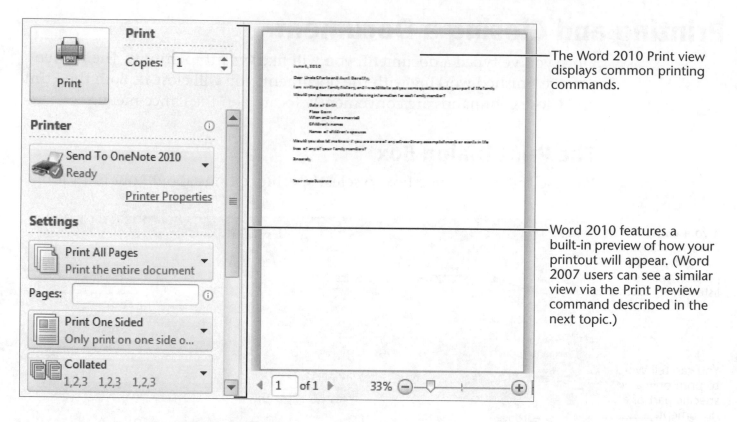

The Word 2010 Print view displays common printing commands.

Word 2010 features a built-in preview of how your printout will appear. (Word 2007 users can see a similar view via the Print Preview command described in the next topic.)

Print Preview

The Print Preview window shows how a document will look when it prints. It is especially useful when printing long documents and those containing intricate graphics and formatting. It is always wise to preview a long or complex document before sending it to the printer.

Preview Window Features   When you display the Print Preview window, you see a Print Preview Ribbon that replaces the regular Ribbon. Following are a few key commands that will be of interest to you:

- The Print command displays the Print dialog box, which you will examine next.

- The Zoom command allows you to specify the magnification of the page and the number of pages you see on the screen at once.

- The Next Page and Previous Page commands allow you to move from page to page in a multipage document.

- The Close Print Preview command returns you to the main Word window.

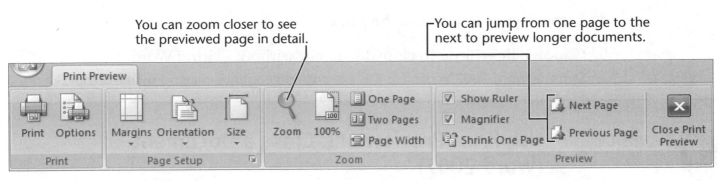

You can zoom closer to see the previewed page in detail.

You can jump from one page to the next to preview longer documents.

Word's Print Preview Ribbon

Closing a Document

When you are finished working with a document, you will close it. If you made changes since your last save, you will be prompted to save your document when you close it. The Close command appears on the Office menu.

 HANDS-ON 3.8A **Use Print Preview and Close a Document (Word 2010)**

In this exercise, you will examine Print view, including its built-in print preview. Then you will close the document.

Word 2007 Users: Skip this version of the exercise and perform the steps in Hands-On 3.8B on page 106.

1. Choose File→Print.

   Word 2010 displays the Print view. Unlike Word 2007, this has a built-in print preview. Notice the Zoom control at the bottom-right corner of the window.

   68% ⊖ ———▽——+—— ⊕ ▣

2. Follow these steps to zoom the print preview in and out:

   Ⓐ Click the Zoom In button three times to gradually zoom in. ⎯⎯⎯

   Ⓑ Click here on the zoom bar to zoom out several levels with a single click. ⎯⎯⎯ 68% ⊖ ———▽——+—— ⊕ ▣

   Ⓒ Click the Zoom to Page button to adjust the zoom so the entire page is visible. ⎯⎯⎯

   Word zooms the page to the highest setting at which the entire page is visible.

3. Click the Print button near the top-left corner of the Print view to print your letter.

   Word sends the letter to the *default* printer. This is the printer Windows uses unless you choose a different one.

4. Retrieve your letter from the printer.

5. Choose File→Close to close document without exiting Word.

Skip the Word 2007 version of this exercise and continue reading the next topic.

 HANDS-ON 3.8B **Use Print Preview and Close a Document (Word 2007)**

In this exercise, you will examine Print Preview window and the Print dialog box, and then you will close the document.

NOTE! The features described below apply specifically to Word 2007. Word 2010 builds the preview window into the Print command view and simplifies the commands available for that view.

1. Follow these steps to see how your document will look when printed:

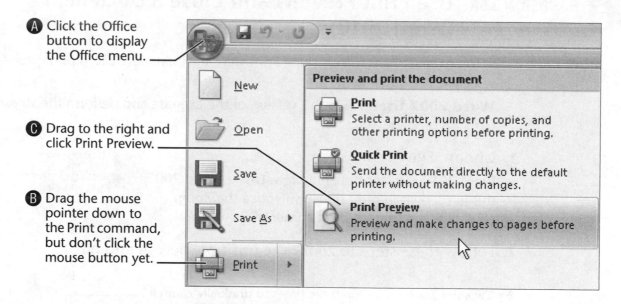

A Click the Office button to display the Office menu.

C Drag to the right and click Print Preview.

B Drag the mouse pointer down to the Print command, but don't click the mouse button yet.

New

Open

Save

Save As

Print

Preview and print the document

Print
Select a printer, number of copies, and other printing options before printing.

Quick Print
Send the document directly to the default printer without making changes.

Print Preview
Preview and make changes to pages before printing.

2. Move the mouse pointer over the document.

Notice that the mouse pointer is shaped like a magnifying glass in the Print Preview window.

3. Click the mouse button to magnify the view.

4. Click again anywhere on the page to zoom back out.

5. Click the Close Print Preview ⊠ button on the Print Preview Ribbon to close this window.

You are now back to viewing your document in the standard Word window.

Print and Close the Document

6. Choose Office →Print.

Word opens the Print dialog box.

7. Click OK to print your letter.

8. Retrieve your letter from the printer.

9. Choose Office →Close.

Word closes the document, leaving a blank window. The Word program is still running, ready for your next command. In the next exercise, you will create a new document.

Starting a New Blank Document

If you have only one document open in Word, when you close it, the Word screen goes blank and there is no document to type in. If you want to type, you need to create a new blank document. The New command is located in the Office menu like the figure at right.

The New Document dialog box defaults to Blank Document as shown in the following illustration.

About Computer Printers

Computer printers can create sharp, colorful pages from documents you type or from web pages you view online. Most home users have either an ink jet or all-in-one printer. Both are described in this section.

Ink Jet Printers   Ink jet printers spray microscopic drops of ink on the page. Most use separate black and color ink cartridges and mix the colors as necessary to print your documents and photos. Compared to the laser printers found in most office environments, ink jet printers are slower, and the cost of printing each page is usually a few cents more. But ink jet printers are also capable of printing digital photographs in photo-realistic color.

 TIP!   When it comes to printing photographs, the paper you use with an ink jet printer makes a huge difference in the quality of the picture.

All-in-One Printers   All-in-one ink jet printers can serve as a copier, a document or photo scanner, and a fax machine. Most all-in-ones have a USB port and a slot into which you can plug your digital camera's storage card.

Image courtesy of Epson America, Inc.

The Epson Expression Premium XP-600 Small-in-One™ Printer makes copies, scans, prints from photo storage cards, and wirelessly connects to tablets and smartphones.

Wireless Printing

Many printers now feature the ability to print wirelessly over your home network or from a mobile device such as a tablet or smartphone. This allows you to send a file to print without a physical connection to the printer. For example, you can print from a computer on the other side of the house. Or you can open a document on a tablet and print it without the use of another computer.

> **!TIP!** Wireless printing capability goes by various vendor-specific names, such as Apple AirPrint™ Epson Connect™, Google Cloud Print™, and HP ePrint™.

Using Word's Proofreading Aids

Two features that help you proofread your documents are the AutoCorrect and the Spell Check features. Although these tools are quite helpful, they are only *aids*. You must still proofread your documents to ensure accuracy.

Working with AutoCorrect

Word has a wonderful feature called AutoCorrect that automatically corrects misspelled words and typos for you as you type. For example, if you type *aboutthe,* AutoCorrect will change it to *about the.* It corrects other errors, too, such as incorrect capitalization and accidentally typing with Caps Lock turned on.

 HANDS-ON 3.9 **Create a Blank Document and Use AutoCorrect**

In this exercise, you will create a blank document and use Word's AutoCorrect feature.

Create a Blank Document

1. Follow the step for your version of Word:
   - **Word 2010:** Choose File→New.
   - **Word 2007:** Choose Office 🔘→New.

   Word displays the New Document view. This shows various options for creating new documents from predesigned templates and a blank document. Notice that the Blank document option is already selected for you.

2. Double-click the Blank Document, or tap the Enter key on the keyboard.

Word creates a new blank document. Notice that a generic name is already suggested in the title bar.

Use AutoCorrect

3. Type **teh** and tap the Spacebar.

When you tap the Spacebar, AutoCorrect fixes the spelling and capitalizes the word if it is the first word of a sentence. Let's try some more.

4. Tap the Enter key to move to a blank line and type **int he** followed by a space.

AutoCorrect fixes the typographical error and capitalizes the word *In*. Word assumes the first word you typed is the beginning of a new sentence.

5. Tap Enter to move to a blank line and then tap Caps Lock at the left edge of your keyboard to turn on this feature.

6. Type the word **Now**, holding down Shift as you type the N.

Because Caps Lock is turned on, it looks like this—nOW.

7. Tap the Spacebar and AutoCorrect fixes the error and turns off Caps Lock.

Using Spell Check

If you make a typo and AutoCorrect isn't sure how to fix it, Spell Check comes to the rescue. Spell Check monitors your spelling as you type and underlines words it suspects are misspelled with a wavy red line. Right-clicking on the underlined word generates a pop-up menu with suggestions of possible correct spellings. Then, you need only choose the correct spelling from the menu, as shown here. (The Mini toolbar also appears, but you can just ignore it.)

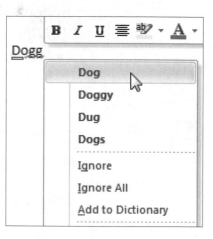

Not Every Misspelling Is Caught   Sometimes Spell Check marks a word as a possible misspelling when it is not. Some proper names fall into that category, although Spell Check has many common proper names in its dictionary and does not mark them. If Word marks a word as incorrect, you can either ignore the underlining (it won't print) or choose Ignore All from the pop-up menu.

!NOTE! Word may also mark an apparent grammatical error with a green (rather than a red) squiggle as in the example at right.

I are going to the store.

 HANDS-ON 3.10 Use Spell Check

In this exercise, you will make some deliberate spelling errors and use Spell Check to correct them. You will also instruct Spell Check to ignore the spelling of a proper name.

Before You Begin: The new document you created in the last exercise should be on the screen.

1. Tap [Enter] to move to a blank line, type **dogg**, and tap the [Spacebar]. Notice the wavy red line under the word.

   In the next step you will perform a right-click rather than a normal (left) click. Simply tap and release the right mouse button to perform this mouse motion. A right-click often displays a pop-up menu similar to the one you will see in step 2.

2. Place the mouse pointer over the misspelled word and click the right (not the left) mouse button to display the pop-up menu.

   In addition to the pop-up menu, the Mini toolbar will also appear. Ignore it for now.

3. Choose the correct spelling of *Dog* from the menu.

   Next you will type a proper name that Spell Check will incorrectly mark as misspelled.

4. Tap [Enter], type **Goodspeed**, and tap the [Spacebar]. Word places a red wavy line under the word.

5. Right-click on the word and choose Ignore All from the menu to remove the red line.

   Word will not mark the name as misspelled again during the current session, meaning it will ignore the term in this document and other documents. Once you exit from Word, Spell Check resets itself so it will treat the word as misspelled when you restart Word.

   If you expect to use the word regularly, you can add it to the dictionary instead. Then, Word would not mark the word as misspelled again.

6. Follow the step for your version of Word:
   - **Word 2010:** Choose File→Close.
   - **Word 2007:** Choose Office [icon]→Close.

7. Choose No when Word asks if you wish to save the document.

Opening a Document

When you have saved and closed a document, you may wish to open it again for several reasons. For example, you may want to revise it or print it. The Open dialog box lets you navigate to your document and open it.

Recent Documents List

Word and Windows 7 give you a couple of ways to easily locate and open documents you've recently opened or created. Word's Recent Documents list appears when you click the File (Word 2010) or Office (Word 2007) orb. You can pin specific documents to this list so they always appear, until you either unpin or remove them from the list.

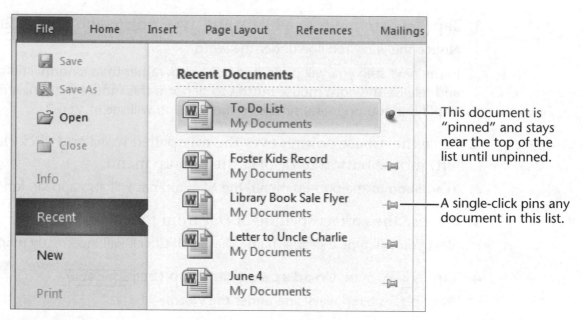

This document is "pinned" and stays near the top of the list until unpinned.

A single-click pins any document in this list.

An example of Word 2010's Recent document list

Win 7 and Recent Documents Win 7 displays recent documents in a *jump list* for Word when it is pinned to the Start menu or taskbar, or when it appears in the recently used programs list. As with Word's File (2010) or Office (2007) command, you can pin frequently used documents to these lists so they never go away.

W Microsoft Word 2010 ▶	Pinned ───────────
	W To Do List
X Microsoft Excel 2010	Recent ───────────
	W Foster Kids Record 📌
Calculator	**W** Library Book Sale Flyer
	W Letter to Uncle Charlie
Sticky Notes	

Win 7 displays a jump list of recent Word documents
and allows you to pin them in place.

HANDS-ON 3.11 Open a Document

In this exercise, you will open the letter you closed in an earlier exercise.

1. Follow the step for your version of Word:
   - **Word 2010**: Choose File→Open.
   - **Word 2007**: Choose Office →Open.

   The Open dialog box appears. It displays the My Documents (or Documents) folder by default. You should see Letter to Uncle Charlie in the file list.

2. Click the Letter to Uncle Charlie file to select it and then click the Open button in the bottom-right corner of the dialog box. Or you can double-click to open the file.

	Letter to Uncle Charlie Microsoft Office Word Docu... 10.3 KB

   The letter opens in the Word window.

About Computer Keyboards

Although computer keyboards have a layout of keys similar to typewriters (the QWERTY layout) they also feature several special keys. For example, some computer keyboards add functionality with keys that help you start an email program or a program to play music. There are also keys that modify other keys that you tap. The following illustration displays a typical computer keyboard and points out the location of some types of keys. However, there are many designs for computer keyboards, and this is just one example.

Photo courtesy of Logitech.

	Key Names	Description
A	Cursor keys	These keys allow you to move the blinking cursor without using the mouse.
B	Ctrl and Alt keys	You hold down one of these keys to modify the next key you tap. For example, hold down Ctrl and tap C to issue the Copy command. This is the same command you could issue using the Copy command on the Ribbon. Many computer users find these keyboard shortcuts quite handy.
C	Function keys	These keys change function depending on the program you are running.
D	Numeric keypad	When you press the Num Lock key at the top of the keypad, these keys function like a 10-key calculator.
E	Windows Key	Tapping this key opens the Start menu.
F	Esc key	You can use this key to switch off some functions. For example, if a program is in full-screen mode, this key will return the view to normal.

Using Cut, Copy, and Paste

Nearly all Windows programs feature the Cut, Copy, and Paste commands. These allow you to move or copy text from one place to another within a document, between documents, or even between different programs. Because they are so closely associated, these three buttons appear together on the Clipboard group of the Home tab. Before you can give a cut or copy command, you must select the text.

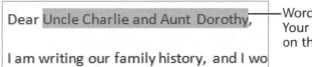

Clipboard group on the Home tab

QUICK REFERENCE: Copying and Moving Text

Command	Description
Cut	Delete my selection and place it in a special area in memory called the Clipboard for pasting.
Copy	Leave my selection where it is and place a copy of it in a special area in memory called the Clipboard for pasting.
Paste	Insert a copy of my most recently cut or copied item at the spot where the cursor is blinking.

Selecting Text

In Word you select (highlight) text in order to do something to it. For example, you would select text to move, copy, replace, or apply formatting (such as **bold**) to it. Selecting text is your way of telling Word, "Apply my next command to this (selected) text." You can select an item as small as a single letter or word, or as large as an entire page or even an entire document.

Dear Uncle Charlie and Aunt Dorothy,

I am writing our family history, and I wo

Word highlights text as you select it. Your next command is performed only on the highlighted text.

Selection Methods   Most of the time, you can simply drag with the mouse pointer to select text. However, Word also allows you to make selections of entire lines or to use the Select All command from the Ribbon. Word has numerous selection methods but you will use just the most basic ones in the next exercise.

Method	Description
Drag with the mouse	• This is the most commonly used method to select text. You position the mouse pointer at the start of the selection and then hold down the left mouse button as you drag to the end.
Use Select All command	• Choose Home→Editing→Select from the Ribbon. • Choose Select All from the menu.

Undoing a Command

 Sometimes you will make mistakes while working on a word processing document. For example, you may delete some text you actually want to keep. Word always keeps track of your recent activities and allows you to undo them. Simply click the Undo button after a mistake.

> **!TIP!** You can click the Undo button several times if necessary to undo multiple commands.

QUICK REFERENCE: Using Cut, Copy, and Paste

Task	Procedure
Use Cut/Copy and Paste	• Select the text you want to move or copy. • Choose Home→Clipboard→Cut ✂ or Copy 📋 from the Ribbon. • Click to place the blinking cursor where you wish to paste the cut or copied text. • Choose Home→Clipboard→Paste 📋 from the Ribbon. • Repeat the preceding two last steps if you wish to repeatedly paste the same item.

HANDS-ON 3.12 Select and Edit Text

In this exercise, you will select, copy, and paste text. You will also replace a selection with new typing and learn about Word's handy Undo button.

Before You Begin: The Letter to Uncle Charlie file should be open in Word.

1. Choose Home→Editing→Select menu ▼ from the Ribbon.

2. Choose Select All from the menu.

3. Choose Home→Clipboard→Copy 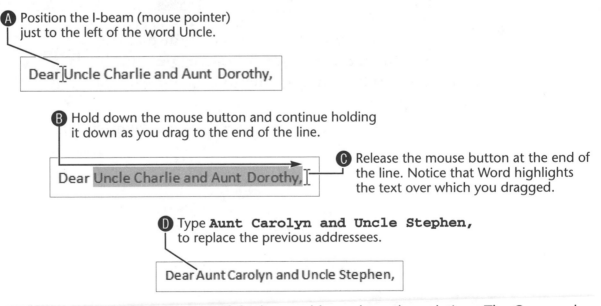 from the Ribbon.

It may seem as if nothing happened, but Word has actually copied your selection to a special place in memory called the Clipboard. It is ready to be pasted wherever you need.

Now you will open a new blank document and paste the letter into the new document.

4. Follow the step for your version of Word:

- **Word 2010**: Choose File→New.
- **Word 2007**: Choose Office →New.

Notice that the New Document dialog box defaults to Blank Document; therefore, you do not need to make any changes here.

5. Double-click the Blank Document, or click once on the Blank Document and tap the Enter key.

Word opens a new document. Right now you have two different documents open in the program. Notice the blinking cursor near the top of the document.

6. Choose Home→Clipboard→Paste from the Ribbon.

Word pastes the entire letter into the blank document. This is a convenient way to start a new version of this letter.

Select and Edit Text

Now you will select the original addressees and replace them with new ones.

7. Follow these steps to change the addressees of the letter:

(A) Position the I-beam (mouse pointer) just to the left of the word Uncle.

Dear Uncle Charlie and Aunt Dorothy,

(B) Hold down the mouse button and continue holding it down as you drag to the end of the line.

(C) Release the mouse button at the end of the line. Notice that Word highlights the text over which you dragged.

Dear Uncle Charlie and Aunt Dorothy,

(D) Type **Aunt Carolyn and Uncle Stephen,** to replace the previous addressees.

Dear Aunt Carolyn and Uncle Stephen,

Now you have a new version of the letter addressed to other relatives. The Copy and Paste commands make it easy to make use of text you've already typed.

8. Click the Save  button on the Quick Access toolbar as shown below.

Word displays the Save As dialog box so you can give the untitled file a name.

9. If necessary, click the Documents link in the left panel to display that folder in the box at the top of the Save As dialog box.

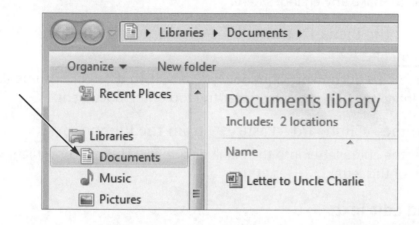

Word displays the destination for your saved document in the address bar.

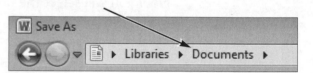

10. In the File Name box at the bottom of the dialog box, type **Letter to Aunt Carolyn** and click the Save button in the bottom-right corner of the dialog box.

Word saves the letter to the My Documents (or Documents) folder.

Select, Copy, and Paste Lines of Text

Now you will select and copy a few lines of text.

11. Follow these steps to select some text:

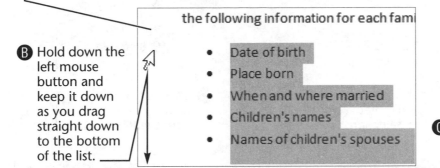

Ⓐ Position the mouse pointer in the margin (not too close to the text) to the left of the Date of Birth text so it appears to be an arrow tilted to the right.

Ⓑ Hold down the left mouse button and keep it down as you drag straight down to the bottom of the list.

the following information for each fami

- Date of birth
- Place born
- When and where married
- Children's names
- Names of children's spouses

Ⓒ Release the mouse button when the last line of the list is highlighted.

12. Choose Home→Clipboard→Copy 📋 from the Ribbon.

Word saves your selection to the Clipboard.

13. Follow these steps to position the cursor where you will paste the copied text:

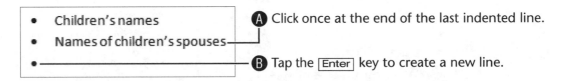

- Children's names
- Names of children's spouses

Ⓐ Click once at the end of the last indented line.

Ⓑ Tap the [Enter] key to create a new line.

14. Choose Home→Clipboard→Paste 📋 from the Ribbon.

Word inserts the copied lines into the letter.

Use the Undo Command

15. Click the Undo ↺ button on the Quick Access toolbar.

Word undoes your Paste command.

16. Click the Undo ↺ button again.

Word undoes the new line you added in step 13.

Use Cut and Paste to Move Text

Next you will change the order of two lines using the Cut and Paste commands.

17. Follow these steps to cut a line of text from the information lines:

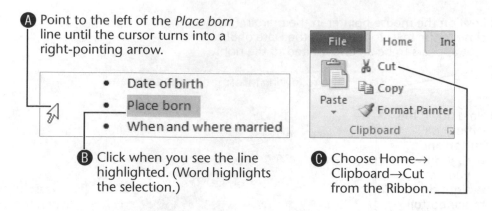

Ⓐ Point to the left of the *Place born* line until the cursor turns into a right-pointing arrow.

Ⓑ Click when you see the line highlighted. (Word highlights the selection.)

Ⓒ Choose Home→ Clipboard→Cut from the Ribbon.

The line of text disappears as Word cuts it to the Clipboard. The lines below the line you cut shift up to fill in the space.

18. Point between the bullet and the word *Date* on the first line in the bulleted list, and then click once to place the blinking cursor just before the word *Date* as shown below:

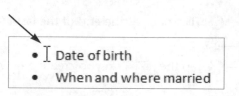

Placing the blinking cursor tells Word where you wish the Paste command to be performed in the next step.

19. Choose Home→Clipboard→Paste ▦ from the Ribbon.

The pasted line jumps into position at the top of the list. That's because the Paste command always *inserts* the pasted item immediately after the location where the cursor was blinking.

Save Your Work and Close the Document

20. Click the Save ⊞ button on the Quick Access toolbar.

It's always a good idea to use the Save command when you finish working with a document.

21. Follow the step for your version of Word:

- **Word 2010**: Choose File→Close.
- **Word 2007**: Choose Office 🔘→Close.

Word closes the window with the letter to Aunt Carolyn. Now the Letter to Uncle Charlie should be visible.

22. Click the Close ⊠ button on the top-right corner of the window. Choose No if Word asks if you wish to save any changes to the document.

Just as some of the ways you learned to work with text in WordPad have also applied to Word, ways you work with Word apply to many other Windows programs. So, in this lesson, you've not just been learning how to work with Word. Commands such as Cut, Copy, and Paste work the same in many other Windows programs you will use in the future. In the next lesson, you will see how these commands allow you to move and copy your document files from one place to another.

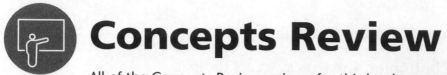# Concepts Review

All of the Concepts Review quizzes for this book are available on the student web page. Your instructor will let you know how to complete the quizzes (in the book or online).

True/False Questions

Page number

1. Tabs on the Ribbon, such as the Home tab, are divided into command groups. **true   false** _____

2. A word underlined with a wavy red line indicates grammatical error. **true   false** _____

3. AutoCorrect automatically corrects many misspelled words for you as you type. **true   false** _____

4. You made changes to a document after originally saving and naming it. Word saves these changes to the file automatically. **true   false** _____

5. When you open the Print Preview window, Word automatically sends your document directly to the printer. **true   false** _____

6. In Word you select (highlight) text in order to do something to it. **true   false** _____

Multiple Choice Questions

7. If nonprinting characters are visible on the screen, tapping ⌶Enter⌶ displays which of the following?
   Page number: _____
   a. An arrow
   b. A paragraph symbol
   c. A dot
   d. A four-headed arrow

8. When you cut/copy text, Word places the selected text into a special place in memory called the _____.
   Page number: _____
   a. cut memory
   b. paste memory
   c. selection
   d. Clipboard

9. You can accept a phrase that AutoComplete proposes by tapping _____.
   Page number: _____
   a. ⌶Tab⌶
   b. ⌶Spacebar⌶
   c. ⌶Backspace⌶
   d. ⌶Enter⌶

10. AutoCorrect does which of the following?
    Page number: _____
    a. Automatically inserts the date in your document.
    b. Corrects grammar errors as you type.
    c. Automatically corrects typos as you type.
    d. Prevents you from having to proofread your documents.

Skill Builders

SKILL BUILDER 3.1 Send a Letter to Uncle Charlie

In this exercise, you will send Uncle Charlie a quick thank you for writing you such a nice letter.

1. Start the Word program using Start→All Programs→Microsoft Office→Microsoft Office Word 2010 or 2007, or look for the Word 2010 or 2007 command in the recently used programs list on the Start menu.

2. Read the following notes then type the letter.

   - Remember to use the word wrap feature. Do not tap Enter until you reach the end of a short line or if you wish to insert a blank line. Do not be concerned if your line endings do not match the following illustration.

   - Use the Delete or Backspace keys if you make a typo.

September 6, 2011

Dear Uncle Charlie,

Just a quick note to say thank you for all of the information you sent It really helps a lot in putting together the Davidson Family History. I look forward to receiving the rest of the material when you get it.

I sure wish I had some of the mushrooms you were talking about. Leo is lucky to live next to you!

Love to you and Aunt Dorothy.

Your niece Suzanne

---

3. Click the Save 🖫 button on the Quick Access toolbar near the top-left corner of the Word window.

   Word displays the Save As window automatically because you have not yet saved this document and given it a name.

4. Make sure the My Documents (or Documents) folder is shown then type **Another Letter to Uncle Charlie** as the new filename.

5. Click the Save button near the bottom-right corner of the Save As dialog box.

   Notice that the name of the document appears in the title bar at the top of the Word window.

6. Choose File→Close or Office 📖→Close to close the document without exiting the Word window.

   The window is empty again.

SKILL BUILDER 3.2A **Preview a Printout (Word 2010)**

In this exercise, you will use the Letter to Uncle Charlie document you created earlier in this lesson to practice using Print Preview and to print.

Word 2007 users: Skip this version of the exercise and perform the steps in Skill Builder 3.2B on page 125.

1. Click File on the Ribbon.

   Notice that because no document is currently open, Word displays the Recent view. This displays your recently opened documents and is the easiest way to locate and open a document you've created or saved in the past day or so.

2. Choose the Letter to Uncle Charlie document in the Recent documents view.

3. Choose File→Print.

   Word displays a print preview on the right side of the Print view.

4. Use the Zoom control at the bottom-left corner of the window to make the preview easier to read.

5. Choose the Home tab on the Ribbon, or tap the [Esc] (Escape) key on the keyboard.

   Word closes the Print view without printing. The Escape key is a common method to cancel a command. Leave the document open.

   Skip the Word 2007 version of this exercise and continue with Skill Builder 3.3.

Use Print Preview (Word 2007)

In this exercise, you will use the Letter to Uncle Charlie document you created earlier in this lesson to practice using Print Preview and to print.

1. Choose Office 🔲→Open.

   Word displays the My Documents (or Documents) folder by default unless another user has changed this setting.

2. Click once with the left mouse button to choose the Letter to Uncle Charlie document, and then click the Open button near the bottom-right corner of the window.

3. Choose Office 🔲→Print ▸→Print Preview to see how the letter will look when printed.

4. Place the mouse pointer over the date at the top of the letter and click to zoom in so you can read it.

5. Click again anywhere on the page to zoom out.

6. Choose Print Preview→Preview→Close Print Preview 🔲 from the Ribbon to close the window.

   Leave the document open.

Copy and Paste Text

In this exercise, you will make a copy of the original letter to Uncle Charlie. Then you will use the Copy and Paste commands to revise the letter. You will add a second page to the document, which will allow several family members' information to be written down.

Before You Begin: The Letter to Uncle Charlie document should be open and the Word window should be maximized.

Save the File with a New Name

Now you will save the file with a new name to make a copy of it. This way, your original Letter to Uncle Charlie document will not be changed.

1. Choose File→Save As or Office 🔲→Save As.

2. Type **Revised Letter** as the new name for the document then click the Save button.

   Notice the new name on the title bar at the top of the Word window.

Revised Letter - Microsoft Word

Copy Some Text

Now you will copy some text that you will paste later in the revised letter.

3. Follow these steps to select some text:

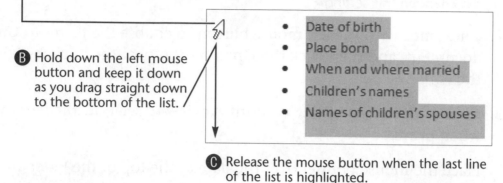

Ⓐ Position the mouse pointer in the margin (not too close to the text) to the left of the Date of Birth text so it appears to be an arrow tilted to the right.

Ⓑ Hold down the left mouse button and keep it down as you drag straight down to the bottom of the list.

- Date of birth
- Place born
- When and where married
- Children's names
- Names of children's spouses

Ⓒ Release the mouse button when the last line of the list is highlighted.

Word highlights your selection, ready to apply your next command to the selection.

4. Choose Home→Clipboard→Copy 🗎 from the Ribbon.
Word saves your selection to the Clipboard.

5. Hold down the Ctrl key and tap the End key to position the cursor at the end of the document. Release the Ctrl key.

6. Tap the Enter key to add a new line to the end of the document.

> **⚠ TIP!** In the next step, you will tell Word to start a new page in your document. You will do this by using a keyboard shortcut. Page breaks like the one you will create in step 7 are a good example of the control a word processor gives you over the appearance of each page.

7. While holding down the Ctrl key, tap the Enter key. Release the Ctrl key.
Word inserts a page break. Now you have a two-page document.

Create a New Family Member Information Section

Now you will add new sections for family member information to the new page. Notice where the cursor is blinking on the page. This is where you will continue typing.

8. Type **Family Member Name:** and tap Enter.

9. Choose Home→Clipboard→Paste 📋 from the Ribbon.
Word pastes the text you selected and copied earlier in the exercise.

Copy and Paste the New Section

10. Drag to select the lines for the new information section you've created.

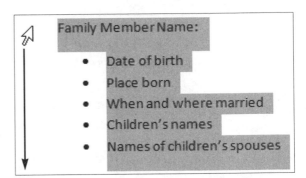

11. Choose Home→Clipboard→Copy ▤ from the Ribbon.

12. Click once with the left mouse button on the last line of the document.

13. Choose Home→Clipboard→Paste ▤ from the Ribbon.

Word pastes the new section into position.

14. Choose Home→Clipboard→Paste ▤ from the Ribbon again.

Word pastes the new section again. You can keep pasting the most recently cut or copied item as many times as you wish.

15. Paste the information two more times.

16. Choose File→Save or Office ▤ →Save to save your changes.

17. Close ▤ the Word window.

Working with Files

When you begin working with a
computer, you will have just a few files to
keep track of. But as your use of the
computer grows, so will the number of files
you must manage. After several months,
you may have several dozen of your own
files. After a year, you may have a hundred
or more files. Fortunately, you can use
folders to keep related files together. (You
can even create folders inside of other
folders.) In this lesson, you will learn how
files are organized on a Windows computer,
how to find and open your own files, and
how to move and copy files to place them
exactly where you want them to be. You will
also learn about the Windows Control Panel
and how it can help you make useful
adjustments to the way the mouse
functions.

LESSON OBJECTIVES

After studying this lesson, you will be able to:

- Describe the Windows Control Panel
- Browse libraries, folders, and files on the computer
- Create new folders
- Move and copy files to new locations
- Delete and undelete (restore) files

Additional learning resources are available at labpub.com/learn/silver/wtwc4/

Case Study: Organizing Files on the Computer

One definition of a computer might be a *big* filing cabinet. What is the function of a filing cabinet? It is essentially a storage device that safeguards documents. For people in an office, a filing system consists of labeling file folders and storing them in each drawer. Guess what? Your computer organizes files in the same way. If you understand how a filing cabinet found in the office of nearly every business works, you already understand the filing method used on your computer.

Reusing a Document

A few weeks ago, Sharon used Word to write a letter to her local homeowner's association. She has not heard back from them and wants to follow up with another letter to which she will attach a copy of her original letter. Because she saved a copy of the original letter in the Documents library, she knows that she can quickly open it to print a new copy and even use some of its information (such as the mailing address) for her follow-up letter. So she opens the Documents library on her computer, locates the original letter, and then opens it in Word to print.

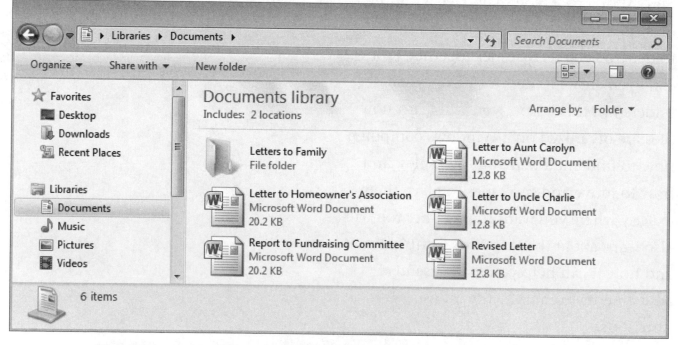

Sharon locates her letter in the Documents library.

Introducing the Windows Control Panel

There are many ways to change the way Windows looks and operates. Many of the controls for changing the properties of Windows can be found in the Windows Control Panel.

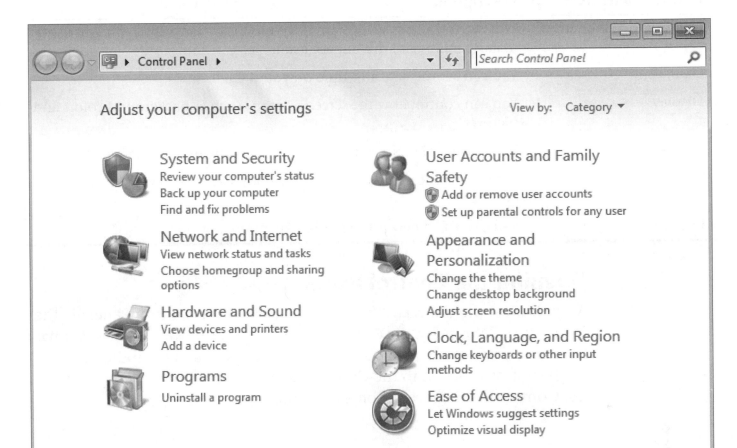

The Windows Control Panel groups various controls into several categories.

Some Common Control Panel Tasks

The following table describes some of the most important Windows features that you can control through the Control Panel.

Control Panel Item	Description
Add/Remove Programs	This setting allows you to uninstall programs you aren't going to use—making more hard drive space available.
Date/Time	You can set the date and time on your PC.
Display	You can control how the screen appears, such as background colors and pictures.
Mouse	This setting allows you to change the way the mouse operates.
Sounds	This controls the various sounds Windows associates with system events.
Printers	You can add a new printer or set the normal printer.

Opening the Control Panel

As with most programs and functions, you open the Control Panel via the Start button. Normally, the control panel displays the *category* view, similar to the figure on the previous page. If you are studying in a computer lab, you might not have access to the Control Panel. However, you can try viewing the Control Panel on your home computer.

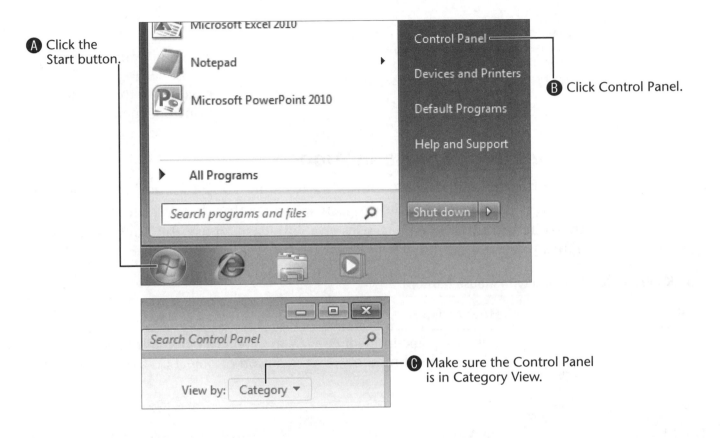

HANDS-ON 4.1 Start the Control Panel

In this exercise, you will examine the many controls available to you in the Control Panel.

1. Follow these steps to view the Windows Control Panel:

Ⓐ Click the Start button.

Ⓑ Click Control Panel.

Ⓒ Make sure the Control Panel is in Category View.

NOTE! Some computer labs do not permit student access to the Control Panel. If you cannot open the Control panel, skip this exercise and also Hands-On 4.2. Instead, you might try these two exercises at home if your computer has Win 7.

The Control Panel displays the Category/Home view. This groups various controls for easy access depending on the task you wish to accomplish.

When you open a category to make new settings with the Control panel, Windows displays its various controls. In the next exercise, you will adjust the mouse properties.

Setting Mouse Properties

The mouse has numerous settings you can adjust. Probably the most important setting for a beginner is the double-click speed. You perform a double click by quickly tapping and releasing the mouse twice in quick succession. You have the option of changing how quickly you must double-click for Windows to recognize it as a double click rather than two slow single clicks. If you're experiencing difficulty double-clicking, slowing down the double-click speed may help.

```
┌─ Double-click speed ────────────────────────────────┐
│  Double-click the folder to test your setting. If the    ┌──────┐
│  folder does not open or close, try using a slower       │      │
│  setting.                                                │      │
│                                                          │      │
│  Speed:   Slow ─────────▯──────── Fast                  └──────┘
│                ' ' ' ' ' ' ' ' ' '                         │
└──────────────────────────────────────────────────────┘
```

The Double-Click Speed is a good example of a mouse setting you can make from the Windows Control Panel.

More About Mouse Motions

You can perform five basic motions with a mouse. Each motion has specific uses in Windows and other programs. You've already used the point, click and drag motions. In this lesson, you will learn to use the double-click and right-click motions.

QUICK REFERENCE: Working with Mouse Motions

Motion		How to Do It	This motion is used...
Click		Gently tap and immediately release the left mouse button.	to "press" a button or select a menu option or object on the screen.
Double-click		Click twice in rapid succession.	as a shortcut for many types of common commands.
Drag		Press and hold down the left mouse button while sliding the mouse. Release the mouse button when you reach your destination.	to move an object, select several objects, draw lines, and select text.
Right-click		Gently tap and immediately release the right mouse button.	to display a context-sensitive menu for the object at which you are pointing.
Point		Slide the mouse without pressing a button until the pointer is in the desired location.	to position the pointer before using one of the four motions above, to select an object on the screen, or to get a menu to appear.

Computer Displays

Computer and tablet displays use millions of tiny points of light (called pixels) to form images. With the popularity of HD (high definition) television, most computer displays use the same wide-screen proportion of 16:9. Tablets and a growing number of desktop computers also have touch-screen capabilities, allowing you to give commands by touching and sliding your fingers across the screen.

How Computers Display Video The more pixels the screen of a computer monitor has, the sharper the image it can display. Displays are therefore rated for the number of pixels they display horizontally and vertically. For example, a 24" display may be rated to display 1920 pixels across by 1080 pixels high (usually abbreviated as 1920x1080). A popular screen resolution for notebook computers is 1366x768.

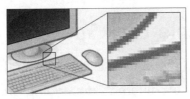

The images you see on a computer screen are actually composed of thousands of tiny points of light (pixels).

Illustration courtesy of Ed 2gs.

Native Resolution Every display has a native resolution, at which it displays best. This is the highest resolution it's capable of. Many displays can be set to a lower resolution, which may make small objects on the screen appear larger. Many computers and tablets have settings to help those with vision problems see the display more easily. For example, it may be possible to change the size of icons on the screen, or the size of text.

Double Clicks

So far, you have used a single click to select items on the screen. You have also used the dragging motion (holding down the left mouse button as you move the mouse) to select text in Word and used the right-click motion to correct a spelling error. You can perform a double click by quickly tapping and releasing the mouse twice in quick succession. A double click is essentially a shortcut.

Example   You want to open a file. You display the My Documents window, locate the file, and then use a double click to open it. You could also select the same file with a single click and then choose File→Open from the menu bar or simply tap the Enter key.

> ⚠️ **TIP!**   Some beginners have difficulty doing a double click at first. If you find a double click difficult, don't worry. Just use a single click to select an item and then tap the Enter key to open it, or give a command from the command bar.

 HANDS-ON 4.2   Change the Mouse Double-click Speed

In this exercise, you will practice adjusting the double-click speed of the mouse.

Your Mouse Properties screens may look a bit different, depending on the brand of mouse you have.

1. Choose the Hardware and Sound command, as shown below.

Windows displays the Control Panel items in this category. There are items for the mouse, keyboard, printers, and other hardware that may be attached to the computer. In the left panel are additional, related commands.

2. Choose Mouse under Devices and Printers, as shown below.

A new window appears to display the mouse properties (settings). Notice the Double-click Setting near the middle of the window. A small folder icon serves as a test area where you can check the double-click speed.

3. Follow these steps to slow the double-click speed:

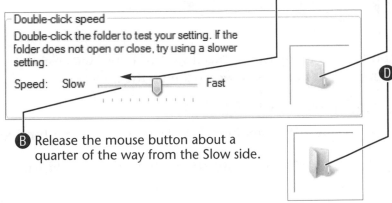

Ⓐ Point the tip of the mouse over the slider control and then hold down the left mouse button and keep it held down as you drag the slider control to the left.

Ⓒ Place the tip of the mouse pointer over the folder icon and then quickly tap and release the left mouse button twice in succession.

Double-click speed

Double-click the folder to test your setting. If the folder does not open or close, try using a slower setting.

Speed: Slow _____⬚_____ Fast

Ⓑ Release the mouse button about a quarter of the way from the Slow side.

Ⓓ If the folder appears "open" like this, you've successfully double-clicked. If it is still closed as it appears in step C, try again to tap and release the left mouse button twice as quickly as you can. If the folder still doesn't open, skip to the next step.

4. If the folder did not open on steps C or D above, repeat step 3, but this time set the double-click speed all the way to the Slow setting. Then try steps C and D again.

5. Practice double-clicking on the practice folder until you feel comfortable with this mouse motion.

   Double-clicking is a skill some beginners have trouble with. If that's the case for you, don't worry. With practice, double clicks will become easier. And it's always possible to perform the same tasks without double clicks.

6. When you are finished, click the OK button near the bottom of the window.

   This closes the Mouse Properties window and the Control Panel is visible.

7. Close [X] the Control Panel window.

View the System Date and Time

Windows normally adjusts its system clock via the Internet. Although you could access this setting from the Control Panel, there's an easier method.

8. Follow these steps to view the Date and Time window:

Ⓐ Click once (do not double-click) the date/time display.

Change date and time settings...

Ⓑ Click once on the Change Date and Time Settings link.

12:26 PM
6/14/2010

Windows displays the Date and Time properties. You can use this window to adjust the date and time, if necessary. (However, in a computer lab, you probably don't have this privilege.)

9. Click the Internet Time tab near the top-left corner of the Date and Time window, as shown below.

It's common to have complex settings displayed under tabs like this. As you can see, your computer sets it's time via a web page on the Internet.

10. Click the Additional Clocks tab.

You could set up one or two additional clocks to display other time zones.

11. Click the Cancel button to close the Date and Time window.

Understanding File Locations

Windows has a well-structured system for keeping your files in order. This allows you to easily open a file you created the day before to print it, make some changes, or even reuse part of the file for some other purpose. Understanding the file structure allows you to do other things, such as find a photo to attach and send along with an email message. (You will learn how to do this in Lesson 8, Sending and Receiving Attachments.)

With a little practice, knowing where your files are will become second nature. But when you are starting out, it may take some thought to keep track of where your files are. This section describes the structure in which all of your files are organized. As you gain experience with the structure, it will become easy to envision where your files are located. This book keeps it all as simple as possible. There is more you that you can do with file locations, but for now let's stick to the basics.

The File Organization Hierarchy

Windows uses a flexible hierarchy that is common to most personal computers. The four levels in the hierarchy are listed in the following table.

Level	Definition	Examples
Drive	This is a physical device on which you store files.	• An internal hard drive • A USB flash drive
Library	This is a collection of folders on the hard drive and possibly other drives connected to your computer. Libraries group multiple folders in one location. Windows creates a personal and public folder for each of its four basic libraries. You can later create your own libraries as your needs change.	• Documents • Music • Pictures • Videos
Folder	This is an electronic location in which you store groups of related files. It is also possible to place folders inside of other folders. Folders are often grouped into libraries.	• A folder to store all files for the Word program • A folder to store letters you typed for a project
File	This is a collection of computer data that has some common purpose.	• A letter you've typed • A picture you've drawn

An Analogy   A traditional file cabinet system is a good analogy for the filing system on a computer. This illustration shows the relationship between a drive, a library/folder, and a file on a computer system and their file cabinet equivalents.

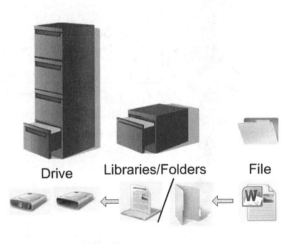

Drive   Libraries/Folders   File

About Libraries

Win 7 introduces the *library* to the file organization hierarchy. Libraries are essentially collections of related groups of files and folders located on one or more storage drives. A library can bring together folders from more than one location on your computer or on a network. Win 7 sets up four basic libraries when it is first installed on a computer. You can also create new libraries if you wish, but for a while, these four libraries should serve your needs just fine.

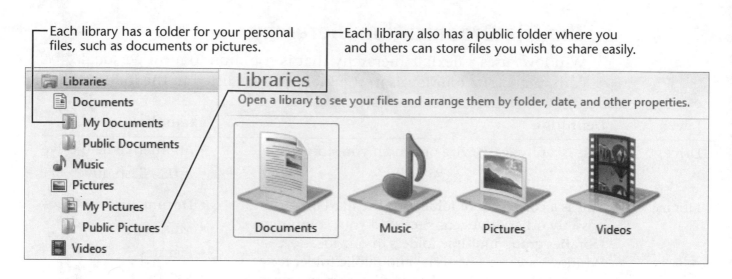

Each library has a folder for your personal files, such as documents or pictures.

Each library also has a public folder where you and others can store files you wish to share easily.

Libraries

Open a library to see your files and arrange them by folder, date, and other properties.

Documents   Music   Pictures   Videos

The Library View   When you view a library, you see *all* of the folders in that library, regardless of where they are located. The Documents library is set up for you when your username is created. It always starts with two folders My [file type] and Public [file type]. The following series of figures shows how the Library view combines the two folder views.

These are the folders in this library.

This Library view displays all files and folders from all folders in the library. It even puts them into alphabetical order as if they were all in the same folder.

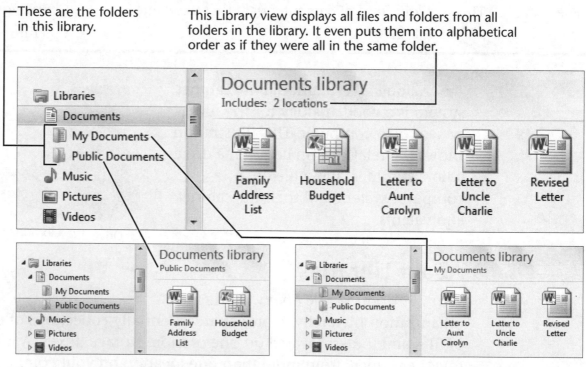

If you wish, you can store files in the Public folder, but you don't have to. Anyone on the computer can open and view files in the Public folder of a library.

This is your main file storage folder. When you save most types of files, Windows puts them in your My Documents folder by default.

Library view example

Using the Library View   The exercises in this lesson will use only the Library view. In every case, whatever you are doing is taking place in your My Documents folder. As you are learning where files are located, it is only necessary to use the Library view. Later, as your needs dictate, you can place files in the Public folders, and even create your own new libraries.

What you see.

Everything you store in the Documents library is actually stored in My Documents.

Where the files are stored when you save them.

 TIP!   Store all of your work in the *Documents* library as you start using the computer. Whenever you save most types of files, Windows stores them in the My Documents folder in the Documents library, unless you specifically indicate a different location. (The exceptions are picture, music, and video files, which Windows will put into their respective libraries.)

When you save a picture created with the Paint program, the program tries to save it to the Pictures library.

Folders Compared to Files

Files and folders are closely related, but quite different from each other. Folders (like the drawers in an office filing cabinet) are simply electronic containers for your files. On a computer, your files contain your work, which you want to preserve and protect. As the number of files you create grows, you can create and use folders to help organize your work. And you can group folders into new libraries as your file and folder collections grow.

A folder you created in the Documents Library.

Your document files grouped inside the folder.

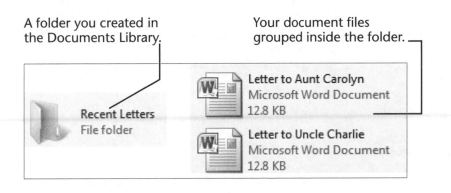

HANDS-ON 4.3 View the Contents of the Documents Library

In this exercise, you will view the contents of the My Documents folder.

1. If necessary, start the computer and log in.

2. Click the Start button then choose Documents near the top-right corner of the Start menu, as shown at right. (The name and picture above Documents will differ from what is shown in the figure.)

   Windows displays the contents of the Documents Library, including your personal My Documents folder. It probably contains files you created in Lesson 3, Using a Word Processor. If it does not, that's OK.

3. Perform the steps in Appendix A, Creating New Documents if you did not perform the exercises in the previous lesson or if the files you created are not in the My Documents folder. Otherwise, continue reading the next topic.

Features of the Documents Library Window

Along with the display of any files and folders inside it, the Documents library window has several other features. The following illustration displays typical features of the Documents library window. (Your screen will probably differ from this figure and that's OK.)

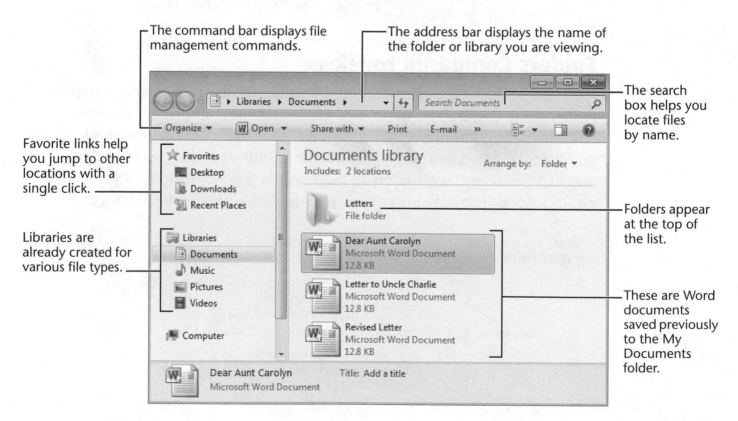

The command bar displays file management commands.

The address bar displays the name of the folder or library you are viewing.

The search box helps you locate files by name.

Favorite links help you jump to other locations with a single click.

Libraries are already created for various file types.

Folders appear at the top of the list.

These are Word documents saved previously to the My Documents folder.

Drive Letter ABCs

A Windows computer assigns a letter to each storage device attached to it. If you attach a new storage device to the computer, Windows automatically assigns the next available drive letter to it. Drive letters are just another way to tell one storage location from another. Windows also labels each storage location with a name. You can usually change the name of a device. For example, you can change the name of your USB flash drive to something easier to identify, such as your first or last name.

User-friendly Displays   Windows helps you visualize where your information is stored. The following illustration shows a typical display of storage devices on a Windows computer.

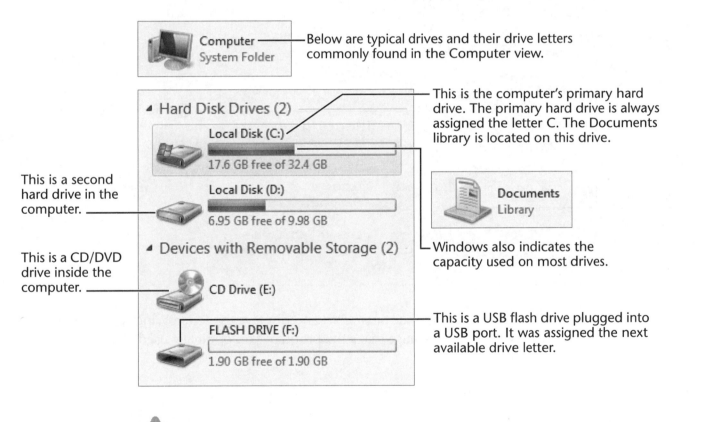

!TIP!   You might want to review the Behind the Screen: Storage Basics section on page 94 for descriptions of these common storage devices.

Opening Files

One reason to use the Documents library window is to locate and open a file you've created previously. There are two ways to open an existing file saved previously: from within the application you used to create the file or from a Documents library (or similar) window. Either method is just as effective as the other.

HANDS-ON 4.4 **Open a File from the Documents Library**

In this exercise, you will practice opening files from the Documents library window.

Before You Begin: The Documents library window should be open on the screen.

Open a File Using the Command Bar

1. Follow these steps to open the Letter to Uncle Charlie document you created and saved in a previous lesson:

Ⓐ Click once (do not double-click) on the icon (not the filename) of the Letter to Uncle Charlie document.

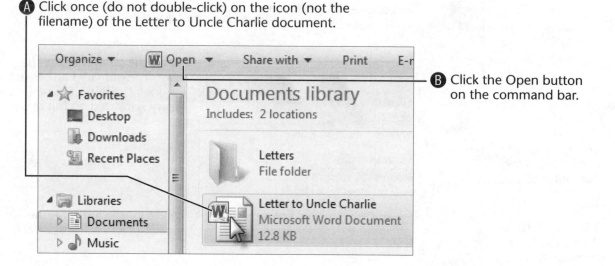

Ⓑ Click the Open button on the command bar.

There is a pause as Windows starts Word and displays the letter. Windows knew to use Word to open the file because that's the program you originally used to create and save the document.

2. Close ⊠ the Word window.

Open a File Using a Double Click

3. Follow these steps to open the same file using a double click:

Ⓐ Point the tip of the mouse pointer over the file icon.

> **Letter to Uncle Charlie**
> Microsoft Word Document
> 12.8 KB

Ⓑ Taking care to hold the mouse steady, tap and release the left mouse button twice in quick succession.

Ⓒ If Word did not start after step B, repeat steps A and B. If the file still does not open, don't worry; simply repeat step 1 to open the file.

Windows once again starts the Word program to display the letter. If you were unable to open the file with a double click, that's OK. It takes practice to use this mouse motion reliably. With further practice, you will be able to double-click whenever you wish.

4. Close ⊠ the Word window.

5. Click once on a clear area of the Documents library window (that is, not on a file or folder).

The file you had opened is deselected (no longer highlighted).

Using Folders

In addition to using the basic Documents library window, you can create new folders of your own to store your files. For example, you may want to create a folder in which to store most of the letters you type or to store photos taken with a digital camera. Windows makes it easy to create new folders whenever you need them. Once you have created a folder, you can store files in it just like you did with the Documents library view in Lesson 3, Using a Word Processor.

Creating New Folders

Win 7 has a command to create a new folder right on the command bar. Many Windows programs include a button that lets you create a new folder from within the program.

> **W** Save As
>
> ◀ ○ ○ ▽ 📄 ▶ Libraries ▶ Documents ▶
>
> Organize ▼   New folder ──

Office 2010 programs such as Word include a button to create a new folder when you save a document.

QUICK REFERENCE: Creating a New Folder

Task	Procedure
Create a new folder	• Open a Documents or Computer window.
	• Display the location where you wish to create the new folder (for example, in the Documents library or your USB flash drive).
	• Click the New Folder button on the command bar.

Naming Folders   You use the same rules to name folders that you use to name files. Refer to the Naming Files Quick Reference table in Lesson 3 (page 96). A folder name can be up to 255 characters long and can use some types of punctuation marks, such as dashes, commas, and ampersands.

Opening Folders

You can use the same techniques to open a folder that you use to open files. You can select a folder by single-clicking and choosing Open from the command bar or by using a double click.

The Back Button

When you open a folder, you go "inside" it. How can you get back to the folder from which you opened it? The easiest method is to use the Back button. Each time you click the Back button, Windows takes you back to the previous view. One or two clicks of the Back button will usually get you back to the Documents library window where you started.

Create and Open a New Folder

In this exercise, you will create a new folder, open it, and then return to the Documents folder.

Before You Begin: The Documents window should be open.

1. If necessary, click on a clear area of the Documents window so no file is selected.

2. Click the New Folder button on the command bar, as shown below.

Windows displays the new folder name. Notice that the folder name is highlighted in blue, indicating that the name is selected for replacement.

3. Type **Letters to Family** as the new folder name, as shown at right, then tap the Enter key.

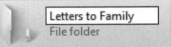

4. Make sure that the folder is still selected and then tap the Enter key once or double-click with the left mouse button to open the folder.

Windows opens the new folder. Notice that the folder is currently empty, since you've not yet saved any files to it. Notice that the folder name appears in the Address bar near the top of the window, indicating that you are viewing the (empty) contents of this folder.

> ▶ Student ▶ Documents ▶ Letters to Family

5. Click the Back button on the top-left side of the window.

You are back to viewing the Documents library. Notice the name on the address bar at the top of the window.

Now that you've learned how to create a new folder, it's time to see how you can place your own files into it.

Software Standards and Ease of Use

In the early days of personal computers, there was a great deal of innovation. Software companies would come up with all sorts of clever ways to make their programs useful and powerful. Unfortunately, what you learned with one program usually had nothing to do with another program. Learning a new program was so difficult that many people used the one or two programs they knew well for tasks the software was never designed for. These days, the situation is quite different. Now, what you learn as you use one program usually works with the next program. The reason for this enhanced ease of learning is *standards*: commonly used conventions that work similarly from one program to the next. The following two examples illustrate how standards make it much easier for beginners to learn basic tasks.

Example 1: Cut, Copy, and Paste The Cut, Copy, and Paste commands you learned in Lesson 3, Using a Word Processor, work in nearly all Windows programs. As you experienced in this lesson, these commands work in a similar fashion to help you move and copy files too, not just text. Let's take a closer look at the similarities. In the following illustrations, notice the Cut, Copy, and Paste commands.

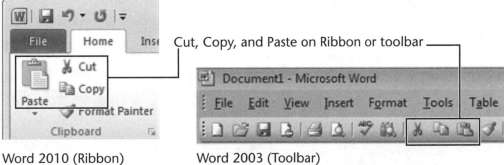

Cut, Copy, and Paste on Ribbon or toolbar

Word 2010 (Ribbon)   Word 2003 (Toolbar)

Cut, Copy, and Paste on command/menu bar

Win 7 Documents Library Window

Win XP

Word 2003

Example 2: Saving Your Work   The Save command is another example of software standards. With few exceptions, Windows programs feature File→Save and File→Save As commands. The first command always replaces the previously saved version of your file with the version that's currently on the screen. The second always allows you to name a file for the first time or to give the file a new name. Let's see how this works with programs you may never have seen before. Look for the Save and Save As commands in the menus for the following four programs.

Word 2010   Word 2007   Word 2003   Windows MovieMaker

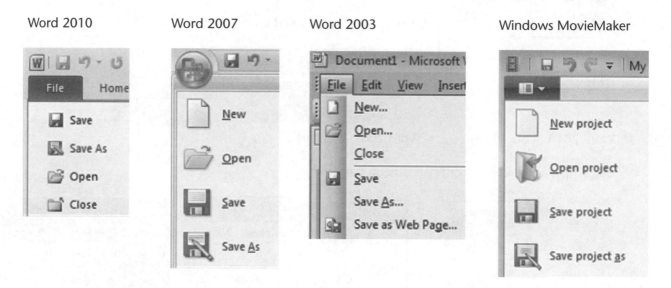

Are the menus different? Yes. Any program's menus will reflect the specific tasks it was designed to help you perform. But all of these menus have Save and Save As. This will be true for about 99 percent of all Windows programs you will ever use.

Conclusion: It Gets Easier from Here   Your first sessions on the computer will be the most difficult; then it starts getting easier—I promise. Go ahead and try using common commands such as Cut, Copy, and Paste you have just learned in these last two lessons when you use a new program. In nearly every case, common commands such as these will work just like it did when you first learned them. And with practice and repetition, these common commands will become second nature to you, just like numerous other everyday activities.

Moving and Copying Files

Once you save a file in a folder (or simply in the Documents library), it does not mean the file has to *stay* in that particular location. You have the option of moving the file into another folder if it suits your needs. The easiest way to move a file to another folder is to simply cut it from its original location and paste it in a new location. The commands used to perform this task are just like the Cut and Paste commands you learned about in Lesson 3, Using a Word Processor.

 TIP! This consistency with common commands such as Cut, Copy, and Paste is one reason why it's much easier to learn how to use a computer than it once was. You can exploit techniques learned in one program to work effectively in other programs, and in Windows itself.

Cut, Copy, and Paste for Files

The following table summarizes how the Cut, Copy, and Paste commands work when you use them in a Documents library window for file management. (Compare this table with the one in the Using Cut, Copy, and Paste section of Lesson 3.)

Command	Description
Cut	Delete the selected file after it is pasted in a new location.
Copy	Leave selected file in place after it is pasted in a new location.
Paste	Place the most recently cut or copied file into the location currently in view.

The Undo Command

New computer users are often concerned about deleting something important or breaking the computer. It is more difficult to disable a working computer than you might think. But, just in case things *do* go wrong, there is often a way to back out of what you just did. The Undo feature you learned about in Lesson 3, Using a Word Processor, is also available from the My Documents window. (Hmm, do you notice a trend here?)

 TIP! It's a good idea to use the Undo command immediately after you realize you've made a mistake or changed your mind about a command.

HANDS-ON 4.6 Move a File to a Different Folder

In this exercise, you will use the Cut and Paste technique to move a document file to the new Letters to Family folder. Then you will use the Undo feature to undo the command.

Before You Begin: The Documents library window should be open on the screen.

1. Click once on the Letter to Uncle Charlie document file.

   Windows highlights the file name and its icon to indicate that the file is selected for your next command.

2. Choose Organize→Cut from the command bar.

   Notice that the icon for the Letter to Uncle Charlie file appears slightly dimmed. This tells you that the file was cut and will be deleted here if you paste it somewhere else.

3. Double-click with the left mouse button on the Letters to Family folder. Or click once on the folder and then tap the ⎡Enter⎤ key if double-clicking does not work.

   Windows takes you to this empty folder. Notice the name of the folder in the address bar. Whenever you wonder exactly what you are viewing in the main (right) panel of a library or folder window, take a quick look at the address bar.

4. Choose Organize→Paste from the command bar.

   The file appears in the folder as Windows pastes it into this new location. Now let's see what happened to the file in the Documents library.

5. Click the Back ⬅ button on the top-left side of the window.

   You are back to viewing the Documents library. Notice the name on the title bar at the top of the window. Notice also that the Letter to Uncle Charlie document file is no longer in this folder. You successfully moved it into your new Letters to Family folder.

Undo the Cut and Paste Command

Let's say that you've changed your mind and do not wish to have the file moved after all. You can simply undo the previous command.

6. Choose Organize→Undo from the command bar.

   The Letter to Uncle Charlie document file reappears in the My Documents library. You have successfully undone the previous cut and paste commands that moved this file.

7. Double-click with the left mouse button to open the Letters to Family folder, or click once on the folder and tap the [Enter] key.

The folder is empty again after the Undo command you performed in step 6.

8. Click the Back ⬅ button on the top-left side of the window.

You are back to viewing the Documents library.

Moving and Copying Multiple Files

Sometimes you may wish to move or copy (that is, cut or copy) more than one file with the same command. In order to do this, you must first select the files you want affected by the Cut or Copy command. Normally, Windows only selects one file at a time whenever you give a single click. However, if you hold down the [Ctrl] (Control) key on the keyboard, Windows adds any additional files you click to the selection. Conversely, if you click on a file that's already selected while holding down the [Ctrl] key, Windows deselects that file.

The [Ctrl] key ——— The [Alt] key

Computer keyboards have special keys near the [Shift] key. (Your keyboard may not match this photo.)

Copying Files with the Copy Command

The Copy and Paste commands work just like the Cut and Paste commands you used in the previous exercise, with one exception. When you copy rather than cut your selection, the original file remains in the folder from which you copied it after you give the Paste command.

HANDS-ON 4.7 Copy Two Files to a Different Folder

In this exercise, you will use the Copy and Paste technique to copy your two letter document files to the new Letters to Family folder.

Before You Begin: The My Documents window should be open on the screen.

1. Follow these steps to see what happens when you select one file and then another file:

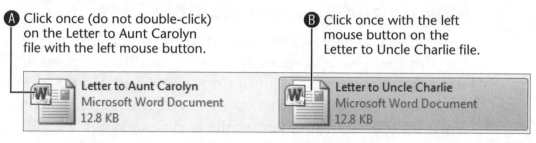

A Click once (do not double-click) on the Letter to Aunt Carolyn file with the left mouse button.

B Click once with the left mouse button on the Letter to Uncle Charlie file.

Letter to Aunt Carolyn Microsoft Word Document 12.8 KB

Letter to Uncle Charlie Microsoft Word Document 12.8 KB

Notice that when you selected the second file in step B, Windows removed the selection from the first file selected in step A. In the next step, you will select both files at the same time by holding down the Ctrl key.

2. Follow these steps to select both document files for copying:

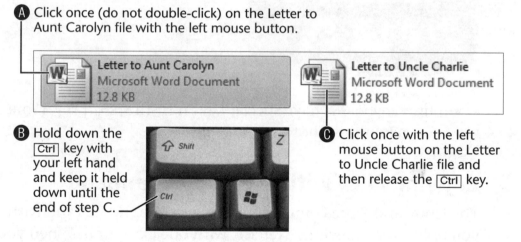

A Click once (do not double-click) on the Letter to Aunt Carolyn file with the left mouse button.

Letter to Aunt Carolyn Microsoft Word Document 12.8 KB

Letter to Uncle Charlie Microsoft Word Document 12.8 KB

B Hold down the Ctrl key with your left hand and keep it held down until the end of step C.

C Click once with the left mouse button on the Letter to Uncle Charlie file and then release the Ctrl key.

Notice that both files are now selected for your next command. Your screen should now appear similar to the following illustration:

Letter to Aunt Carolyn Microsoft Word Document 12.8 KB

Letter to Uncle Charlie Microsoft Word Document 12.8 KB

3. Choose Organize→Copy from the command bar.

Windows copies both files to the Clipboard for pasting. Notice that this time the document icons are not "dimmed" the way they had been when you used the Cut command in the previous exercise.

4. Double-click with the left mouse button on the Letters to Family folder. Or you can click once on the folder and then tap ⌈Enter⌉.

The folder is still empty after the Undo command you used at the end of the previous exercise.

5. Choose Organize→Paste from the command bar.

Both files appear in the folder as Windows pastes them into this new location. Since we used the Copy command, both files should also still be in the Documents library. Let's go back and see.

6. Click the Back button.

Notice that both files are still in the Documents library. Leave the My Documents window open since you will use it again in the next exercise.

Deleting and Restoring Files

As you use the computer to create new files, there may come a time when some of them will no longer be needed. Windows makes it easy as well as safe to delete unneeded files while also giving you a method to undo deletions even days after they were made. The key to this is the Recycle Bin.

The Windows Recycle Bin

When you delete a file on the hard drive—such as any file in the My Documents folder—the deleted file is not yet deleted forever. Where has the file gone? It is actually still on the hard drive! Windows does not physically delete the file until it needs the space for other files. You can still retrieve a file that has been deleted it by mistake.

!WARNING! Files deleted from USB flash drives *are not* sent to the Recycle Bin. You cannot restore (undelete) files deleted from these devices as described in this topic. The Restore command does work as described here on files stored on your computer's hard drive (in the Documents library, for example).

An Analogy   The Recycle Bin in Windows is much like the recycle bin you use for household recyclables. What day are your trash and recyclables picked up in your community? If Friday is trash day and you place an item in your household recycle bin on Monday, can you still retrieve that item on Thursday? Of course! The Windows Recycle Bin works the same way. It allows you to retrieve files and folders placed in the bin, returning them to a folder so they will be available to you in the future.

Restoring Deleted Files

You know that files placed in the Recycle Bin are not really gone. Placing files in the Recycle Bin can be compared to throwing an item in the recycle bin you have at home. Until the trash is picked up the item can be retrieved. In the same way, files deleted in Windows Explorer and put in the Recycle Bin can be returned (or restored) to their former location (the folder they were originally in). One way to restore a file is to display the contents of the Recycle Bin, select the file you wish to undelete, and then click Restore this Item in the task panel on the left side of the window.

Restore this item

Emptying the Recycle Bin

By design, the Recycle Bin holds your recently deleted items until it gets "full." After a certain proportion of space on your hard drive is taken up with old, deleted files, the Recycle Bin automatically deletes the oldest files inside it to make room for newly deleted files. If you wish, you can also empty the Recycle Bin yourself. Simply open the Recycle Bin and click Empty the Recycle Bin in the task panel of the left side of the window.

Empty the Recycle Bin

Delete and Restore a File

In this exercise, you will delete a copy of one of your letter files then open the Recycle Bin to view and restore this file.

Before You Begin: The Documents library should still be open on the screen.

Delete a Document File

1. Click once with the left mouse button (do not double-click) on the Letter to Uncle Charlie file.

2. Choose Organize→Delete from the command bar.

   Windows should display a prompt asking you to confirm deletion of the file. (It's very rare for this default option to be switched off.) Some details about the file to be deleted are also displayed.

   Delete File   ✕

   Are you sure you want to move this file to the Recycle Bin?

   Letter to Uncle Charlie
   Type: Microsoft Word Document
   Size: 12.8 KB
   Date modified: 6/4/2010 4:16 PM

   [Yes]   [No]

   ---

3. Choose Yes to confirm deletion of the file, or skip to the next step if the confirmation prompt was switched off.

   The file disappears as Windows moves the document from My Documents into the Recycle Bin. Now, you will open the Recycle Bin to see where the file has gone.

Open the Recycle Bin

4. Click once on the Minimize ⊟ button on the Documents window.

   Windows hides the My Documents window, leaving the Desktop fully visible.

5. Double-click the Recycle Bin icon on the Desktop, or click once on the Recycle Bin with the left mouse button and tap ⌷Enter⌷.

   A window displaying the contents of the Recycle Bin appears. Depending on files others have deleted, you may see just the Letter to Uncle Charlie document or numerous documents in the Recycle Bin. There may be so many documents that it will be difficult to find your file, but we will.

6. Follow the appropriate step:
   - Click once with the left button on the Letter to Uncle Charlie file if it is visible.
   - Tap the [L] key on the keyboard (the first letter of the filename) until the Letter to Uncle Charlie file appears highlighted. (Windows will move to each file with a name beginning with the letter you press.)

   The Letter to Uncle Charlie file is highlighted, ready for your next command.

7. Click Restore This Item on the command bar , as shown below.

   The file disappears from the Recycle Bin. Windows has restored it to the Documents library (from which you deleted it in step 3).

8. Close  the Recycle Bin window.

   The Desktop should be clear again. Now you will use the taskbar to restore the Documents library to the screen and confirm that the Letter to Uncle Charlie file has been undeleted.

9. Click the Documents library button on the Windows taskbar, as shown at right.

   The previously minimized Documents library window reappears.

10. Look for the Letter to Uncle Charlie file in the folder. It should be visible again.

11. Close  the Documents library window.

Organizing Digital Photos

Most computers come with a program that helps you transfer photos from your digital camera or smartphone. However, unless you transfer photos frequently, they probably won't be organized in a way that makes photos from specific events easy to identify. Your skills with file management will work with photo organization as well.

Organizing Folders Chronologically To organize the photos, you'll want to use folders. But how should you name the folders? Naming the folders by year, followed by the month and event is a good method. The months work best as two-digit numbers. So, the photos you took in February 2012 would go into a folder named 2012-02-[Event Name]. For example: 2012-02-Concert Photos. Now when you scan a list of folders, every event will be in chronological order.

Using year-month prefixes, folders for photos arrange in a neat chronological order.

Cutting and Pasting Once you create a folder, you can cut and paste photos into it. This method works like the commands you used with Word in Lesson 3, Using a Word Processor. Cutting a file will move it upon pasting; just like text in Word. You can use the cut and paste commands to move groups of photos for a specific event into a folder of their own.

Understanding Cloud Computing

Cloud computing is the running of programs and use of files that are housed on a storage drive somewhere on the Internet (the *Cloud*) rather than on your computer's local storage system. As with cloud storage, the physical location of your files doesn't really matter. Cloud computing takes the same concept of portability and applies it to the programs you run and the way you access your work (files).

Cloud Applications   A *cloud application* is an Internet-based program that loads onto your computer for temporary use. For example, you can run a cloud-based word processor from any computer. You don't have to install the program; it just runs from within your Web browser. Although cloud applications tend to lack the more sophisticated features of a traditional local drive-based application, they can perform basic tasks just fine.

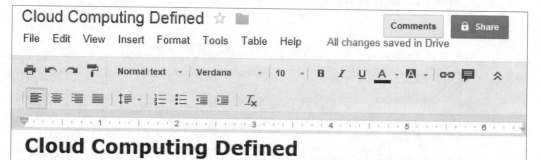

The word processor built into Google Drive is an example of a cloud application. Its basic controls will be familiar to any user of traditional word processing programs.

Sharing Files   The ability to share files easily is a significant benefit of Cloud storage. Because the file exists on a server somewhere in the Cloud, anyone with a link or some other form of permission can access it. To share a file with someone, you send them a link and/or password.

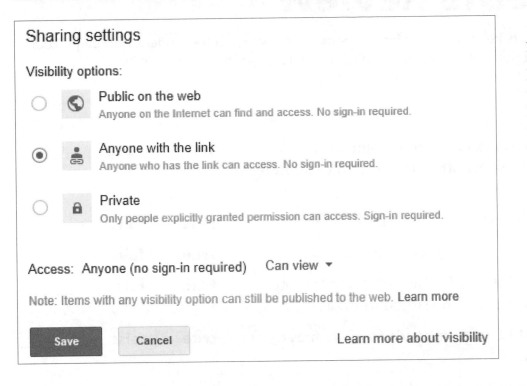

Sharing settings

Visibility options:

○ 🌐 **Public on the web**
Anyone on the Internet can find and access. No sign-in required.

◉ 👤 **Anyone with the link**
Anyone who has the link can access. No sign-in required.

○ 🔒 **Private**
Only people explicitly granted permission can access. Sign-in required.

Access: Anyone (no sign-in required) Can view ▾

Note: Items with any visibility option can still be published to the web. **Learn more**

Save Cancel Learn more about visibility

A dialog for Google Drive allows you to set how a file is shared. In this example, sending a link to someone gives them immediate access to the file.

Synchronization between Devices Another benefit of cloud computing is the ease with which you can make the same information available on all of your electronic devices. For example, from your smartphone you can view a phone directory created on your computer. If you make a change to the directory on one of your devices, the updated version can automatically synchronize to your other devices.

Using a service such as Dropbox, the same file can appear on all your devices from a single Cloud-based location.

Concepts Review

All of the Concepts Review quizzes for this book are available on the student web page. Your instructor will let you know how to complete the quizzes (in the book or online).

True/False Questions

Page number

1. Managing files on a Windows computer is similar to managing a filing system in an office that uses file cabinets and folders.   **true**   **false**   _____

2. The Documents library is located on the hard drive.   **true**   **false**   _____

3. You can control the double-click speed of the mouse.   **true**   **false**   _____

4. You cannot store folders inside of other folders in the My Documents folder; only files can be stored in folders.   **true**   **false**   _____

5. You can use the Cut and Paste commands to move files from one location to another.   **true**   **false**   _____

6. You must move or copy files one at a time.   **true**   **false**   _____

Multiple Choice Questions

7. What happens when you delete a file on the hard drive?
   Page number _____
   a. The file is immediately erased.
   b. The file is marked for future deletion.
   c. The file is placed in the Recycle Bin.
   d. The file is permanently deleted.

8. When can you create a new folder?
   Page number _____
   a. When you move a file
   b. When you copy a file
   c. While you browse files in the My Documents window
   d. All of the above

9. What does the Back  button on the My Documents window do?
   Page number _____
   a. Takes you back to the most recently used program
   b. Takes you back to the previous folder you were browsing
   c. Undoes your most recent command
   d. None of above

10. The Documents library _____.
    Page number _____
    a. is located on the hard drive
    b. stores your own files
    c. can contain other folders
    d. All of the above
    e. Only a and b

SKILL BUILDER 4.1 **Browse My Documents**

In this exercise, you will open the My Documents folder and open a document file saved in the Letters to Family folder you created previously.

1. If necessary, start the computer and log in.

2. Click Start and then choose Documents from the right panel.

   Windows displays the contents of the My Documents folder.

3. Click the Maximize button if the Documents window is not already maximized.

   - If the window is already maximized, the middle window sizing button will appear with the restore button like the figure at right. In this case, you can skip directly to step 4.

   If it did not already, the My Documents window now fills the screen, except for the Windows taskbar at the very bottom of the screen.

4. Double-click to open the Letters to Family folder icon (not the name of the folder), or click once on the folder icon and then tap the [Enter] key if you have trouble double-clicking.

   Windows displays the contents of the folder. The two document files you copied to the folder should be visible.

   The address bar displays the current folder location.

   ▸ Libraries ▸ Documents ▸ Letters to Family

5. Double-click to open the Letter to Aunt Carolyn document, or click once to select the document and then tap the [Enter] key to open it.

   There will be a pause as Windows starts the Word program to display your document.

6. Close ☒ the Word window. Choose No if Word asks if you wish to save any changes to the document.

   You are back to viewing the Letters to Family folder.

7. Click the Back ⬅ button to return to viewing the My Documents folder.

   Leave the My Documents window open. You will create a new folder here in the next Skill Builder exercise.

Create and Rename a Folder

In this exercise, you will create a new folder in the My Documents folder.

Before You Begin: The My Documents window should be open. Follow step 2 in Skill Builder 4.1 if you don't recall how to open a My Documents window.

1. Click the New Folder button on the command bar.

   Windows displays a new folder. Notice that the folder name is highlighted, ready for you to type the new name.

2. Type **Practice** as the new folder name and then tap the [Enter] key. You can use the [Backspace] key if necessary to correct any typos.

   Windows displays the folder with the new name.

Rename the Folder

3. Follow these steps to rename the folder:

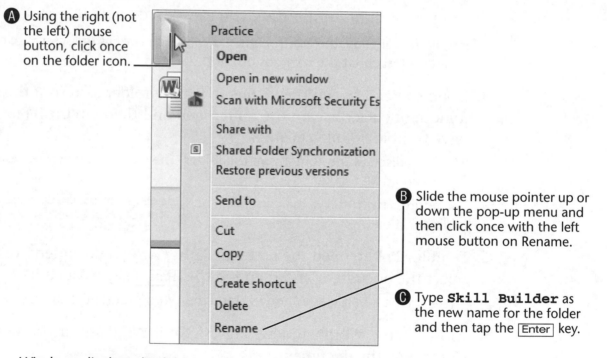

Ⓐ Using the right (not the left) mouse button, click once on the folder icon.

Ⓑ Slide the mouse pointer up or down the pop-up menu and then click once with the left mouse button on Rename.

Ⓒ Type **Skill Builder** as the new name for the folder and then tap the [Enter] key.

   Windows displays the folder with the new name. It's easy to rename a folder if necessary.

4. Double-click to open the Skill Builder folder, or click once on the folder and then tap the [Enter] key if you have trouble double-clicking.

   The folder is empty since you have not yet saved, moved, or copied any files to it.

5. Click the Back [←] button to return to viewing the My Documents folder.

   Leave the My Documents window open.

6. Click once to select the Skill Builder folder and then tap the ⌈Delete⌉ key on the keyboard, or choose Organize→Delete from the command bar.

Windows will ask you to confirm deletion of this folder. Since you know it is empty, it is safe to delete the folder. (And anyway, you could undelete it from the Recycle Bin if necessary unless it's on your USB flash drive.)

7. Choose Yes to confirm deletion of the folder.

The folder disappears into the Recycle Bin, from which you could undelete it if you felt the deletion was a mistake.

SKILL BUILDER 4.3 ## Copy Files to a USB Flash Drive

In this exercise, you will copy files from the My Documents folder to a USB flash drive.

To Perform This Exercise: You need a USB flash drive (sometimes called a thumb drive or a pen drive). Your computer must also be equipped with a USB port.

Before You Begin: The My Documents window should be open. Follow step 2 in Skill Builder 4.1 if you don't recall how to open a My Documents window.

1. Follow these steps to select two document files for your copy command:

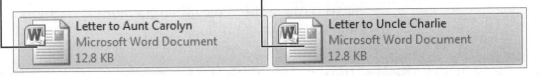

Ⓐ Click once with the left mouse button on the document icon to select the Letter to Aunt Carolyn document file.

Ⓑ Hold down the ⌈Ctrl⌉ key on the keyboard and then click once with the left mouse button on the document icon to select the Letter to Uncle Charlie document file.

Letter to Aunt Carolyn	Letter to Uncle Charlie
Microsoft Word Document	Microsoft Word Document
12.8 KB	12.8 KB

Ⓒ Release the ⌈Ctrl⌉ key.

Windows displays a highlight on the two files you selected.

2. Choose Organize→Copy from the command bar.

Windows copies the file information to the clipboard for use when you give the Paste command in a later step.

3. Close ⎯⎯⎯X⎯⎯⎯ the My Documents window.

Windows will open a new window to display the contents of the USB flash drive when you complete step 5.

4. Plug the USB flash drive into an available USB port on the front or rear of the computer.

There will be a pause as Windows examines the contents of the USB flash drive. Then a window will appear asking what you wish to do with this new drive.

5. If necessary, use the scroll bar on the right side of the window to view the bottom of the list and then choose Open Folder to View Files Using Windows Explorer and click the OK button.

The address bar displays the current folder location. The flash drive name may differ from the one shown in the figure.

 !NOTE! The name and drive letter displayed for the USB flash drive will probably differ from the figures above. Windows assigns drive letters as it needs them, and they do not affect your ability to view or copy files on the flash drive..

This USB flash drive has a name set for it by the manufacturer.

6. Choose Organize→Paste from the command bar.

There will be a brief pause as Windows copies the files to the USB flash drive. If some one else has already copied the same files to this flash drive, Windows will ask if you wish to overwrite the old versions of the files on the flash drive with the new versions you are copying from the hard drive.

 !NOTE! You may see a light flashing on the USB flash drive. This tells you that files are being read from or written to the drive. It is important never to remove the drive while the light is flashing. It might cause the loss of files on the drive.

7. Click the Yes to All button with the left mouse button if Windows asks if you wish to overwrite other versions of the files on the flash drive. Otherwise, read the comment below and continue to the next step.

When the Paste command is completed, you will see the files in the window.

8. Follow these steps to safely eject your flash drive:

Ⓐ Click the Show Hidden Icons button.

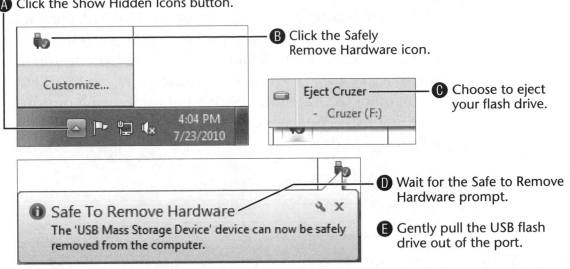

Ⓑ Click the Safely Remove Hardware icon.

Ⓒ Choose to eject your flash drive.

Ⓓ Wait for the Safe to Remove Hardware prompt.

Ⓔ Gently pull the USB flash drive out of the port.

Searching for Files

Sometimes you will have trouble finding files on your system. This won't be a problem in this course because you are working with just a few files in the My Documents folder. But, what if you had to keep track of a hundred files? Searching for a file in this situation could feel like finding the proverbial needle in a haystack. Fortunately, Windows has an excellent Search utility to help you quickly locate files. With additional search options, you can also locate files of specific types or files that were created or last modified within a specific range of dates.

There is a Search box on all Folder and Computer windows.

The search word(s) you used are highlighted.

A preview of the text in a document appears in the search window.

A right-click on the file displays a command to open the folder where it is located.

Documents library
Search Results

Arrange by: Top results ▼

Letter to Aunt Carolyn
Dear Aunt Carolyn and Uncle Stephen, I am writing our family history, and I would like to ask you some questio...
C:\Users\Studer

Date modified: 6/5/2010 2:03 PM
Size: 12.8 KB
Authors: Student

Open
Edit
New
Print

Letter to Unc
June 4, 2010 Dea writing our fam
C:\Users\Studer

d: 6/4/2010 4:16 PM

dent

Rename

Open file location

Properties

QUICK REFERENCE: Finding a File or Folder

Task	Procedure
Find a file on Win 7	• Open a Folder or Computer window. • Type all or part of the name of the file in the Search box at the top-right corner of the window.

SKILL BUILDER 4.4   Search for Files

In this exercise, you will use Window's search utility to search for files on your exercise diskette.

1. Choose Start→Documents to open the Documents folder.

2. Type **letter** in the search box on the top-right corner of the Documents window.

   Windows displays a list of search results. Depending on files others have created on your computer and where your own files are stored, you may see a large or small number of search results. However, the search utility should have found your Letters to Family folder and the letter files you moved in the lesson.

3. Double-click one of the files or folders in the search results to open it.

   Windows opens the file or folder.

4. Close ▐ X ▌ the program window or folder window.

5. If necessary, close ▐ X ▌ the search results window.

The Internet

In this unit, you will go online! In Lesson 5, you will be introduced to the Internet and Internet Explorer. You will navigate with the address bar, links, and navigation buttons. In Lesson 6, you will search for websites using the instant search box and keywords. You will also use Internet Explorer's tabbed browsing feature. Other topics in this lesson include bookmarks and favorites, the history view, and printing web pages. In Lesson 7, you will work with webmail to create, proofread, and send an email message. Other topics in this lesson include working with email folders, receiving new messages, replying to messages, and signing out of webmail. In Lesson 8, you will send and receive email attachments. You will also download files from the web and learn about viruses and internet security. This unit includes many WebSims, web-based simulations of tasks performed on the web.

The Internet

Browsing Web Pages

The World Wide Web (or "the web") is the richest information resource in human history. There are tens of millions of websites in the world, and you can navigate to any of them with just a few keystrokes and clicks. The web organizes information onto pages connected by links, which you click to navigate to other web pages. You view web pages with an application program called a web browser. One of the most popular web browsers is Microsoft's Internet Explorer, which comes installed with all versions of Windows. In this lesson, you will learn the basics of browsing web pages with Internet Explorer.

LESSON OBJECTIVES

After studying this lesson, you will be able to:

- Define the Internet
- Navigate to web pages by typing in the browser's Address bar
- Describe how a computer connects to the Internet
- Navigate in a website via hyperlinks
- Navigate using the browser's controls
- Browse web pages in full-screen view

Additional learning resources are available at labpub.com/learn/silver/wtwc4/

Case Study: Using an Online Encyclopedia

Josie has browsed the web off and on since she first learned to use a computer. She's pretty amazed by the incredible variety of interests and information she finds on the web. In fact, she starts to wonder if the web isn't a watershed of human progress on a par with writing, the sailing ship, or perhaps even the wheel. Josie wants to learn more about the origins of this technology, so she goes to a website a friend recommended, a place called Wikipedia. It's an online encyclopedia that people all over the world are creating and adding to every day. The friend gives Josie Wikipedia's web address (also called a uniform resource locator, or URL). Josie types the address into the Address bar of her web browser, and soon she's found an article.

Browsing the article, Josie discovers that spots in the articles called *hyperlinks* let her swiftly jump to all sorts of related topics. Connections to past and recent events and discoveries abound in most every paragraph.

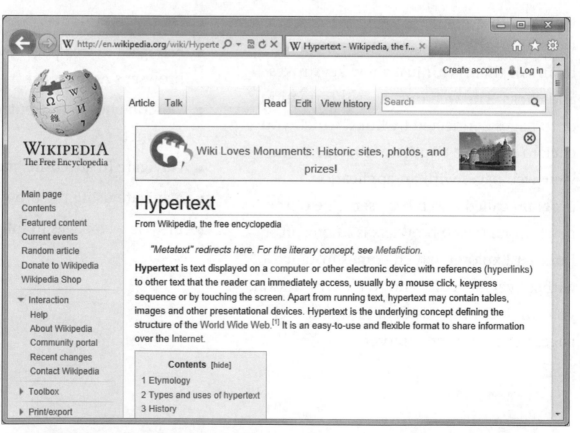

The Wikipedia.org website contains tens of thousands of articles in a vast online encyclopedia.

Defining the Internet

The Internet is the world's largest computer network. It is an interconnected system of computers residing on every continent. These computers "talk" to each other with a common set of rules (called *protocols*). Every computer on the Internet has the capability to send information to any other computer that is also connected to the Internet.

The Internet supports many services for global communications. The two most commonly used services on the Internet are the *web* and electronic mail (*email*). However, the Internet also supports many other types of services.

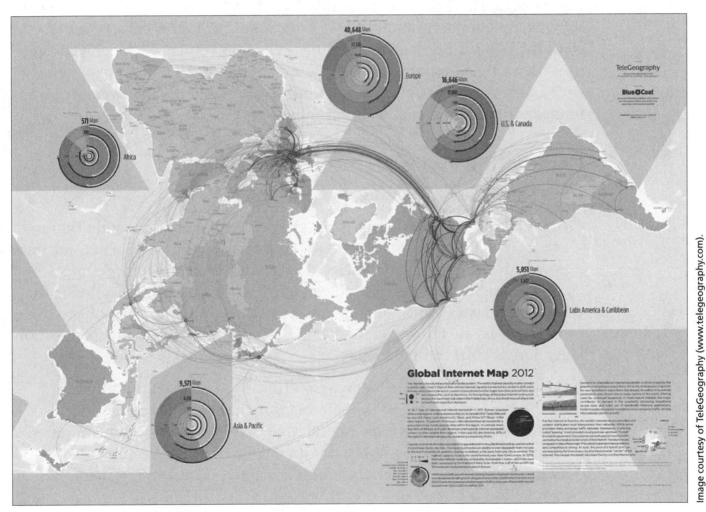

A connectivity map shows the major Internet network lines throughout the world.

Image courtesy of TeleGeography (www.telegeography.com).

Connecting to the Internet

In order to use Internet services, your computer must have a connection to the Internet. This connection usually comes to your computer via a telephone line, television cable, or a corporate network. Nearly all home connections make use of an *Internet service provider* (also called an ISP).

Internet Service Providers

A company that sells Internet connections is called an Internet Service Provider (ISP). There are national ISPs that service virtually any location in the country. There are also numerous local ISPs that offer regional coverage only. Many telephone and cable TV companies now offer ISP services. National ISPs include America Online (AOL) and PeoplePC. When you sign up with an ISP, you pay a monthly subscription fee. The ISP provides you with an email address, the information, and possibly the hardware required to make the Internet connection.

Connection Types

There are four primary means of Internet connection:

- **Broadband Modem**—This is a high-speed Internet connection that is available in most non-rural areas and is increasingly available in rural areas as well. It uses a TV cable or Digital Subscriber Line (DSL) modem to connect to the Internet. The advantage of a broadband connection is that it is much faster than a dial-up modem connection. Most broadband connections are always on, which means you have an Internet connection as soon as your computer starts.

- **Corporate/Academic Network**—This is the most commonly used method of connecting to the Internet from a school or business office. This connection works over a Local Area Network (LAN). Your computer communicates over the LAN with other computers in the network also connected to the Internet. Like most broadband connections, a LAN connection is always on.

- **Wireless (WiFi)**—This type of connection is available in airports, hotels, public meeting places such as libraries and cafes, and business offices. Many home users are also setting up wireless access to the Internet. Wireless connections are a means for rural areas to have broadband Internet access where cable TV and DSL connections are not available. You may encounter two types of wireless connections:

    o **Public**—Your computer can detect and immediately connect to this type of wireless connection.

    o **Encrypted**—This type of wireless connection requires a security password to use. Some airports and cafes offer daily, weekly, or monthly subscriptions that give you this connection.

- **Dial-up Modem**—This is a fading method of connecting to the Internet from a home. It depends on a device called a dial-up modem to connect your computer to an ISP. When your modem dials up to the ISP's computer, you have access to the Internet through the ISP's connection. When you disconnect your modem connection to the ISP, you lose your Internet connection until the next time you dial up.

Sharing an Internet Connection

If your home has more than one computer or if you have a visitor with a notebook computer, it is easy to share the Internet connection between them. The two most popular methods are listed below:

- **Wireless Router**—A wireless router broadcasts a wireless signal that can reach throughout a normal-sized home. You can share a home wireless connection with multiple computers throughout the house. You can even print to a printer attached to the network via the router or another computer. A wireless router also allows wired connections to nearby computers. Some broadband modems also serve as a wireless router.

Photo courtesy of Buffalo Technology (USA).

- **Wired Router**—A wired router is a small hardware device that allows you to run network cables to each computer. You can plug your Internet connection into the router to share it with any computer on the network.

HANDS-ON 5.1 Check Your Internet Connection

In this exercise, you will check which type of Internet connection is running on your computer.

> **!NOTE!** Some computer labs do not allow access to the commands below. If you find that a step does not work, skip the rest of this exercise and continue reading the next topic. (Also, you can try this exercise on your home or office computer.)

1. Click Start > Computer and then choose Network from the left panel.

   A Network window appears to display your computer's network.

2. Click the Network and Sharing Center button on the toolbar.

| Organize ▾ | Network and Sharing Center | Add a printer | Add a wireless device |

The Network and Sharing Center appears to display your Internet connection.

3. Close [X] the Network and Sharing Center window.

Using Internet Explorer

Internet Explorer (IE) is an application program—similar to a word processor or spreadsheet—but it is designed for viewing and navigating web pages on the Internet. There are several ways to launch Internet Explorer. When you start the browser, it will begin searching for a page on either the Internet or your hard drive.

QUICK REFERENCE: Starting Internet Explorer

Task	Procedure
Via the Start menu	Choose Start > All Programs > Internet Explorer.
Via the taskbar	Click the taskbar pinned Internet Explorer button on the Windows taskbar.

> **!NOTE!** This book concentrates on the use of Internet Explorer 9, which comes installed with all new Win 7 computers and may also be installed on Win Vista computers (but not Win XP).

Other Browsers

Internet Explorer is one of the most popular web browser programs, there are many others you can install and use in its place. These include Firefox, Chrome, and Safari. Most of these browsers have similar features to Internet Explorer. You can download and install them directly from the web.

The Homepage

When you launch Internet Explorer, the first page you see displayed is the *homepage*. Internet Explorer allows you to set any page on the web as your homepage. The homepage you are viewing now may be the Microsoft Network (MSN) website, or it may be set to a page for your educational institution.

 NOTE! Later in this lesson, you will learn how to set your own homepage.

HANDS-ON 5.2 **Start Internet Explorer**

In this exercise, you will start the Internet Explorer browser program.

1. Click the Internet Explorer icon on the taskbar beside the Start button or choose Start > All Programs > Internet Explorer.

The browser window appears and displays the homepage.

2. Click the Maximize ▣ button if the browser window does not fill the screen. Leave the browser window open. You will be using it throughout this lesson.

Internet Explorer Window Features

Like many other application programs, Internet Explorer has menus and a toolbar that allow you to give commands, such as to navigate back and forth between web pages, print, or return to the homepage. The following figure displays some of the most significant features of the Internet Explorer window. Depending on how Internet Explorer is set up on your computer, there may be additional features visible as well. You will use many of these features in this lesson.

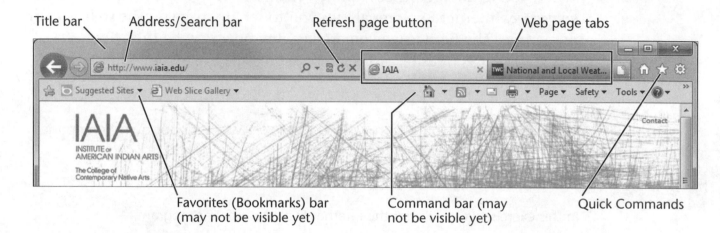

Navigating with the Address/Search Bar

Internet Explorer 9 introduces an integrated address and search bar. When you type a valid web address (see next topic, below) Internet Explorer displays that web page. When you type something else in the address/search bar, Internet Explorer performs a search with the currently set search engine (see the Searching from the Address Bar section of Lesson 6).

Typing Web Addresses

In order to navigate the web, you need to tell your browser which sites you wish to view. Every page on the web has a unique identifying address, called a URL. When you enter a URL in the address/search bar, the browser loads the web page found at that address.

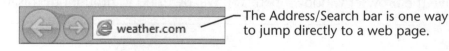
The Address/Search bar is one way to jump directly to a web page.

 NOTE! From now on the Address/Search bar will simply be called the "Address bar." Special search features of this bar will be covered in Lesson 6.

URLs

A URL (pronounced "you are el") is essentially an address for a web page. Similar to residential addresses, URLs contain several parts that help your browser find the exact page you are looking for. Every URL contains a domain name, for example. A URL may also contain file and folder names that point to a specific web page. If page names and folder names are part of a URL, each is separated by a forward slash (/).

The parts of a URL are shown in the following illustration:

| http:// | labpub.com | learn/silver/wtwc4/ | index.htm |
| Protocol | Domain name | Folder names | Page name |

NOTE! When you type a URL in the Address bar, you can leave out the *http://* protocol portion of the URL because the browser adds this automatically.

The Refresh Button

⟳ The Refresh button reloads any web page currently displayed. Use the Refresh button when it appears that a web page did not load completely or it is out-of-date.

HANDS-ON 5.3 ## Navigate with the Address Bar

In this exercise, you will navigate to the National Park Service web page, the student web page, and a linked page from the student web page.

1. Click once in the Address bar to highlight the current address as shown at right (the highlighted URL will differ from the one shown here).

The current address turns blue to show it is highlighted. Now it will be replaced by whatever you type. (There is no need to use the Backspace or Delete key.)

2. Type **nps.gov** in the Address bar as shown at right and then tap Enter.

The National Park Service web page appears. The .gov domain name at the end of the URL lets you know that this is a governmental website (the official National Park Service website) and not a commercial site.

3. Click once to highlight the current address, type **google.com** in the Address bar, and tap Enter.

The Google search engine website appears. You will learn more about using Google in Lesson 6, Searching for Websites.

Navigate to a Web Page

Now you will navigate to a specific web page. Be sure to type the URL below exactly as it is written. Incorrectly typing even a single letter can cause you to miss the page.

4. Click once in the Address bar (to highlight the current address), type **labpub.com/learn/silver/wtwc4/broadband.htm** exactly as shown, and tap Enter.

A web page about broadband Internet connections appears. This page is one of several that support this book. Now you will go to the student page for this book by deleting part of the URL.

5. Follow these steps to modify the current URL:

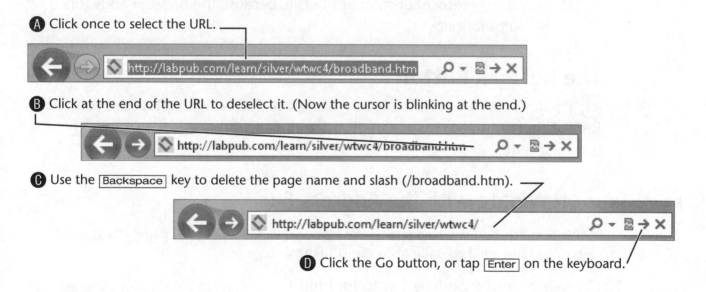

Ⓐ Click once to select the URL.

Ⓑ Click at the end of the URL to deselect it. (Now the cursor is blinking at the end.)

Ⓒ Use the Backspace key to delete the page name and slash (/broadband.htm).

Ⓓ Click the Go button, or tap Enter on the keyboard.

The default student web page appears. When you don't indicate a specific page in a URL, Internet Explorer displays the default page found in the address.

Behind the Screen

Internet Domains

About Domains A *domain* is a computer network connected to the Internet. A domain may consist of a single computer or hundreds of computers networked together. Every computer connected to the Internet is part of a domain. Most domains use a domain name to make them easy to identify. The most basic identifier for a domain is its top-level domain.

Top-level Domains The characters that follow the period at the end of a domain name indicate the top-level domain a website belongs to. There are many types of top-level domains. When domain names were first created, several top-level domains were designated. Additional top-level domains have been added to the list over the years. The following table lists several different top-level domains and the types of organizations they usually represent.

Top-level Domain	Description	Examples	Organization Name
.com	A commercial website	microsoft.com sears.com	Microsoft, Inc. Sears, Roebuck & Co.
.edu	An educational institution	berkeley.edu sfcc.edu	U.C. Berkeley Santa Fe Community College
.org	A nonprofit organization	npr.org amnesty.org	National Public Radio Amnesty International
.gov	A government agency	irs.gov state.gov	Internal Revenue Service US Secretary of State
.jp	An organization based in Japan	japantimes.co.jp yahoo.co.jp	Japan Times Publications Yahoo! Japan

Example Josie views some web pages about national parks in the American Southwest. She notices that the domain names that end in ".gov" are official National Park Service websites. Web pages that end in ".com" are nearly always commercial websites independent of the national parks.

Smart Address Bar

Internet Explorer's Address bar incorporates Autocomplete technology to help you enter URLs of previously visited websites more quickly. As you type a URL, the Address bar checks it against your previous browsing history, and favorites (bookmarks), looking for possible matches. It displays the potential matches as you type.

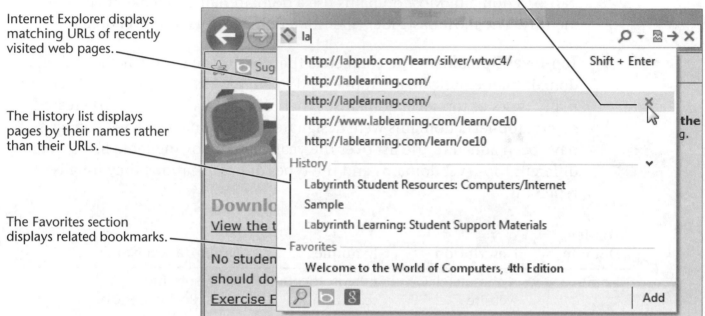

You can delete misspelled URLs in the list.

Internet Explorer displays matching URLs of recently visited web pages.

The History list displays pages by their names rather than their URLs.

The Favorites section displays related bookmarks.

Recently Viewed Pages

Internet Explorer also displays all recently visited web pages. This feature allows you to view the list, then immediately select a page from the list to navigate back to the page.

The Autocomplete ▼ menu button displays recently visited web pages.

Navigate Recently Entered URLs

In this exercise, you will navigate to the book web page via AutoComplete.

1. Follow these steps to use the Smart Address Bar:

A Click the Home button to return to the homepage.

B Click once on the URL in the Address bar and type the following: **labpub**. (Internet Explorer's AutoComplete feature will enter the .com automatically, as shown here.)

C Choose the broadband.html item in the AutoComplete list.

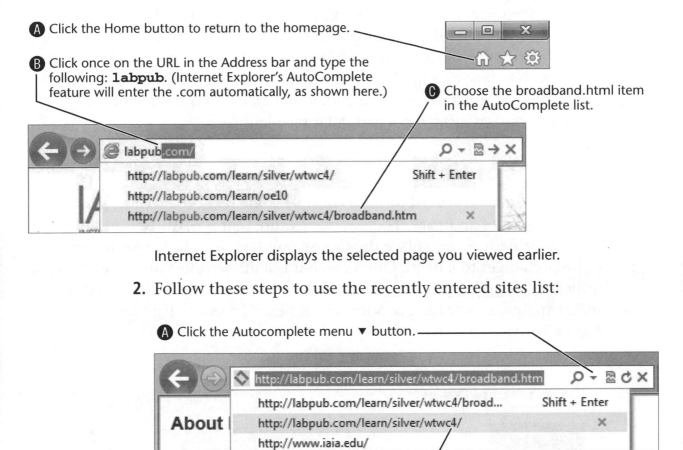

Internet Explorer displays the selected page you viewed earlier.

2. Follow these steps to use the recently entered sites list:

A Click the Autocomplete menu ▼ button.

B Choose the wtwc4 item.

Internet Explorer displays the student web page.

Navigating with Links

After URLs, a *link* (short for *hyperlink*) is the most basic tool for web navigation. A link is essentially an object on a web page that can point to some other location on the same page, a different page, or even a different website. Web pages with links are examples of *hypertext*. Ted Nelson coined this term in 1963 while a sociology student at Harvard. He envisioned a book with hypertext connections to all human knowledge. Links usually navigate you to a web page or a specific location on a web page. Some links may perform other functions, such as generating an email message that is addressed automatically to a particular recipient.

Varieties of Links

A link can take on several forms. It may be some text on a web page or an image or part of an image. There is one feature that is consistent for *all* forms of links. Whenever you place the mouse pointer over a link, the mouse pointer changes to a hand. On many, but not all, websites links are often indicated by underscored text. However, not all links are underscored, and many are buttons or images. Some examples of links are displayed on the following page.

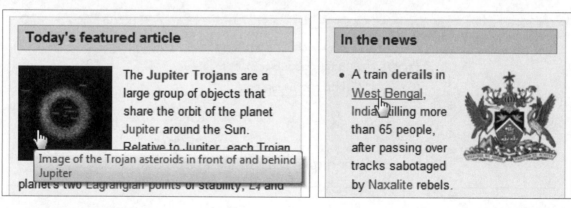

Anything on a web page that causes the pointer to change to a hand functions as a link. A picture and some underscored text on these web pages each serve as links.

⚠️ **TIP!** When in doubt, point at a potential a link. If the pointer changes to a hand 👆, you know you're pointing at a link.

About WebSims

In the following exercise, you will perform the steps on a special type of web page. A *WebSim* is a **simulation** of a real website. Because most websites change over time, these instructions might not work on the "live" version of the site. A copy of the actual website is stored on the website for this book and will always work exactly according to the exercise instructions.

 !NOTE! All WebSim pages are clearly identified with the word *Simulation* in a corner of the WebSim screen. Most of the links on WebSim pages are disabled. Only links used in the exercise are active.

Click the Forward button if a step does not work.
This will get you to the next step in most cases.

Many (but not all) WebSims have a control similar to this one.

 HANDS-ON 5.5 Navigate with Links

WebSim

In this exercise, you will look up *hypertext* in Wikipedia.org, and then you will use links to navigate to related topics.

Before You Begin: The student web page should be open in Internet Explorer.

1. Click the Navigate with Links link on the student web page.

   A new Internet Explorer window appears, and there will be a pause as a special WebSim web page loads. The new Internet Explorer window is maximized to make as much room available to display the WebSim.

   As the WebSim starts, the Wikipedia homepage appears. It displays the various languages in which you can view its articles.

2. Click in the search box, type **hypertext** as shown at right, and tap the Enter key.

   | hypertext | English |

   The Wikipedia article devoted to this topic appears. Notice the words that appear in blue in the first paragraph and the Contents box below it. Each of these words is a link.

3. Follow these steps to navigate with a link:

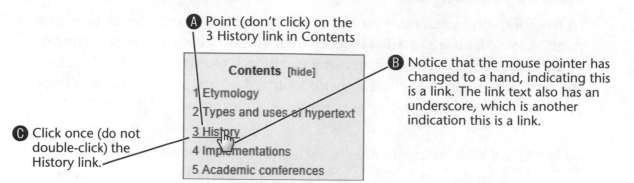

Ⓐ Point (don't click) on the
3 History link in Contents

Ⓑ Notice that the mouse pointer has changed to a hand, indicating this is a link. The link text also has an underscore, which is another indication this is a link.

Ⓒ Click once (do not double-click) the History link.

Contents [hide]

1 Etymology
2 Types and uses of hypertext
3 History
4 Implementations
5 Academic conferences

The History section of the article immediately appears. This part of the article also features numerous links, each marked in blue.

4. Click the Vannevar Bush link in the second paragraph of the History topic. (The line that begins "In 1945, …")

This link jumps you to a brief biography of the American academic whose essay "As We May Think" pioneered many ideas that we now use daily on the web.

5. Click the Continue to Next WebSim button.

The title of the next WebSim appears since it begins where this one leaves off. Read the next topic until you reach the next Hands-On exercise.

Browsing Controls

Web pages may or may not have navigation controls (such as *next* and *previous* links) built into them. Fortunately, your web browser has basic navigation controls that are always available. These basic navigation controls allow you to navigate reliably in any type of website. They also have some features that ordinary links lack.

Basic Navigation Buttons

The most basic navigation controls on Internet Explorer are the Forward and Back buttons. Normally, the Back/Forward buttons jump you one page at a time. However, you can also make multipage jumps, rather than having to click back page-by-page.

Back/Forward
buttons

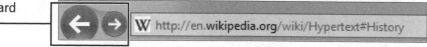

W http://en.wikipedia.org/wiki/Hypertext#History

Making Multipage Jumps

The Back button allows you to jump several pages at once. This can be much faster than clicking the Back/Forward buttons repeatedly. For example, you can jump from deep within a website back to its homepage with a single jump.

A right-click on the Back button displays a list of recently-visited pages.

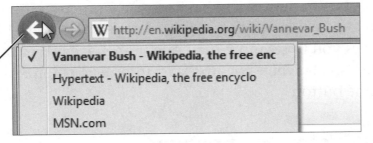

HANDS-ON 5.6 Navigate Back and Forward

WebSim

In this exercise, you will navigate back and forth through web pages you've already visited.

Before You Begin: The Navigate Back and Forth exercise should be displayed. If it is not, go to the web page for this book and then click the Navigate Back and Forth link.

Notice that the Forward button is presently grayed out. This is because you cannot move "forward" until you have moved back at least one page.

1. Click the Back ← button.

   Internet Explorer returns to the display of the previous web page. Now the Forward button is colored and active.

2. Click the → Forward button.

   Internet Explorer returns to the web page you moved back from in step 1. Notice that the Forward button is grayed-out again, since there's once again no page you've moved back from.

3. Follow these steps to jump back several pages:

Ⓐ Right-click (don't left click) on the Back button.

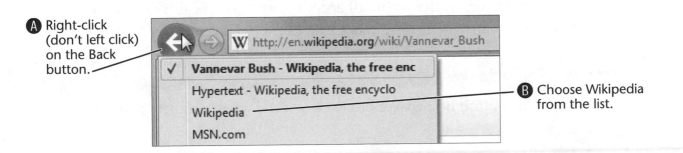

Ⓑ Choose Wikipedia from the list.

Internet Explorer jumps you back to the Wikipedia homepage. However, this is the simulation version of the page, so in the next step you will close the simulation window.

4. Hold down the Ctrl key and then tap **W** on the keyboard to close the WebSim Internet Explorer window.

The student web page is visible again.

The Home Button

The Home 🏠 button jumps you back to your homepage (the page the browser displayed when you first started Internet Explorer). Internet Explorer allows you to set more than one homepage. All of these homepages open simultaneously when you first start Internet Explorer or whenever you click the Home button.

Setting a Custom Homepage

You do not have to use the homepage originally programmed for Internet Explorer. For example, a computer vendor may program its own website as the homepage on a new computer. You can change the homepage whenever you wish and set a web page as an additional homepage.

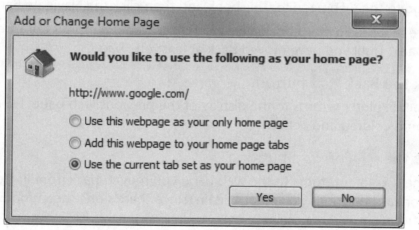

The Add or Change Home Page dialog box lets you choose to create multiple homepages or to use just one.

Multiple Homepages Example   Josie likes to check the news headlines of her local newspaper, her webmail account, and the local weather when she first starts web browsing. She sets these three websites as her homepages.

| 🌐 (4 unread) - rstolins - Yah... ✕ | 🌐 Local news briefs - The Santa... | 🌦 87508 Weather, Current Con... | 🏠 ⭐ ⚙ |

Josie's Home button homepages display when she starts Internet Explorer.

Task	Procedure
Add a new homepage	• Display the web page you wish to use as a homepage. • Right-click (don't left-click) the homepage 🏠 button and then choose Add or Change Home Page from the pop-up menu. • Choose whether to set current page as the only homepage or add it as an additional homepage and click Yes.
Change your homepage to a set of tabs	• Open the set of pages you wish to use as your new homepages, each in its own tab on the same Internet Explorer window. • Right-click (don't left-click) the Home 🏠 button and then choose Add or Change Home Page from the pop-up menu. • Choose Use the Current Tab Set As Your New Home Page, and then choose Yes.

HANDS-ON 5.7 Set a Custom Homepage

In this exercise, you will set a new page as your homepage and then reset the homepage to the original homepage.

Set an Additional Homepage

1. Make sure that the Welcome to the World of Computers book page is displayed.

2. Follow these steps to add this to your homepages:

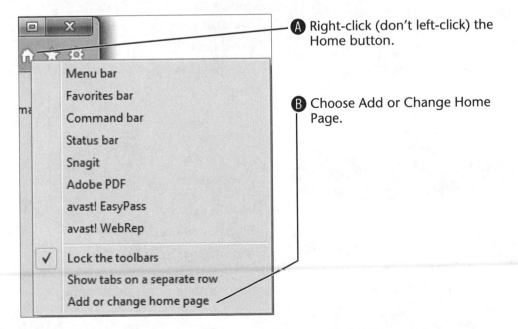

Ⓐ Right-click (don't left-click) the Home button.

Ⓑ Choose Add or Change Home Page.

A dialog box appears asking how you wish to add this homepage.

3. Choose the Add This Webpage to Your Home Page Tabs option and click Yes.

Internet Explorer adds the page to the Home button.

View Multiple Homepages

4. Close the Internet Explorer window.

5. Choose Start > Internet to restart Internet Explorer, or click its button on the Taskbar.

Notice that there are two tabs opened in Internet Explorer when you start the browser. Each homepage opens automatically in its own tab.

> **!NOTE!** If someone else has already defined any additional homepages, there might be more than two tabs visible in Internet Explorer.

6. Click the second tab to display the book web page.

Internet Explorer displays the newly added homepage. You will learn more about tabbed browsing in the next lesson.

Re-set Your Homepage

7. Follow these steps to re-set your Home page button to display only a single home page:

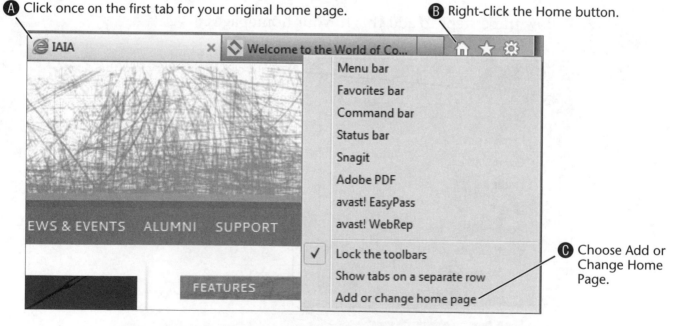

Ⓐ Click once on the first tab for your original home page.

Ⓑ Right-click the Home button.

Ⓒ Choose Add or Change Home Page.

Internet Explorer asks you to confirm removing this homepage.

8. Choose the Use this Webpage as Your Only Home Page option as shown below, then click Yes.

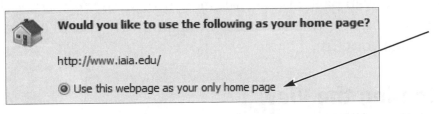

Would you like to use the following as your home page?

http://www.iaia.edu/

◉ Use this webpage as your only home page

Internet Explorer re-sets the homepage to just a single page. However, the other home page tab will still be visible in the Internet Explorer window until you navigate away from it.

9. Click the second tab to display the book web page again.

⌖ IAIA   ◇ Welcome to the World of ... ✕

10. Click once on the Home 🏠 button to display the home page.
Internet Explorer displays the homepage again.

11. Click the Back ← once to return to the book web page.
The student web page should be visible again.

Viewing Web Pages

Once you find the web page you wish to read, Internet Explorer and your mouse have controls to bring parts of it into view and make it easier to read.

Mouse Scroll Wheel

Most modern mice have a scroll wheel between the left and right mouse buttons. Rolling the wheel with your index finger intuitively scrolls the web page up and down. In addition to the scroll wheel, many mice have additional controls to control web pages similar to the following figure.

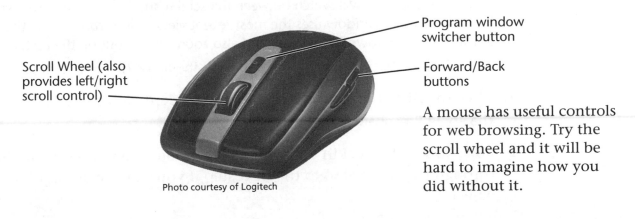

Program window switcher button

Scroll Wheel (also provides left/right scroll control)

Forward/Back buttons

A mouse has useful controls for web browsing. Try the scroll wheel and it will be hard to imagine how you did without it.

Photo courtesy of Logitech

Full-screen View

Even with Internet Explorer's compact browser controls, you may wish to see more of a web page and less of the controls. The *full-screen* view reduces the browser controls to a bare minimum, allowing you to concentrate on the web page content.

Zooming the View

You can also adjust the scale of text and images on most web pages to make them easier to view. For example, you can magnify the size of text on an article that has small print. The zoom changes the size of images on the page as well. You can zoom the view in and out using the keyboard.

QUICK REFERENCE: Adjusting the View of a Web Page

Task	Procedure
Scroll a web page using the mouse	• Click once over the part of the web page you wish to scroll. • Roll the scroll wheel up and down with your forefinger.
Shift into/out of Full Screen view	• Tap the F11 function key on the keyboard. • Tap the F11 function key again to toggle out of full-screen mode.
Scale web page text larger and smaller	• Hold down the Ctrl key on the keyboard. • Use Ctrl + + to zoom in or Ctrl + - to zoom out.
Navigate a web page using the keyboard	• Tap the Home key to jump to the top of the page. • Tap the End key to jump to the bottom of the page. • Tap the PgUp and PgDn keys to jump one screen up or down.

HANDS-ON 5.8 Adjust the View of a Web Page

In this exercise, you will switch between full-screen and normal view. You will also see how the browser window uses the most recent view mode. You will use the scroll wheel to move up and down in the page and also zoom in and out on the text.

Before You Begin: The student web page should be displayed in Internet Explorer.

1. Click the About Broadband link on the student web page.
   The About Broadband web page appears.

2. Roll the scroll wheel in the center of the mouse to scroll up and down through the page. Skip to the next step if your mouse doesn't have a scroll wheel.

Navigate with the Keyboard

3. Tap the `Home` key on the keyboard to jump to the top of the page.

4. Tap the `PgDn` key a few times to get to the bottom of the page.

5. Tap the `PgUp` key once to scroll up one screen.

6. Tap the `End` key on the keyboard to jump to the bottom of the page.

7. Tap the `Home` key on the keyboard to jump back to the top of the page.

Zoom the View

8. Hold down the `Ctrl` key on the keyboard and then tap the `+` (plus sign) key twice to zoom in. Release the `Ctrl` key.

> **!TIP!** The `+` key is usually beside the `Backspace` key on the keyboard.

The view zooms closer each time you tap `Ctrl`+`+`.

9. Use `Ctrl`+`-` (minus sign) to zoom out again.

Toggle Full-Screen Mode

10. Tap the `F11` function key on the top row of the keyboard; make sure your mouse pointer is not near the top of the web page.

Internet Explorer shifts to full-screen mode. The Address bar and other controls disappear, leaving maximum space to display the web page.

11. Tap the `F11` function key again to toggle back to the normal view.

12. Tap the `F11` function key again to toggle back to full-screen view.

Close and Open Internet Explorer in Full-screen Mode

13. Point over the picture and wait until the Address bar disappears.

14. Point above the title near the top of the page so that the pointer turns into an arrow.

The Address bar and other controls reappear in black rather than their normal colors. You can always get them to reappear by pointing at the top of the page.

15. Follow these steps to close Internet Explorer in full screen mode:

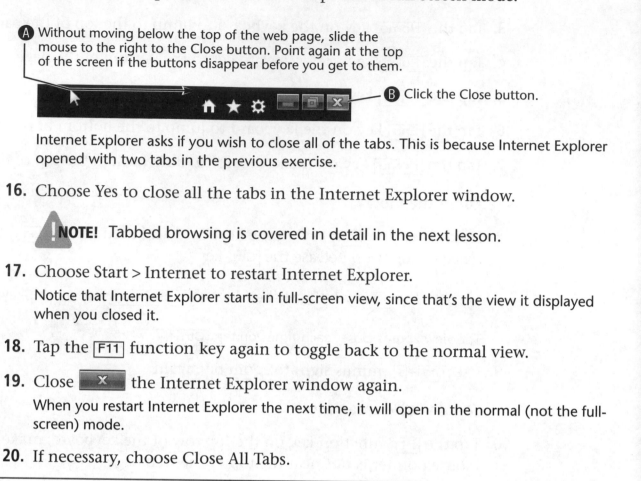

Ⓐ Without moving below the top of the web page, slide the mouse to the right to the Close button. Point again at the top of the screen if the buttons disappear before you get to them.

Ⓑ Click the Close button.

Internet Explorer asks if you wish to close all of the tabs. This is because Internet Explorer opened with two tabs in the previous exercise.

16. Choose Yes to close all the tabs in the Internet Explorer window.

!NOTE! Tabbed browsing is covered in detail in the next lesson.

17. Choose Start > Internet to restart Internet Explorer.

Notice that Internet Explorer starts in full-screen view, since that's the view it displayed when you closed it.

18. Tap the F11 function key again to toggle back to the normal view.

19. Close ☒ the Internet Explorer window again.

When you restart Internet Explorer the next time, it will open in the normal (not the full-screen) mode.

20. If necessary, choose Close All Tabs.

Concepts Review

All of the Concepts Review quizzes for this book are available on the student web page. Your instructor will let you know how to complete the quizzes (in the book or online).

True/False Questions

Page
number

1. A URL is essentially the address of a website.   **true**   **false**   _____

2. The Forward button navigates you to the next web page on a site.   **true**   **false**   _____

3. You can navigate forward and back only one page at a time.   **true**   **false**   _____

4. You can change the web page displayed by Internet Explorer's Home button. **true**   **false**   _____

5. When you type a URL, you must always include http://.   **true**   **false**   _____

6. You can set more than one homepage in Internet Explorer.   **true**   **false**   _____

Multiple Choice Questions

7. A link can be a _____.
   a. word or text phrase on a web page
   b. a button on a web page
   c. an image on a web page
   d. All of the above

8. A URL is very similar to _____.
   a. a highway sign
   b. a computer terminal
   c. a mailing address
   d. None of the above

9. Internet Explorer's Smart Address Bar feature _____.
   a. lists the names of recently visited web pages similar to the name you are typing
   b. allows you to choose URLs from a list
   c. appears below the Address bar
   d. All of the above

10. The Forward button _____.
    a. is always active
    b. takes you forward to a new next page on a website
    c. only works after you use the Back button
    d. jumps you to the next homepage

Skill Builders

Browse National Parks

WebSim In this exercise, you will visit the National Park Service website and view information about some parks.

1. Start Internet Explorer.

2. Click in the Address bar, enter the URL **labpub.com/learn/silver/ wtwc4** and then tap the Enter key.

   The web page for this book appears.

3. Click the Browsing National Parks link.

   The first part of this exercise will be a WebSim.

   The National Park Service website appears. Notice the long green navigation bar below the main image. This provides navigation links to various main sections of the website. Virtually all websites have some sort of navigation bar or scheme that's readily apparent on the homepage.

4. Click the Find a Park link on the left side of the navigation bar.

   This page offers different ways to locate a park. Let's use the map method.

5. Click the Select a State from the Map Below link.

   A map of the U.S. appears.

6. Click the State of New Mexico on the map.

   The map zooms to a detail view of New Mexico.

7. Follow these steps to view information about a site on the map:

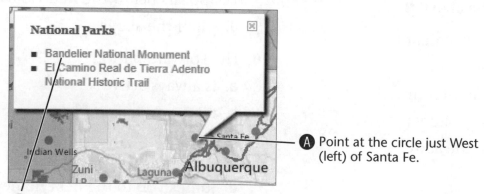

Ⓐ Point at the circle just West (left) of Santa Fe.

Ⓑ Click the Bandelier National Monument link.

Some brief notes for this site appear.

8. Click the Bandelier National Monument title link at the top of the pop-up box and then click the scroll bar on the right side of the WebSim window.

The Bandelier site's web page appears. Notice the navigation links along the left side of the page.

9. Follow these steps to navigate to a virtual tour of the national monument:

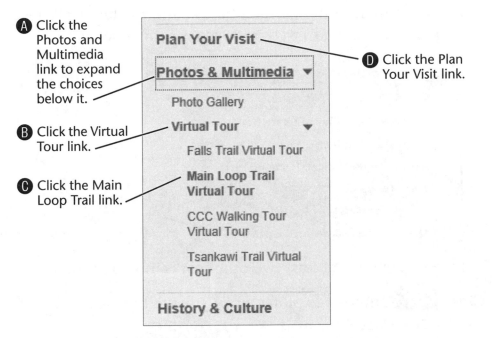

A Click the Photos and Multimedia link to expand the choices below it.

B Click the Virtual Tour link.

C Click the Main Loop Trail link.

D Click the Plan Your Visit link.

The Photos and Multimedia items collapse, and the Plan Your Visit section expands. Many websites have dynamic navigation menus such as this to help you locate the web pages and information you wish to view.

Browse the Live National Park Service Website

10. Click the National Park Service logo in the top-left corner of the page.

A new browser window opens to display the homepage of the National Park Service website.

Many websites feature a link like this that always returns you to the homepage.

 NOTE! You are now viewing the live National Park Service website. (Notice the URL in the Address bar.) For the rest of this exercise, the site may look and act differently from the WebSim in the previous steps.

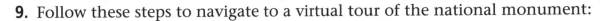

U.S. National Park Service - Experience

http://www.nps.gov/index.htm

11. Try navigating the site on your own using the following guidelines:

- Choose a park near where you live.

- Visit some of the pages that show maps and features of the park.

- Use the scroll wheel, PgDn , and Home keys to move up and down on each page.

- Use a right-click on the Before button and the Recent Pages list to jump back to the main NPS website page (as shown below).

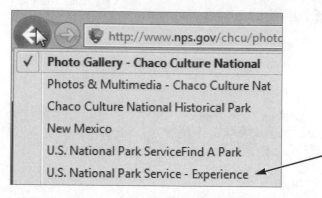

- Browse pages for at least two other parks in your area.

12. Close Internet Explorer when you are finished.
The WebSim window reappears.

13. Close the WebSim window.
The student web page reappears.

SKILL BUILDER 5.2 Browse Web Pages

In this exercise, you will navigate to web pages with the Address bar.

Live Links: These are live web links. It is possible for a link to have changed locations or to have shut down since this book was printed. A link may also be down temporarily due to technical problems. If you try a link and it does not work, go on to another link.

1. If necessary, launch Internet Explorer.

2. Navigate to the homepage of a website on the following list by typing its URL in the Address bar. If you see an error message, check for a typo in the Address bar and try again.

> **!NOTE!** Notice that some of the URLs below use a "www" at the front. Usually, you can omit the www. However, if the site you expect does not appear, try adding www. to the front of the URL.

Website	URL
Smithsonian Institution	`www.si.edu/`
Library of Congress	`lcweb.loc.gov/`
Project Gutenberg	`gutenberg.org`
National Aeronautics and Space Administration	`www.nasa.gov/`

3. If you find a website that interests you, feel free to navigate the site for a few minutes. Look for links on the page in the forms of navigation bars, images, and underscored text.

4. Navigate to at least one other website that interests you and try browsing that site.

LESSON 6

Searching for Websites

The growth of the web has been explosive. In June 1993, there were approximately 130 websites on the Internet. Nobody knows exactly how many websites and web pages are available on the Internet today, but by mid-2008, there were more than a trillion unique URLs (web addresses) available on the web. While highly useful information is available on the web, its very volume makes finding what you need difficult. Good search techniques will help you quickly locate the most useful web pages. In this lesson, you will use the most significant aid to finding information on the web: the Internet search engine and Internet Explorer's Instant Search feature.

LESSON OBJECTIVES

After studying this lesson, you will be able to:

- Describe what an Internet search engine does
- Perform a basic instant search
- Use Internet Explorer's tabbed browsing feature
- Use favorites to mark and navigate to websites
- Navigate using the History panel
- Print a web page

Additional learning resources are available at labpub.com/learn/silver/wtwc4/

Case Study: Planning a Rail Trip

Spring break is approaching, and Terry wants to travel. He calls a cousin, and they decide to visit the Grand Canyon together. Neither of them has visited the Grand Canyon before, so there's no literature close at hand. Terry goes on the web to find out what's available at the Grand Canyon, where to stay, and what to see. He knows that the best way to find information on the web is to use a search engine. With the choice of a few key words, Terry discovers some good general information and learns about a railroad with daily trains traveling into and out of the Canyon.

Internet Explorer's Address bar also serves as an instant search box, making it easy to quickly search with your favorite search provider.

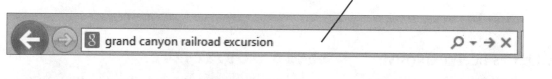

Tabbed browsing lets Terry open several web pages in the same Internet Explorer window.

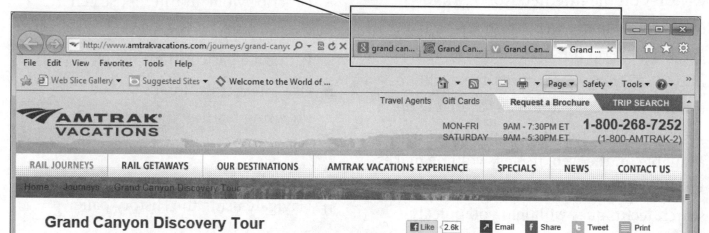

Searching from the Address Bar

You are connected to the Internet, and your web browser is running. Now how do you find pages with the information you wish to view? Unless you want to rely only on URLs that you've memorized or links sent to you via email, you need to perform a *search*. There are numerous services (called *search engines*) available on the web to help you search for web pages.

About Search Engines

An Internet search engine is a website designed to help you locate and navigate to web pages that contain the information you desire. Search engines typically display a list of search result links, which you use to navigate to sites that meet your search criteria. As you will see, there are many types of search engines; the search engine you select can determine the success or failure of your searches. This topic introduces basic techniques for locating web pages.

> **!NOTE!** Most of the exercises in this lesson use the Google.com search engine because it is an excellent general search engine that is easy to use. The techniques you use to work with Google.com will also work well with other search engines.

Address Bar Search

The Address bar gives you immediate access to your favorite search engines.

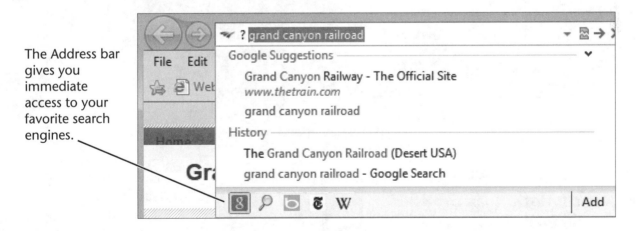

Internet Explorer features an integrated Address/Search bar. Previously, users had to navigate to a search engine's web page in order to use it for a search. Now you can type one or more words into the Address bar and immediately see search results from the search provider of your choice.

NOTE! The Address/Search bar will always simply be referred to as the Address bar throughout this lesson.

Choosing a Search Engine

No single search engine is ideal for every type of search. Some search engines may consistently produce search results highly relevant to the actual information you are seeking. Other search engines may perform a search so complete you don't have time to make your way through all of the hits and yet may be perfectly suited to searching for a very obscure piece of information. Over time you will likely begin to favor one search engine in particular, though there may be occasions when you seek additional search engines because the one you usually use does not provide the results you need.

Adding Search Providers

You can add search providers to the Internet Explorer's Address bar, making it easy to switch from one to another as your search needs dictate. For example, you might use Google as a general search engine and then switch to a different search engine to run a more complete search. The Internet Explorer Gallery has many categories of search providers to choose from. For example, there are search providers for shopping, news, music, and other specialized search needs.

The Internet Explorer Gallery displays search providers you can add to the Address bar.

Accelerators

In addition to search providers, Internet Explorer also allows the installation of accelerator add-ons. These can take information from web pages and transform it into an instant search.

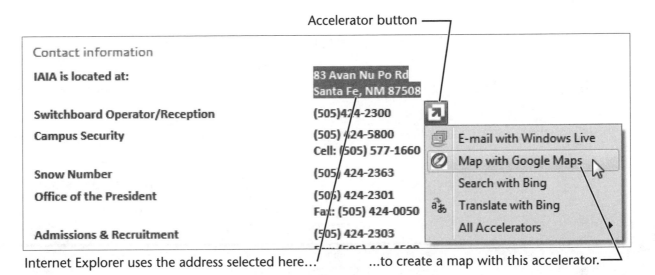

Accelerators can perform searches from content you select on a web page.

⚠ NOTE! Skill Builder 6.3 gives you the opportunity to try out an accelerator.

Setting a Default Search Provider

You can tell Internet Explorer to use a particular search provider by *default*. This means any keyword search in the Address bar will use this provider unless you choose a different provider. You can alter your default search provider at any time.

Task	Procedure
Perform an instant search	• Type one or more search keywords into the Address bar and then tap $\boxed{\text{Enter}}$.
Change the default search provider	• Click the Tools button 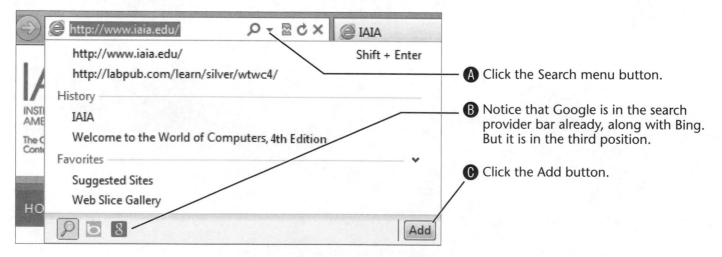 • Choose Manage Add Ons. • Choose Search Providers in the left panel. • Right-click the desired search provider, then choose Set as Default. • Click the Close button at the bottom-right corner of the window.
Add a new search provider	• Click the Address bar search menu button. • Click the Add button at the bottom-right corner of the drop-down box.

HANDS-ON 6.1 Add a Search Provider

WebSim

In this exercise, you will add a new search provider to the Instant Search box.

1. Start Internet Explorer. If necessary, Maximize the window.

2. Navigate to the student web page: `labpub.com/learn/silver/wtwc4`

3. Click the Add a Search Provider link.

   As it starts, Internet Explorer is already running in the WebSim.

4. Follow these steps to add a new search provider:

http://www.iaia.edu/

http://www.iaia.edu/   Shift + Enter
http://labpub.com/learn/silver/wtwc4/
History
IAIA
Welcome to the World of Computers, 4th Edition
Favorites
Suggested Sites
Web Slice Gallery

Add

Ⓐ Click the Search menu button.

Ⓑ Notice that Google is in the search provider bar already, along with Bing. But it is in the third position.

Ⓒ Click the Add button.

Internet Explorer displays a new tab with the first of several pages listing popular search providers. To the left is a navigation panel displaying various categories of providers.

5. Click the scroll bar on the right side of the window to simulate scrolling down.

6. Choose Most Popular from the navigation bar at the top of the search provider list.

The Internet Explorer Gallery displays the most popular search provider choices.

7. Point (don't click) over the New York Times on the first line of the list.

A rating for the search provider appears. As with many ratings you see on the Web, this one should be taken with a grain of salt. However, it may help you spot particularly ineffective search providers.

8. Click the New York Times.

The search provider's Internet Explorer Gallery page appears.

9. Click the Add To Internet Explorer button.

An Add Search Provider dialog box appears.

10. Click the Add button.

Internet Explorer adds the New York Times to the Address bar search.

11. Click the Search button on the Address bar as shown below.

Notice that the New York Times has been added to the search provider list. You can now switch to this provider at any time.

12. Click anywhere on the web page to dismiss the Search list.

Set the Default Search Provider

Now you will set the search provider that Internet Explorer always uses when you first start the program.

13. Follow these steps to display the Add Ons window:

Ⓐ Click the Settings button.

Ⓑ Choose Manage Add-Ons.

The Manage Add-Ons window appears.

14. Follow these steps to change the default search provider setting:

Ⓐ Choose Search Providers.

Ⓑ Right-click (don't left-click) on Google.

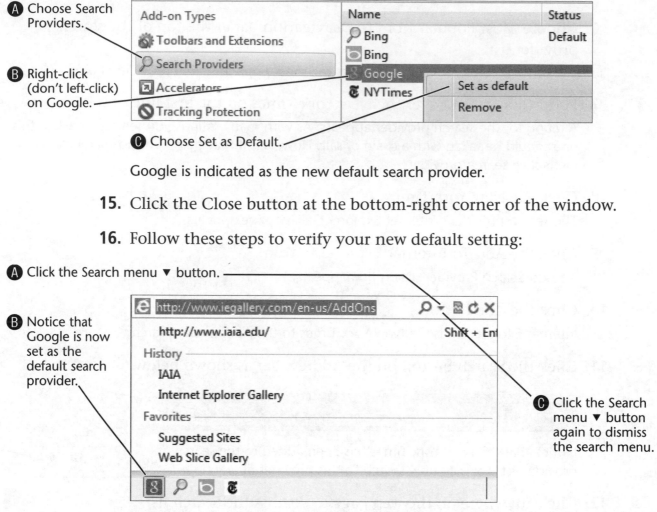

Ⓒ Choose Set as Default.

Google is indicated as the new default search provider.

15. Click the Close button at the bottom-right corner of the window.

16. Follow these steps to verify your new default setting:

Ⓐ Click the Search menu ▼ button.

Ⓑ Notice that Google is now set as the default search provider.

Ⓒ Click the Search menu ▼ button again to dismiss the search menu.

17. Click the Continue to Next WebSim button.

The next WebSim loads into Internet Explorer, ready for the next exercise. Continue reading the next topic.

Performing Basic Keyword Searches

A basic keyword search asks the search engine to find web pages with a specific word or several specific words. Basic searches are quick and easy to execute and will often yield the information you are seeking. Search results are typically reported as a list of search results with a short summary of each page. Sometimes a search may yield no results at all, while other times you may get millions of results—more than you could possibly browse.

Selecting Search Words

The more words you include in a keyword search, the more likely it is that the search results will be relevant to your needs. However, you don't want to start out with so many search words that you miss websites that did not include some of the search words but would still be of interest. When you perform a keyword search with more than one word, most search engines will show you the pages that contain all the words first, then pages that contain only a few of the words.

 TIP! Every Internet search engine has its own rules and conventions (called syntax) for searching. However, the two rules described in the following Quick Reference table work with most Internet search engines.

QUICK REFERENCE: Typing Basic Search Words—Rules

Rule	Examples
Use capital letters only when typing proper nouns. If you type more than one proper name in a search, separate each name with a comma.	Mahatma Gandhi, Grand Canyon
If you wish to search for an exact phrase, enclose the phrase in quotation marks.	"global warming trends" "hybrid automobile"

How Internet Search Engines Work

All Internet search engines maintain some type of database of web pages and their content. When you perform a search, the search engine uses its database to list all web pages that meet your search criteria. Search engines differ in the techniques they use to locate websites and add them to their databases.

Search engines can be broken down into three primary categories based on their method of indexing the content of the web.

- **Full-text**—Some search engines index every word of every web page they encounter. While this yields a very complete search, it is likely that many hits won't relate to the specific topic for which you are searching. On the other hand, you are guaranteed a very complete search. The Hotbot.com search engine uses the full-text indexing technique.

- **Computer-generated**—Some search engines review the first page or part of the first page of a website and then use programming to assign the web page to specific search key words. The Google search engine employs this technique, using data such as the popularity of a website to assign its order in the search results list.

Metasearch Engines

The web also has search engines that search other search engines. Essentially, a *metasearch* engine sends your search to several search engines and other resources with a single command. This approach takes advantage of the strengths of several search engines simultaneously. However, you may end up with more search results than you bargained for.

This metasearch engine searches four popular search engines simultaneously.

Search Result Order

Different search engines usually list the same sites in a different order. There are a few factors that can affect the order of sites in the search results list.

- **Content of the page**—The text on the web page can make a difference in the order a site is listed. The search engine reviews the homepage to determine the level of relevance of the site to your search terms.

- **Search relevance rating**—Each search engine has its own system for rating the relevance of a website to the terms you used in your search. How this relevance rating is processed will change the order of sites in the search results list.

- **Content of the meta-tag for a page**—Many web pages have some hidden code (called a meta-tag) that contains search keywords. Some search engines use this information to determine the order of the web page in a search results list.

- **Sponsored links/money**—Yes, it's true. Many websites pay a search engine to give them a higher position in the search results list. The logic is that the first sites in the search results list are much more likely to be browsed. Conversely, if a web page is deep in the list, it is much less likely that a searcher will make it that far down the list to view the page.

Ads related to grand canyon   Why these ads?

Visit The **Grand Canyon** | NationalParks.org
www.nationalparks.org/
Take A Trip The **Grand Canyon** And Do Trip Research With Our Online Guide

Grand Canyon Rim to Rim | fsguides.com
www.fsguides.com/
Rim to Rim hiking tours since 1999. Professional, knowledgeable guides
Grand Canyon Tours - Utah Hiking Tours - Havasu Falls - Yosemite

Grand Canyon Tours | Papillon.com
www.papillon.com/Grand_Canyon_Tours
Book Your **Grand Canyon** Tours Online with Papillon & Save Up to 40%!
Helicopter Tours from Las Vegas - Airplane Tours from Las Vegas

Grand Canyon National Park - National Park Service
www.nps.gov/grca/
Jul 31, 2012 – Official National Park Service site. News and events, information on camping and lodging, facilities and fees, maps and volunteer openings.
Plan Your Visit - Lodging - Fees & Reservations - Directions

Grand Canyon - Wikipedia, the free encyclopedia
en.wikipedia.org/wiki/Grand_Canyon

Three sponsored (paid) links push their websites to the top of Google's search results. The paid links appear before the much more popular National Park Service website (the first unpaid result). Not all search engines mark sponsored links.

Search Suggestions

Internet Explorer's search suggestions feature displays likely searches as you type in the Address bar. This feature works by sending your keystrokes to the active search provider. Due to privacy issues, this feature doesn't work until you choose to turn it on with one or more search providers. You can also turn this feature off when you don't want to use it.

A search provider displays an invitation to turn on search suggestions.

HANDS-ON 6.2 **Search with the Address Bar**

WebSim

In this exercise, you will search on a specific keyword via the Address bar.

Before You Begin: The Address Bar Search WebSim should be open. If it is not, go to the student web page and then click the Address Bar Search link.

The WebSim begins with an Internet Explorer browser window open.

1. Follow these steps to perform a quick search for the Grand Canyon:

Ⓐ Start typing **gran** in the Address bar.

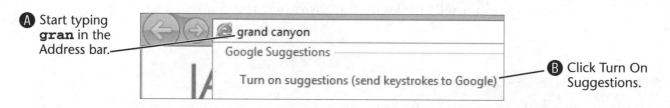

Ⓑ Click Turn On Suggestions.

Google displays search suggestions based on what you've just typed. Notice that it's already suggesting Grand Canyon. It does this because the words Grand Canyon are very popular search keywords.

2. Choose Grand Canyon from the Google Suggestion list.

The first page of Google's search results appears. Notice that this initial search found over 72,000,000 (!) results.

3. Choose Images from the left side of the search results.

Google displays images located by your search.

4. Choose Maps from the left side of the search results.

Google displays a map of the Grand Canyon.

Notice that the left panel of search categories has disappeared.

5. Click the Back ← button.

   You return to the Images page, and the search categories list reappears on the left.

6. Choose Web from the left side of the search results.

   You are back to the original search results. Next, we'll look at the details of interpreting search results.

7. Click the Continue to Next WebSim button.

Interpreting Search Results

Most search engines display basic information about each result turned up by a search. This helps you select the results most likely to have the content you want. This is one area where search engines can differ quite a bit. The following figure displays features of a search results list from the Google search engine.

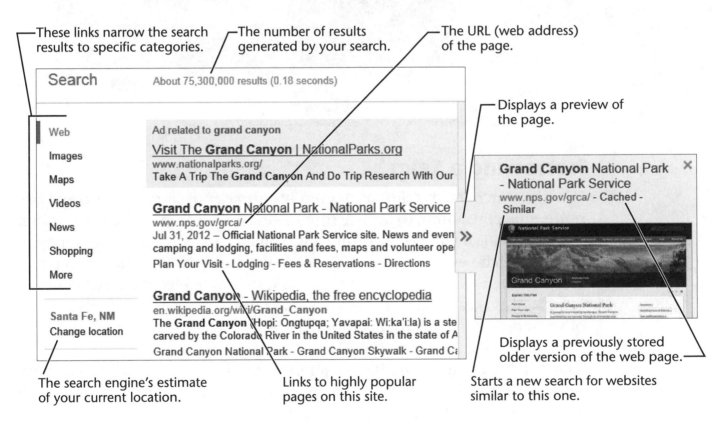

These links narrow the search results to specific categories.

The number of results generated by your search.

The URL (web address) of the page.

Displays a preview of the page.

The search engine's estimate of your current location.

Links to highly popular pages on this site.

Starts a new search for websites similar to this one.

Displays a previously stored older version of the web page.

Searching for Specific Types of Results

Good search engines also allow you to search for specific types of results. For example, you can search specifically for images or maps of a particular locale. You tried this at the end of the previous Hands-on exercise.

Search engines let you search for specific categories of search results.

Pointing over an image displays some details.

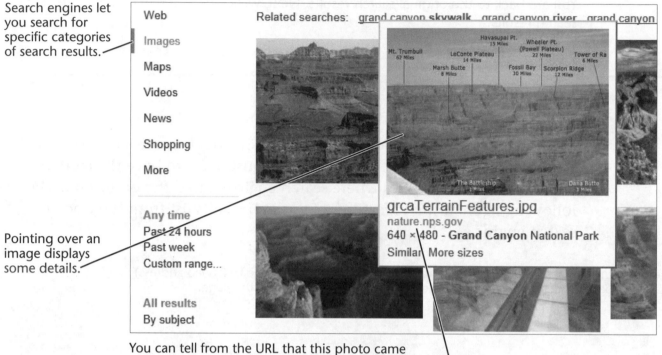

You can tell from the URL that this photo came from the official National Park Service website.

Narrowing a Search

When a search yields millions or even just thousands of results, it could be quite time-consuming to browse through even a fraction of the pages to find the information you need. Fortunately, you can easily narrow a search by adding search keywords. This means that you can conduct a broad search first and then add more keywords to the search to reduce the number of results. This is called narrowing your search because a narrower cross-section of websites will match your additional keywords.

Example   Since Terry and his cousin have decided to take a rail trip into the Grand Canyon, Terry decides to narrow his search to pages that contain references to railroad and railway trips.

HANDS-ON 6.3 **Narrow a Search**

WebSim

In this exercise, you will add keywords to narrow a search for visits to the Grand Canyon by railway.

Before You Begin: The Narrow a Search WebSim should be open.

In the next step, you could narrow your search in the Search box or in the Google web page showing the search results. Be sure to use the Google web page as shown.

1. Follow these steps to add words to your search:

Ⓐ Start typing **railway** **e**. (Google displays search suggestions as you type.)

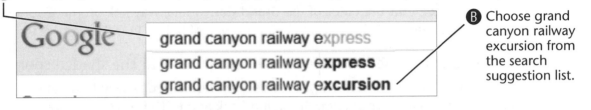

Ⓑ Choose grand canyon railway excursion from the search suggestion list.

Google displays the results of your narrowed search. The number of results has gone down from more than 71 million to 28,300. Notice that there are three sponsored (paid) links in the shaded region at the top of the list, and more sponsored links to the right. These paid links are a major income generator for Google and other search engines.

2. Click the scroll bar on the right, and then click the first unshaded link: Grand Canyon Railway – The Official Site.

The linked web page appears.

3. Click Explore on the new web page then choose Schedule & Route.

Navigate Back and Forward

4. Click the scroll bar on the right side of the page to simulate scrolling down the page.

Notice that the Forward ➡ button is dimmed. This is because you can only move forward again once you have moved back.

5. Click the Back ⬅ button.

You return to the first page you viewed on the site. Notice that the Forward button is no longer undimmed. Once you move back, it's possible to move forward.

6. Click the Forward ➡ button.

You return to the page you moved back from. It's also possible to jump back several pages with a single command. Let's do that next.

7. Follow these steps to perform a multipage Back command:

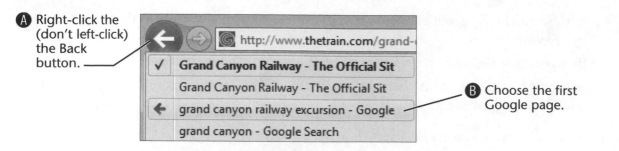

Ⓐ Right-click the (don't left-click) the Back button.

Ⓑ Choose the first Google page.

Internet Explorer jumps you back to the search page in one step.

Notice that the color of the Grand Canyon Railway link on the Google search page has changed. This is Internet Explorer's way of telling you that you've visited this link.

8. Click the second Grand Canyon Railway in the shaded sponsored links area.

Going back and forth between search results is one way to go about finding the information you need. But going back and forth between different sites is difficult and a bit tedious. There is another method to open web pages that makes this type of search much more effective: tabbed browsing. Let's learn about this feature now.

9. Close ▭X▭ the WebSim window.

The book web page reappears since it is no longer covered by the WebSim page.

Using Tabbed Browsing

Tabbed browsing is the capability to open multiple web pages within the same browser window. Instead of going back and forth between web pages or having to open multiple browser windows, you can open a new tab for each page you wish to view. You can also open a new tab and start a new search or navigate to a new web page via the Address bar.

Your search results ⎯⎯⎯⎯⎯⎯⎯⎯⎯⎯⎯⎯⎯⎯⎯⎯⎯ The currently viewed tab ⎯⎯

| ⧉ grand canyon railway excur... | 🦅 Grand Canyon Arizona Tour... | v Grand Canyon Railroad Exc... | 🦅 Grand Canyon Railroad ... ✕ |

Opening Links in a New Tab

You can open links in new tabs by using a right-click rather than a left-click. A right click opens a pop-up menu with the option to open the link in a new tab or in a new browser window.

Grand Canyon Railway — The Official Site
www.thetrain.com/
The Official Site for Gra...
train tours to Grand Car...

| Open |
| Open in new tab |

Right-clicking a link displays Open in New Tab in a pop-up menu.

TIP! When you want to view several results from a search, use the right mouse button to open each search result in its own tab.

 HANDS-ON 6.4 **Open Links in Tabs**

WebSim In this exercise, you will open links in new tabs and then switch from one tab to another.
Before You Begin: The student web page should be open.

1. Click the Open Links in Tabs link on the student web page.
   A simulation of Google search results appears.

2. If necessary, Maximize ▣ the new Internet Explorer window.

3. Follow these steps to open a search result in a new tab:

Ⓐ Right-click (don't left-click) the Grand Canyon Railway – The Official Site link.

Grand Canyon Railway – Offical Website f...
www.thetrain.c | Open |
Book Your Gra | Open in new tab |

Ⓑ Choose Open in New Tab from the pop-up menu.

Internet Explorer opens a new tab for this web page. However, you are still viewing the search results in the original (leftmost) tab.

4. Scroll down the page, then right-click the Grand Canyon Railroad Excursion – Sedona & Flagstaff Rail Tours link and then choose Open in New Tab from the pop-up menu.
   Another new tab appears at the top of the web page.

5. If necessary, scroll down the page and then open the Grand Canyon Discovery Tour link in a new tab.
   You could actually open a dozen or more new tabs, but these three new ones will do.

Navigating Tabs

You can switch from one tab to the next using the mouse or convenient keyboard commands. It's also easy to close a tab once you are finished viewing it. Internet Explorer can even help you open recently closed tabs for another look.

QUICK REFERENCE: Using Tabbed Browsing

Task	Procedure
Open a link in a new tab	• Right-click the link you wish to open. • Choose Open in New Tab from the pop-up menu.
Close a tab	• Point over the tab you wish to close. • Click the tab's Close ☒ button, or use Ctrl+W from the keyboard.
Close all tabs but one	• Right-click the tab you wish to keep. • Choose Close Other Tabs from the pop-up menu.
Close all tabs	• Close ☒ the Internet Explorer window. • Choose Yes if you are asked to confirm closing the tabs.
Switch to a new tab using the keyboard	• Use Ctrl+Tab to switch to the next tab. • Use Ctrl+Shift+Tab to switch to the previous tab.
Open a new tab	• Click the New Tab ▢ button on the tab bar, or use Ctrl+T from the keyboard.
Open a recently closed tab	• Right-click on a tab. • Choose Recently Closed Tabs from the pop-up menu. • Choose the tab you wish to re-open.

HANDS-ON 6.5 Navigate Tabs

WebSim

In this exercise, you will use various techniques to navigate between tabs.

Before You Begin: The search results page should be open, and there should be four tabs visible. Repeat Hands-On 6.4 on page 219 if you did not continue from the previous exercise.

1. Click once on the Grand Canyon Railway tab as shown below.

The web page for this tab appears immediately. One advantage of opening web pages in new tabs is that the pages can load in the background while you choose additional pages to open. This can be helpful if you access the Internet via a slow connection.

NOTE! In the next step, hold down one key and then tap the other key. Do not try to hold down both keys at the same time.

2. Hold down the Ctrl key with the thumb on your left hand, tap the Tab key on the left side of the keyboard with your index finger, and then release the Ctrl key.

   Internet Explorer jumps you to the next available tab. This keyboard method can be a very handy way to navigate tabs without having to reach for the mouse.

3. Use Ctrl+Tab again to jump to the next tab.

   Now you are at the end of the tabs for this Internet Explorer window. The next time you jump to a new tab, you will start over with the first tab.

4. Use Ctrl+Tab one more time to jump to the next tab.

   The Google search tab appears. Now you could perform a new search, or choose additional links to open in new tabs.

    NOTE! Do not try to hold down all three keys at once in the next step.

5. Hold down both the Ctrl and Shift keys and then tap the Tab key again. Release the Ctrl and Shift keys.

   Internet Explorer jumps you back to the previous tab.

Close and Re-open Tabs

6. Point at the second to the last tab in the tabs group, then click the x to close that tab as shown at right.

   Internet Explorer closes that tab.

7. Follow these steps to close all but one tab in the tab group:

Ⓐ Right-click the currently displayed tab.

Ⓑ Choose Close Other Tabs from the pop-up menu.

All of the other tabs immediately disappear.

8. Follow these steps to re-open the tabs you just closed (and any others you might have opened in this particular Internet Explorer window).

A Right-click the currently displayed tab.

B Choose Recently Closed tabs from the pop-up menu.

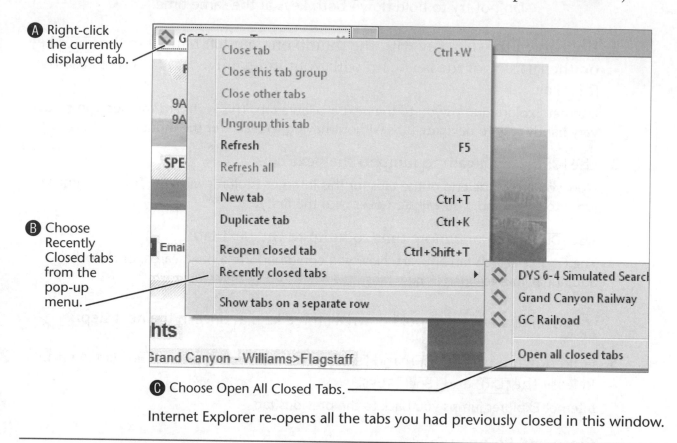

C Choose Open All Closed Tabs.

Internet Explorer re-opens all the tabs you had previously closed in this window.

Bookmarking Favorite Websites

A *favorite* (also called a *bookmark*) is a way to mark a web page so you can open it quickly in the future. Favorites make it easy to locate the web pages you browse most often. For example, you can use a favorite to view the local weather report or to check your favorite online news source.

The Favorites Bar

Internet Explorer has a toolbar to display favorites bookmarks. Use the Favorites bar to get one-click access to the websites you visit regularly. The Favorites bar may not be visible when you start using Internet Explorer.

 NOTE! Depending on how your computer lab is set up, favorites may not yet be visible on your screen. If not, you will make it visible in the next Hands-on exercise.

Creating Favorites

Any time you are viewing a web page you think you will visit often, you can create a new favorite for it using either the mouse or keyboard. If you have several web pages open in tabs, you can create a folder of favorites that you can open with a single click.

You can add all currently displayed tabs to a folder in your Favorites list with a single command.

Hidden Controls

In order to maintain as clean and uncluttered look as possible, Internet Explorer hides some familiar toolbars and menus. These are hidden when the program is first installed (such as a new Windows computer), but you can call them up easily.

A right-click on the Title bar (above the tabs) displays a pop-up menu for Internet Explorer settings.

In this exercise, you will add a favorite for a single web page and for a group of currently displayed tabs and then navigate within Favorites.

Before You Begin: If you did not continue this exercise from Hands-On 6.5 on page 220, you must first repeat Hands-On 6.4 on page 219. (There is no need to repeat the Hands-On 6.5 exercise.)

Add Favorites

1. Follow these steps to add a single web page to Favorites:

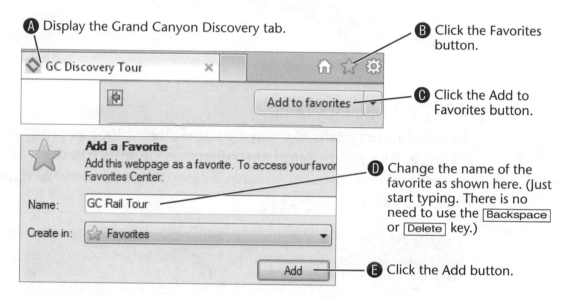

Ⓐ Display the Grand Canyon Discovery tab.

Ⓑ Click the Favorites button.

Ⓒ Click the Add to Favorites button.

Ⓓ Change the name of the favorite as shown here. (Just start typing. There is no need to use the [Backspace] or [Delete] key.)

Ⓔ Click the Add button.

If someone else has added the same favorite, you may see a prompt from Internet Explorer asking if you wish to overwrite the old favorite with this new one.

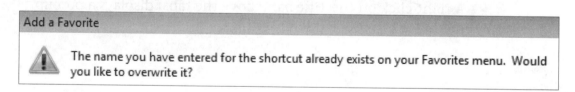

Add a Favorite

⚠ The name you have entered for the shortcut already exists on your Favorites menu. Would you like to overwrite it?

2. Choose Yes to confirm overwriting the previous favorite with the same name if a prompt appeared at the end of Step 1.

Internet Explorer adds the web page to your Favorites list. Now you will add all of the currently displayed tabs to your Favorites.

3. Follow these steps to add the entire tabbed group to Favorites:

(A) Click the Favorites button.

(B) Click the Add to Favorites menu ▼ button.

(C) Choose Add Current Tabs to Favorites.

Add to favorites...	Ctrl+D
Add to Favorites bar	
Add current tabs to favorites...	

Discovery T... ✕

Add to favorites ▼

Folder Name: Grand Rail Trip

Create in: ⭐ Favorites

Add

(D) Type a Folder (group) name for the favorites group here.

(E) Click the Add button.

Display Hidden Controls

Next you will display some Internet Explorer controls that might be hidden in your current computer setup.

4. Follow these steps to display the Command bar.

(A) Right-click (don't left-click) on the Title bar area above the web page tabs.

DYS 6-4 Simulated Searc

Menu bar
Favorites bar
Command bar
Status bar

(B) Choose Command bar from the pop-up menu, or click anywhere else if the Command bar control is already checked.

Internet Explorer displays the Command bar, on the upper-right side of the window. This contains buttons for several types of common commands.

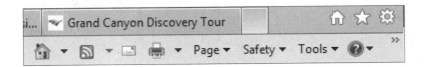

si... ▾ Grand Canyon Discovery Tour   🏠 ⭐ ⚙

🏠 ▾ 🔊 ▾ ⬜ 🖶 ▾ Page ▾ Safety ▾ Tools ▾ ❓▾ »

5. Right-click on the Title bar, and then choose the Favorites bar, or click anywhere else if there is already a checkmark beside the Favorites bar command.

Internet Explorer displays the Favorites bar, just below the Back/Forward buttons. You can place buttons on this bar for single-click access to websites you visit frequently.

6. Click the Add To Favorites bar button just below the Back button as shown at right.

Internet Explorer adds a button for the currently displayed webpage to the Favorites bar.

Navigate with Favorites

Now you will open a new browser window and navigate with your new favorites.

7. Follow these steps to open a new Internet Explorer window:

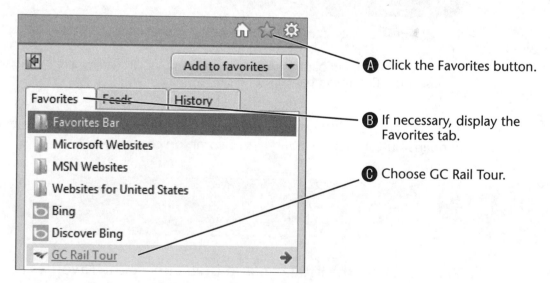

Ⓐ Click the Page menu ▼ button on the Command bar.

Ⓑ Choose New Window from the menu.

Internet Explorer opens a new browser window. This new window displays the same web page you were viewing when you gave the New Window command.

> **!NOTE!** For the rest of this book, a command like this will be written: Choose Page > New Window from the Command bar.

8. Click the Home 🏠 button on the Command bar.

This returns you to the homepage.

9. Follow these steps to navigate to a favorite:

Ⓐ Click the Favorites button.

Ⓑ If necessary, display the Favorites tab.

Ⓒ Choose GC Rail Tour.

Internet Explorer immediately displays the web page.

10. Go Back to the homepage.

Now you will open the tab group favorite you created in step 3.

11. Follow these steps to open the entire tab group with one command:

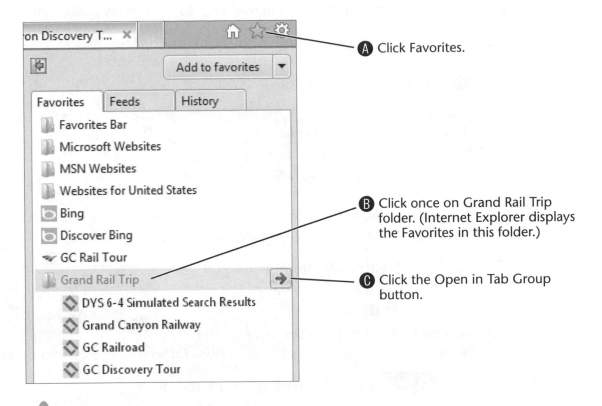

A Click Favorites.

B Click once on Grand Rail Trip folder. (Internet Explorer displays the Favorites in this folder.)

C Click the Open in Tab Group button.

!NOTE! If another student performed this exercise without deleting the tab group, more than four tabs may open.

12. Follow these steps to close a single tab:

A Display the first Grand Canyon tab.

B Click the tab's Close button.

Internet Explorer displays the next tab in the tab group.

Close a Tab Group

After you open several tabs, you may wish to close them again with a single command.

13. Follow these steps to close all but one open tab:

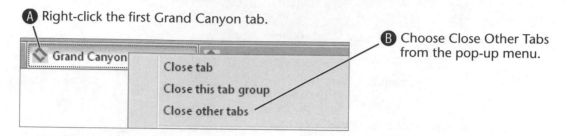

(A) Right-click the first Grand Canyon tab.

(B) Choose Close Other Tabs from the pop-up menu.

Internet Explorer immediately closes the other tabs, leaving you with the one you right-clicked to issue the Close Other Tabs command.

14. Click the button for the website you created on the Favorites bar previously, as shown at right.

Internet Explorer displays the Favorite. The Favorites bar is a great place to put buttons for websites you visit most often.

15. Close ☒ the Internet Explorer window.

The first window you worked with (and its open tabs) should now be visible.

The Favorites Center

The Favorites Center panel displays all of your available favorites. You can open the panel briefly to choose a favorite and it will close when the favorite opens, or you can "pin" the Favorites Center panel so it remains open until you close it.

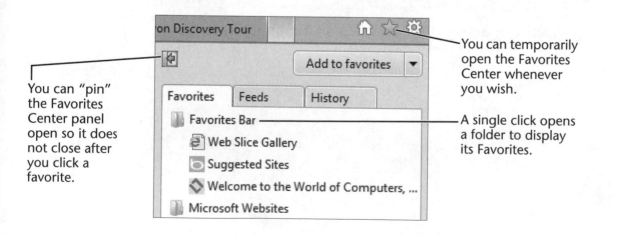

You can "pin" the Favorites Center panel open so it does not close after you click a favorite.

You can temporarily open the Favorites Center whenever you wish.

A single click opens a folder to display its Favorites.

Organizing Favorites into Folders

When you create a favorite, you have the option of placing it in an existing folder in your Favorites list or creating a new folder. This allows you to group favorites so you can find them more easily.

Add a Favorite Add this webpage as a favorite. To access your favorites, visit the Favorites Center. Name: Santa Fe New Mexican Create in: Newspaper Web Sites ▼ New Folder	The New Folder option allows you to create a new folder for a favorite, or you can choose an existing folder in the Create In list.

NOTE! Skill Builder 6.4 gives practice with organizing favorites.

Deleting Favorites

When you no longer need a favorite, it's easy to delete it. You can also delete an entire folder of favorites by deleting the folder.

QUICK REFERENCE: Creating and Using Favorites

Task	Procedure
Create a favorite for a single web page	• Display the web page for which you wish to create a favorite. • Click the Favorites button, then click the Add to Favorites button; or, use Ctrl+D from the keyboard.
Create a favorite for a group of pages	• Open each web page for the group in its own tab. • Click the Favorites button, then click the Add to Favorites ▼ menu button and choose Add Current Tabs to Favorites.
Navigate to a favorite	• Click the Favorites button • If necessary, display the Favorites tab in the Favorites panel. • Click the favorite you wish to open.
Open a folder of favorites	• Click the Favorites button, then choose the folder with the favorites you wish to open. • Click the Open Tab Group ⇨ button for the folder.
Delete a favorite or folder of favorites	• Click the Favorites button. • Right-click the favorite or folder you wish to delete, then choose Delete from the pop-up menu.
Pin the Favorites panel open	• Click the Favorites button. • Click the Pin the Favorites Center ⬅ button.

Using the History View

The History view in the Favorites panel displays all of the web pages you've visited. This can be handy when you want to quickly revisit a web page you've seen before. By default, the History view keeps track of web pages you've viewed up to 20 days before. You can increase or decrease this setting if you wish.

Changing the History View

There are several ways to view your browsing history. By default, the History view displays browsing history by date. You can alter this view as your needs dictate. For example, you might want to display your history in order starting with the most recently viewed pages, or you could display the entire history by website. You can even perform a search on items in your browsing history.

You can view your browsing history in a variety of ways.

 HANDS-ON 6.7 **Use the History View**

Web Sim

In this exercise, you will use the History view to navigate previously viewed web pages.

Before You Begin: The Internet Explorer window displaying four tabs should be open. Repeat Hands-On 6.4 on page 219 if you did not continue from Hands-On 6.6 on page 224. (There is no need to perform Hands-On 6.5 or Hands-On 6.6.)

1. Click the Favorites ☆ button.

Since you most recently used the Favorites panel to navigate favorites, this is what it displays until you shift to History view.

2. Follow these steps to display the History view and pin it to the side of the Internet Explorer window.

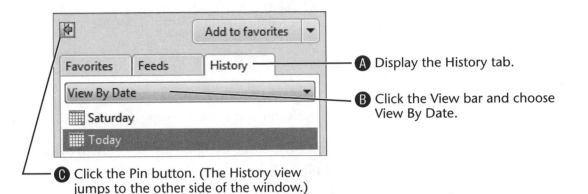

A Display the History tab.

B Click the View bar and choose View By Date.

C Click the Pin button. (The History view jumps to the other side of the window.)

Internet Explorer may display a list of days and weeks, or it may display a list of the websites visited on the currently expanded day/week.

3. Follow these steps to navigate to a web page in History:

A Click Today if a list of web pages does not appear below it as shown here. Otherwise continue to step B.

B Click once on the labpub (labpub.com) folder to expand the display from this website.

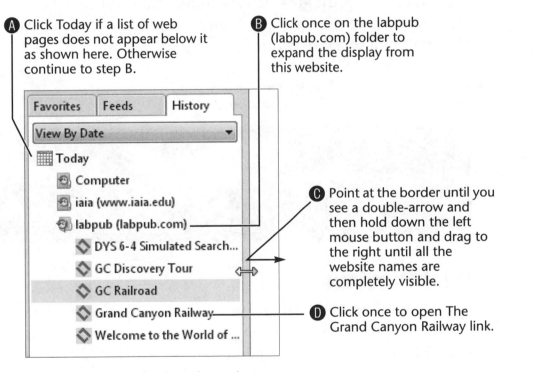

C Point at the border until you see a double-arrow and then hold down the left mouse button and drag to the right until all the website names are completely visible.

D Click once to open The Grand Canyon Railway link.

Internet Explorer displays the web page.

4. Right-click (don't left-click) the GC Discovery Tour item and then choose Open in New Tab from the pop-up menu as shown below.

Internet Explorer opens the favorite in a new tab, while leaving the currently displayed web page in view.

5. Close the History view, as shown at right.

Now you are viewing webpages in the full screen again.

6. Close the Internet Explorer window.

Internet Explorer asks if you wish to close all of the tabs on the window.

7. Choose Close All Tabs to confirm closing all of the tabs in the window.

You should now be back at the web page for this book.

Printing Web Pages

You may often wish to print a web page when you view it. Modern websites make it easy to print an article, without also printing all the navigation and other features of the webpage. Many articles will have an easy way to share it via email or a social network.

Many websites feature links like these to help you send, print, or share the currently displayed article.

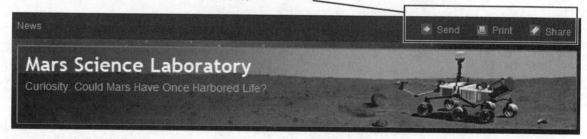

Print Preview

Quite often, printing a single web page may require several printed pages. You may want to preview how the page will print and choose the best way to print it. For example, you could limit the printout to pages that contain items of interest as they appear in the Print Preview window.

TIP! Many websites include a Print link on a page (such as for an article) that allows the page to print more efficiently. For example, the print mode may (or may not) omit online advertisements around the article.

Task	Procedure
Display a print preview	• Click the Print 🖨 ▾ menu ▾ button on the Command bar and then choose Print Preview.
Print a web page directly	• Click the Print 🖨 button on the Command bar.
Print only a selected portion of a web page	• Drag to select the portion of the web page you wish to print. • Click the Print 🖨 ▾ menu ▾ button on the Command bar and then choose Print. • Choose the Selection option in the Page Range section of the Print menu and then click Print.

HANDS-ON 6.8 Print a Web Page

WebSim

In this exercise, you will preview and print a web page.

Before You Begin: The book web page should be open in Internet Explorer.

1. Click the Print a Web Page link.

A simulation of the Mars Rover Curiosity website appears. Let's take a look at one of the news articles on this mission.

2. Click the NASA Curiosity Rover Begins Eastbound Trek on Martian… link.

The article appears. Let's say that after looking it over you want to print a copy.

3. Click the Print link near the top-right corner of the page as shown at right.

Internet Explorer opens a new window displaying just the article. This is good, since it leaves out the navigation spaces that you wouldn't want to print anyway.

4. Click the Print button near the top of the new page.

The Print dialog box appears, set to print with the default printer.

5. Click the Print button near the bottom of the dialog box.

The WebSim displays an image of what the printout would look like.

6. Click the Close Printout button.

7. Click the Close button as shown at right to close the article print page.

You are back to viewing the original article.

Use Print Preview

What if a website doesn't thoughtfully provide a Print link like the one you just used? You can select what you want to print and tell Internet Explorer to print only your selection.

8. Click the Continue WebSim link.

A new webpage appears from a website that doesn't provide a Print link for its articles. To get a good printout, you will select only the part of the page you wish to print.

9. Follow these steps to use the Shift +Click method to select a section of text on the web page:

Ⓐ Click once just left of the date at the start of the article. ——

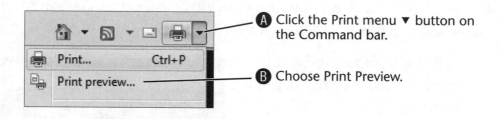

Ⓑ Hold down the Shift key, then click once near the end of the article. Then release the Shift key.

Internet Explorer selects any text and pictures between your two clicks.

10. Follow these steps to open a Print Preview of the web page.

Ⓐ Click the Print menu ▼ button on the Command bar.

Ⓑ Choose Print Preview.

Internet Explorer displays a preview of the page as it will print. Notice that items above and below the article are going to print with the current setting.

11. Follow these steps to tell Internet Explorer to print only your selection.

Ⓐ Click the Select Content menu ▼ button on the Toolbar bar.

Ⓑ Choose As Selected On Screen.

Internet Explorer changes the printout to include only what you selected previously. The additional (unnecessary) parts of the page won't print.

12. Close ▬x▬ the Print Preview window.

13. Close ▬x▬ the WebSim window.

14. Close ▬x▬ the student web page window, or leave it open if you are going directly to the Skill Builder exercises.

Concepts Review

All of the Concepts Review quizzes for this book are available on the student web page. Your instructor will let you know how to complete the quizzes (in the book or online).

True/False Questions

			Page number
1. You can save all of the tabbed web pages in an Internet Explorer window as a tab group favorite.	**true**	**false**	_____
2. In general, the more results you get on a search, the better.	**true**	**false**	_____
3. The Address bar allows searches only with the default search provider you have chosen.	**true**	**false**	_____
4. You can open a link in a new tab.	**true**	**false**	_____
5. You can print a selected portion of a web page rather than the entire page.	**true**	**false**	_____
6. You cannot add a search provider to the Address bar that does not appear in the Add Search Provider page.	**true**	**false**	_____

Multiple Choice Questions

7. Adding search words to reduce the total number of results is called _____.

    Page number: _____
    a. narrowing the search
    b. widening the search
    c. compressing the search
    d. performing an advanced search

8. If a web search provider is not listed on a Search Providers page _____.
    Page number: _____
    a. you can add it to the Address bar search providers anyway
    b. you cannot add it to the Address bar search providers
    c. you must add it as a Topic search provider
    d. None of the above

9. Adding a favorite for a website allows you to _____.
    Page number: _____
    a. change the homepage that appears when you start Internet Explorer
    b. designate a new Address bar search provider
    c. navigate to the site without typing its URL in the address bar
    d. None of the above

10. The quickest way to close many open tabs in Internet Explorer while keeping the window open is to _____.
    Page number: _____
    a. close each tab individually
    b. close the browser window and open a new one
    c. use the Close Other Tabs command
    d. use the Close All Tabs command

Skill Builders

SKILL BUILDER 6.1 Add New Instant Search Providers

In this exercise, you will add another Instant Search provider.

NOTE! Since this exercise is performed on *live web pages*, the instructions or screen may vary from the detailed instructions here.

1. If necessary, start Internet Explorer.

2. Click the Search ⌕ ▾ menu ▾ button and then choose Add at the bottom-right corner of the drop-down menu.

   The web page with popular search providers appears.

3. Follow these steps to find the Wikipedia search provider:

Ⓐ Choose Most Popular.

Ⓑ Look for Wikipedia Visual Search in the first or second lines of the provider list.

NOTE! Reminder: these are live web pages and the list and the item for Wikipedia may differ from the figure above.

   The Wikipedia Visual Search page appears.

4. Click the Add to Internet Explorer button.

   An Add Search Provider window appears.

5. Click the Add button.

   Internet Explorer installs the new search provider. Or you may see a prompt that Wikipedia is already installed.

6. Click OK if you see a prompt that this search provider is already installed.

7. Click the Search 🔍▾ menu ▾ button and then choose Wikipedia as shown at right.

Now Wikipedia will temporarily be your Address bar search provider until you choose another one, or until you close all Internet Explorer windows and open a new one (at which point your default search provider will appear in the Instant Search box).

Search with Various Search Providers

⚠ NOTE! In the next step, Internet Explorer might add a URL to the end of a single keyword search that's part of a recently visited page. If you see a URL appear when you type your search word, tap the ⌷Delete⌷ key on the keyboard to remove the unwanted URL and leave just your search word. (This won't happen if you use more than one search keyword.)

The unwanted URL appearing after the search word...

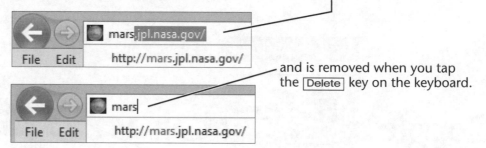

and is removed when you tap the ⌷Delete⌷ key on the keyboard.

8. Enter one or more search words about a topic you find interesting. It could be related to a hobby, technology, history, or most any other topic. Tap the ⌷Enter⌷ key to perform the search.

Wikipedia displays an article it thinks is most closely related to your search word(s), or it may display a list of articles.

9. Click the Search 🔍▾ menu ▾ button and then choose a different search provider.

10. Repeat your search with the same keywords, or try different keywords.

A different set of search results appears from the newly chosen search provider.

Compare Search Engines

In this exercise, you will attempt identical searches with two different search engines and compare the search results. There may be significant or minor differences in the results. The search engine that most reliably finds the types of web pages you are looking for is usually the one you will use first.

Search with One Search Provider

1. Think of a topic on which you would like to perform a web search. For example, you might want to search for a travel destination, a product purchase, or a current news item.

2. Choose two or three search words closely related to your topic and write them on the line.

    _____

3. Choose a search provider from the Address bar Search $\boxed{\mathcal{P} \,\text{-}}$ ▼ menu. If necessary, repeat the steps in Skill Builder 6.1 to add more search providers to the Address bar.

4. Enter the search words you selected in step 2 above and review the first page of search results.

5. Right-click a search result in the list that looks closely related to your topic and then choose Open in New Tab from the pop-up menu.

    Internet Explorer opens the web page in a new tab (but you are still viewing the search results). This makes it easy to return to your search results later.

6. Display the tab for the web page you opened in the previous step. Spend a few minutes browsing this website. Does it contain useful information related to your topic?

7. Display the search results tab and then open another search result in a new tab.

8. Review the web page in the new tab.

Search with Other Search Providers

9. Display the search results tab again using the leftmost tab.

10. Choose a different search provider from the Address bar Search menu.

   Search results for the same keywords appear. The search results you see may closely match your previous search or may be quite different.

11. Open two tabs with search results that look the most promising.

12. Try a third provider such as Wikipedia and open two of its search results in tabs.

   ⚠️**TIP!**   In the next step, use the Ctrl+Tab keyboard shortcut for switching tabs without the mouse.

13. Go from tab to tab, comparing your search results.

14. On the line, write down which search engine you feel came up with the most useful results for your search.

   _____

15. Right-click any tab and then choose Close Other Tabs from the pop-up menu.

Use an Accelerator

Accelerators are a new feature in Internet Explorer. These make it easy to select words on a web page and then perform a specific type of search or other command. In this exercise, you will use an accelerator.

1. If necessary open a new Internet Explorer window.

2. Navigate to the homepage for the school or college you are attending.

3. Find a page on the website with the school or college address. Usually an "About" or "Contact Us" link on the homepage leads you to the school's address.

    NOTE! In the next step, you will select the address much like you would in a word-processing document. Then you will use a map accelerator to create a new map of the address.

4. Once you've found the address, follow these steps to use an accelerator to quickly generate a map to the school or college:

Ⓐ Point at the very beginning of the *address* (not the name) with your mouse until the I-beam appears, as shown here.

Ⓑ Hold down the left mouse button and keep it held down as you drag to the end of the address. Release the mouse button when you have made the selection.

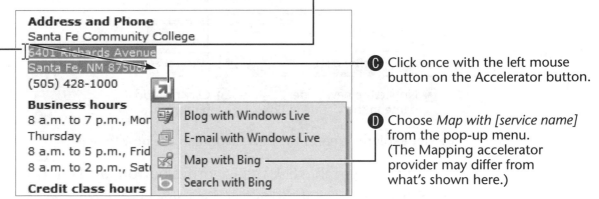

Ⓒ Click once with the left mouse button on the Accelerator button.

Ⓓ Choose *Map with [service name]* from the pop-up menu. (The Mapping accelerator provider may differ from what's shown here.)

A new tabbed page appears to display the map created with the address you selected. Your school or college should appear near the middle of the map.

5. Feel free to use the map scale or other controls to adjust your view of the map. If you're not sure how these controls work, ask a classmate or your instructor for help.

   Every mapping system is different. But the controls are fairly basic.

6. Close ☒ the browser tab with the map, or hold down the Ctrl key then tap **W** from the keyboard.

SKILL BUILDER 6.4 **Practice with Favorites**

In this exercise, you will organize new favorites into folders, delete a favorite, and rename a favorite.

1. If necessary, open an Internet Explorer window.

2. Make sure the Internet Explorer window is Maximized ⬜.

3. Use the Address bar to search for web pages related to a personal interest.

4. Using the Right-click+Open in New Tab technique, open three links found by your search in new tabs.

   Bichon Frise Page
   www.akc.
   A cheerful
   inquisitive
   | Open |
   | Open in new tab |

5. Display one of the web pages discovered in your search.

6. Click the Favorites button and then click Add to Favorites.
   This time, you will create a new folder in which to store the favorite.

7. Follow these steps to create a new favorite in a custom folder:

Ⓐ If desired, edit the default name for the favorite.

Ⓑ Click the New Folder button, give the folder an appropriate name, and click the Create button.

Name: Bichon Frise - Cute dog photos|

Create in: Bichon Links ▼   New Folder

Ⓒ Notice the new folder name in the Create In box.

Ⓓ Click the Add button.

Internet Explorer creates the new favorite in the new folder.

8. Display another tab, click the Favorites button, and choose Add to Favorites.
   Notice that Internet Explorer displays the name of new folder you just created as the Create In setting. You could choose a different folder here if you wish, but in this case you'll continue with the new folder.

9. Follow these steps to add the favorite to your new folder:

Ⓐ If desired, edit the default favorite name.

Name: Bichon USA site

Create in: Bichon Links ▼

Add ——— Ⓑ Click the Add button.

Add a Tab Group to Favorites

10. Click the Favorites button again, click the Add to Favorites menu ▾ button, and then choose Add Current Tabs to Favorites.

Notice that this time the Favorites folder appears in the Create In box.

11. Give the favorite the name **[Topic] Pages**.

12. Choose your new folder name from the Create In list and then click Add.

Open Favorites from the New Folder

13. Right-click any web page tab, then choose Close Other Tabs from the pop-up menu.

14. Click the Favorites button; then, display the Favorites tab.

15. Click the new folder you just created then click a link in the folder.

The web page opens. The Favorites bar disappears since it was not pinned.

16. Click the Favorites button and then Pin ◄ the Favorites panel to the Internet Explorer window.

The Favorites panel jumps to the left side of the window. It will remain open until you close it.

17. Follow these steps to open the tab group in your new folder:

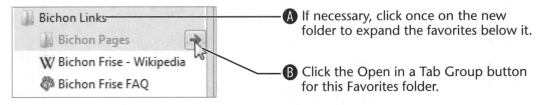

A If necessary, click once on the new folder to expand the favorites below it.

B Click the Open in a Tab Group button for this Favorites folder.

Internet Explorer opens all of the favorites in the folder.

Delete Your New Favorites Folder

18. Right-click the new folder you created (not the additional Pages folder inside of it), and then choose Delete from the pop-up menu.

Internet Explorer asks you to confirm the deletion.

19. Choose Yes to confirm deletion of the custom Favorites folder and all of the favorites within it.

You can use this same technique to delete individual favorites, too.

Sending and Receiving Email

Email is a service on the Internet that lets you send and receive messages online to anyone in the world. The use of email is now as common as the telephone. Web-based email (webmail) services give you access to your email from any web browser anywhere in the world. With a webmail account, you can send and receive email messages as well as send and receive computer files like documents, images, and virtually any other type of information. In this lesson, you will learn the basics of sending, receiving, and replying to email messages using a webmail account.

LESSON OBJECTIVES

After studying this lesson, you will be able to:

- Compare Webmail to traditional email access
- Send an email message
- Receive and reply to email messages
- Describe phishing

Additional learning resources are available at labpub.com/learn/silver/wtwc4/

Case Study: Traveling with Webmail

Donna has used email at work, but now wants an email account of her own. She signs up for a free webmail account that allows her to send and receive email from computers at school, the library, and other locations in addition to her home computer. Donna plans to travel later this year and is pleased that she will also be able to access her email from any of the Internet cafes that have popped up in most foreign countries as well as around the United States.

Donna checks her webmail account from the library and sees her breakfast meeting is still on.

Introducing Webmail

Along with the web, email is one of the two most popular of all Internet services. Email is simply the capability to send a message to a specific individual's email address anywhere in the world. An email message can also have one or more computer files (attachments) sent along with it. With email you can send and receive messages, send one message to a whole group of recipients, and exchange documents and images.

Types of Email Service

Two types of email service are used by most home Internet users:

- **POP Email**—One or more post office protocol (POP) email accounts are provided as part of your Internet service by most ISPs. Most POP email accounts are accessed with a program such as the full Outlook program that comes with the Microsoft Office suite. There are also third-party email programs such as Eudora and Mozilla Thunderbird. Microsoft also makes a free simplified email program available to all Windows users.

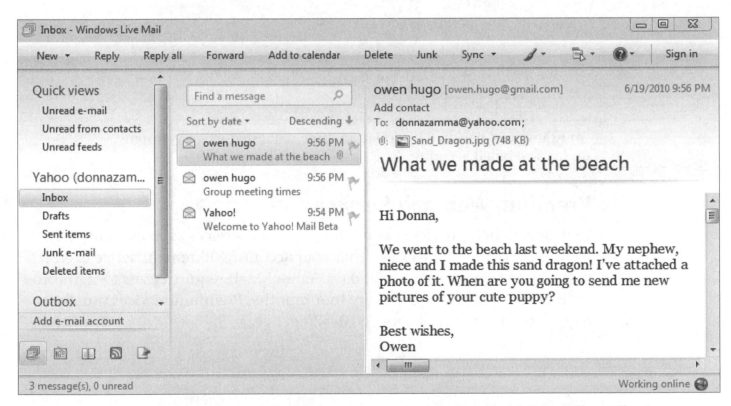

Windows Live Mail—a free program you can download from Microsoft—is an example of a POP email program. You can also use a program like this with a premium webmail service.

- **Webmail**—Webmail accounts such as Yahoo! Mail, Google Gmail, and Hotmail are typically free. You usually access them through a web browser rather than an email program. With a webmail account, you can access your email from any web browser anywhere in the world.

Some links to popular email services are available on the web page for this book.

Signing Up for a Free Webmail Account

Numerous websites offer free webmail service. In most cases, you merely need to choose an account name and password and provide some personal information. Once you sign up and your account name is confirmed, you can immediately begin sending and receiving email messages. Most free webmail accounts require that you sign in to check your email at least once every 30 days.

1. Tell us about yourself...		
My Name	Donna	Last Name
Gender	Female ▾	
Birthday	October ▾	29 · Year
I live in	United States ▾	
Postal Code	02420	

An example of personal information often requested when you sign up for a webmail account

Premium Webmail Services

Several webmail providers also offer premium services such as additional storage space and a guarantee that your account will remain active even if you do not sign on to it for 30 days. Yahoo! Mail requires users to sign into their account at least once every four months. Premium services usually require the payment of about $10–$20 per year.

Signing In to Webmail

Webmail accounts provide special web pages designed for sending and receiving email. The web pages include views of folders in which your email messages are stored, pages in which you compose new messages, and pages for setting various webmail service options. The following figure displays an example of a typical webmail display on the Yahoo! Mail service.

These buttons are to check incoming mail and compose new email messages.

A toolbar lists various email commands/actions.

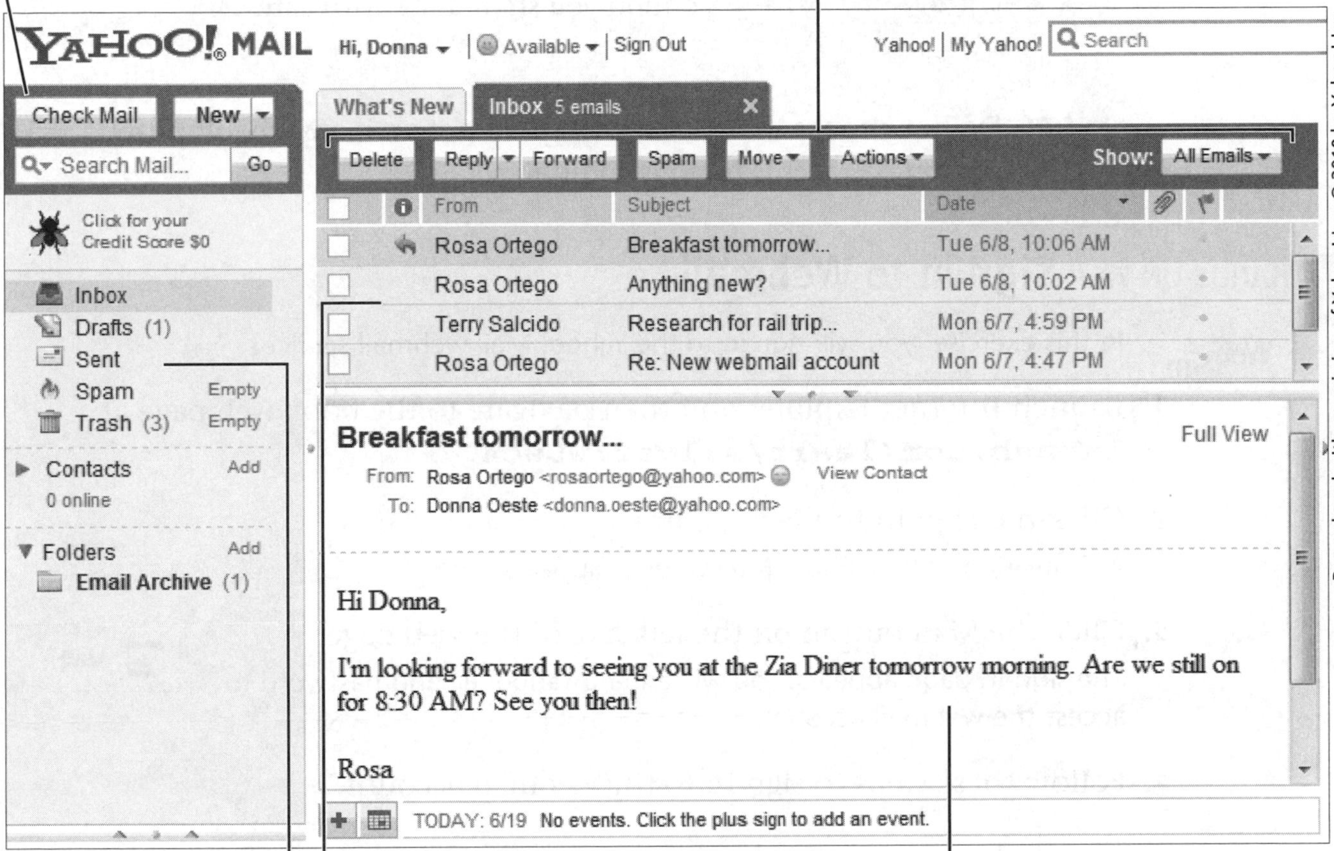

These folders contain your email messages.

These messages are in the currently selected folder (Inbox).

The View panel displays the currently selected message.

Signing In

To access your email page, you must sign in. This requires you to enter your account name and password. It is also possible to tell the webmail service to sign you in automatically from a particular computer, such as the one you use at home. This saves you the task of signing in each time you access webmail from your personal computer.

 Keep me signed in
for 2 weeks unless I sign out. Info
[Uncheck if on a shared computer]

Many webmail services allow you to remain signed in continuously, an option you should use with care.

!TIP! Do not choose the automatic sign-in option if any unauthorized person has access to your computer.

HANDS-ON 7.1 ## Sign in to Webmail

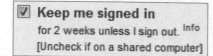 In this exercise, you will sign in to the Yahoo! Mail webmail service.

1. Launch Internet Explorer and then navigate to the book web page at **labpub.com/learn/silver/wtwc4**.

2. Click the Sign in to Webmail link.

   A simulation of the Yahoo! Mail website appears.

3. Click the Mail button on the left side of the web page.

   The sign-in page appears. You will enter a Yahoo! ID and password to access the webmail account.

4. Follow these steps to sign in to the webmail account:

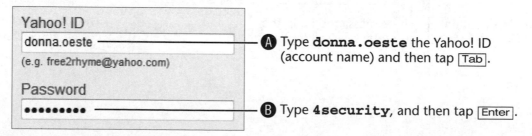

   The Yahoo! Mail page appears.

5. Click the Continue to Next WebSim button then continue reading the next topic below.

Sending an Email Message

Sending an email message is easy. If you know how to use a word processor, you know more than enough to create and send an email message. This section will walk you through the steps of sending your first email message with webmail.

Email Addresses

When you sign up for a webmail account, you are given an email address. This address uniquely identifies your email account. An email address looks similar to, and functions much like, the URL for a web page. The following illustration shows the parts of a typical email address.

donna.oeste@yahoo.com

User ID   Separator   Domain name

!TIP! Like web page URLs, an email address cannot contain spaces. All email addresses include the "at" (@) symbol.

AutoComplete

Yahoo! Mail features an AutoComplete feature for email addresses that works similarly to what you experienced typing URLs in the Internet Explorer address bar. It suggests similar email addresses to whatever you begin to type. If you see the addressee's email address as you begin typing in the To box, just click the desired address and add it as an addressee. The suggested address is entered into the Address box. This feature can help you avoid mistakes typing email addresses.

As you type, the AutoComplete feature may suggest one or more email addresses similar to what you begin typing in the To box.

Spell Check

Yahoo! Mail has a spell check feature to check the spelling before you send your message. Like any spell checker, this may miss some correct spellings as well as some types of misspellings, so always review the message for typos yourself before you click that Send button.

Send Verification

Unfortunately, some individuals try to use webmail services to send spam (junk email). Because of this, some webmail systems may require you to enter a verification code when you send a message. The verification code requirement makes your account impractical for use in spamming. After you have used your email account for awhile, this requirement may disappear.

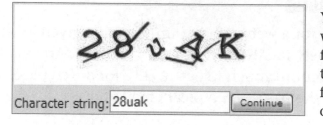

Character string: 28uak   [Continue]

Yahoo! Mail may ask for verification when you send a message after you first create a new account. The lines through the characters are there to foil automated recognition and typing of the code.

HANDS-ON 7.2 Compose and Send an Email Message

WebSim

In this exercise, you will compose a new email message and send it to a special email address at Labyrinth Learning. This email address will automatically send a reply message to you.

Before You Begin: The Compose and Send an Email WebSim should be displayed.

1. Follow these steps to address the message and give it a subject:

Ⓐ Click the New Mail Message button.

Ⓑ Address the message to **rosaortego@yahoo.com.**

Ⓒ Tap the [Tab] key twice to jump to the Subject box.

| Check Mail | New ▾ |
| Q▾ Search Mail... | Go |

APRs Hit 3.62%
See New Rate!

- ✉ Inbox (1)
- 🗐 Drafts
- 🖃 Sent
- 🔥 Spam   Empty
- 🗑 Trash   Empty
- ▶ Contacts   Add

What's New | Inbox 1 message | ✕ | ✉ New

[Send] [Attach] [Save Draft] [Spelling ▾] [Cancel]

To: rosaortego@yahoo.com

Cc:

Subject: New webmail account

Times New Roman ▾   12 ▾   **B** *I* <u>U</u>

Ⓓ Type **New webmail account** as the subject.

Ⓔ Tap the [Tab] key again to jump to the body of the message.

You are now ready to type the body of the message. However, we are going to let the WebSim do the typing for you.

2. Read the following guidelines and then click the keyboard icon to have the WebSim type the body of the message for you.

- Just as with a word processor, when you type to the end of the message box, a new line is started for you automatically.

- When typing an email message, follow the same rules for using the $\boxed{\text{Enter}}$ key as you would in a word-processing program. If you insert unnecessary returns into your message, your recipient may find it difficult to read.

The WebSim types out the body of the message.

Check Spelling

3. Click the $\boxed{\text{Spelling}}$ button near the top of the message.

Yahoo! Mail places a red squiggly line below any word its dictionary does not recognize. In this case, it thinks that *webmail* is not a correct spelling. In this case, you will ignore the misspelling prompt to match the version of this word used in the book. First, you will dismiss the tip box that appears over your message.

4. Follow these steps to respond to the misspelling indicator:

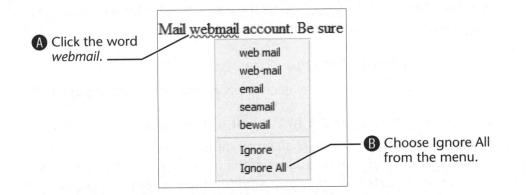

A Click the word *webmail.*

B Choose Ignore All from the menu.

Yahoo! Mail unmarks the word. If it were repeated in the message, all of the other markings of this word would be unmarked as well.

It's always a good idea to scan your messages for typos before you send them off. Remember that just because a word isn't marked by the spell checker, it doesn't mean the word is spelled correctly. (Example: I red the book.)

Send Your Message

5. Click the Send button on the toolbar near the top of the message as shown at right.

   Yahoo! Mail displays a Message Sent confirmation.

   It also notices that you've never sent a message to this addressee before and displays a prompt to add the addressee to your contacts list (address book).

6. Follow these steps to add the address to your contacts list:

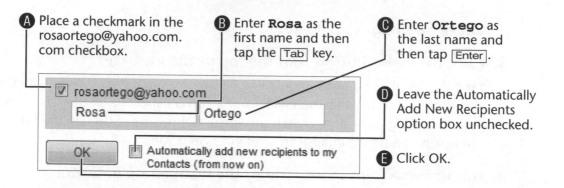

Ⓐ Place a checkmark in the rosaortego@yahoo.com. com checkbox.

Ⓑ Enter **Rosa** as the first name and then tap the [Tab] key.

Ⓒ Enter **Ortego** as the last name and then tap [Enter].

Ⓓ Leave the Automatically Add New Recipients option box unchecked.

Ⓔ Click OK.

   Yahoo! Mail adds Rosa Ortego to the contacts list. This will make it easier to address messages to this contact in the future.

View Your Sent Message

Yahoo! Mail keeps a copy of each message you send. Let's take a look.

7. Choose the Sent folder in the Folders panel as shown at right.

   Yahoo! Mail displays a list of all email messages you have sent. The message you just sent should be at the top of the list. The Sent mail folder stores every message you send from this webmail account automatically. Thus, there is no need to CC: (carbon copy) yourself to have a copy of an email message you've sent.

8. Click once on the New Webmail Account item in the Sent Items section of the page.

9. Click the Continue to Next WebSim button then continue reading with the next topic.

Getting from Here to There

The Internet supports a great many services, the web and email being the two most popular. Email messages use the worldwide Internet computer network to transit continents and oceans in a matter of seconds in many cases. The system is also highly democratic. No matter who sends it, an email message uses the same means and travels at the same speed.

How Email Reaches Its Destination

When you send an email message, the following process takes place to move your message to its destination.

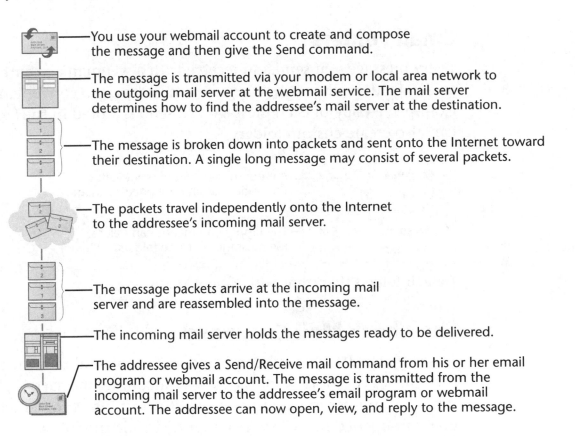

You use your webmail account to create and compose the message and then give the Send command.

The message is transmitted via your modem or local area network to the outgoing mail server at the webmail service. The mail server determines how to find the addressee's mail server at the destination.

The message is broken down into packets and sent onto the Internet toward their destination. A single long message may consist of several packets.

The packets travel independently onto the Internet to the addressee's incoming mail server.

The message packets arrive at the incoming mail server and are reassembled into the message.

The incoming mail server holds the messages ready to be delivered.

The addressee gives a Send/Receive mail command from his or her email program or webmail account. The message is transmitted from the incoming mail server to the addressee's email program or webmail account. The addressee can now open, view, and reply to the message.

Using the Inbox

When messages arrive, they are placed in your Inbox. You can access the Inbox from the Folder list or the Inbox tab. The Inbox holds all messages sent to you until you move them to other folders or delete them.

What's New	Inbox 3 emails	✕	Mobile | Options ▼ | Help ▼

Delete	Reply ▼	Forward	Spam	Move ▼	Actions ▼	Show:	All Emails ▼

☐	ⓘ	From	Subject	Date	▼
☐		**Terry Salcido**	**Research for rail trip...**	Mon 6/7, 4:59 PM	
☐		Rosa Ortego	Re: New webmail account	Mon 6/7, 4:47 PM	
☐		Yahoo!	Welcome to Yahoo!	Sun 6/6, 11:08 AM	

The Inbox displays all of your incoming messages.

Email Folders

Every message you send and receive with a webmail account is stored in a folder. Folders allow you to organize messages into convenient categories. For example, a copy of each message you send is stored in the Sent folder. You can also create custom folders.

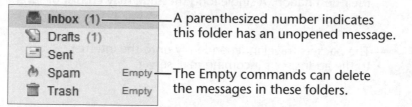

Inbox (1) ———— A parenthesized number indicates this folder has an unopened message.
Drafts (1)
Sent
Spam   Empty ——— The Empty commands can delete the messages in these folders.
Trash   Empty

Default folders that come with Yahoo! Mail

The Check Mail Command

Check Mail The Check Mail command in Yahoo! Mail tells the service to check the mail server for new messages. Any incoming message is placed into your Inbox. A number in parentheses next to your Inbox folder tells you how many unopened messages are currently inside the Inbox.

Receiving Messages

When you first sign in to your webmail account, it displays a note about any new messages in your Inbox. However, new messages can arrive after you sign in. The Check Mail command refreshes the view of the Inbox and displays any new messages. Some incoming messages may end up in the Spam folder, however, depending on their content.

New Message Notification   Yahoo! Mail can display a New Message alert and icon if you are running the Yahoo! Messenger instant messaging service. There is also a Yahoo! Toolbar add-in for Internet Explorer. Of course you can also use the Check Mail button to check for new messages manually from time to time.

Yahoo! Mail can display a new mail message notification on the bottom of the Window.

Reading Incoming Messages

You can read messages in the message preview panel below the Inbox or open a message in place of the Inbox. You can also sort your incoming messages alphabetically by sender, by subject, or by the date each message was received.

	From	▲	Subject	Date
☐	**Rosa Ortego**		**Breakfast tomorrow...**	Tue 6/8, 10:06 AM
☐	**Rosa Ortego**		**Anything new?**	Tue 6/8, 10:02 AM
☐	Rosa Ortego		Re: New webmail account	Mon 6/7, 4:47 PM
☐	**Terry Salcido**		**Research for rail trip...**	Mon 6/7, 4:59 PM
☐	Yahoo!		Welcome to Yahoo!	Sun 6/6, 11:08 AM

When you click a heading on an Inbox column, Yahoo! Mail sorts messages by that heading.

HANDS-ON 7.3 Check for New Messages

WebSim In this exercise, you will check for replies to your first message.

Before You Begin: The Check for New Messages WebSim page should be displayed.

1. Follow these steps to check for incoming email messages:

Ⓐ Click once on the Check Mail button.

Ⓑ Notice that the Inbox appears and displays any new messages as well as all previously received messages.

Check Mail	New ▾
Q▾ Search Mail...	Go

| What's New | Inbox 5 emails | ✕ | Breakfast tomorrow... |

| Delete | Reply ▾ | Forward | Spam | Move ▾ | Actions ▾ |

- 📥 Inbox (2)
- 📝 Drafts (1)
- 📧 Sent
- 🔥 Spam　　Empty
- 🗑 Trash　　Empty

Contacts　　Add

▼ Folders　　Add

☐	ⓘ	From	▲	Subject
☐		Rosa Ortego		Breakfast tomorrow...
☐		**Rosa Ortego**		**Anything new?**
☐		Rosa Ortego		Re: New webmail account
☐		**Terry Salcido**		**Research for rail trip...**
☐		Yahoo!		Welcome to Yahoo!

Breakfast tomorrow...

From: Rosa Ortego <rosaortego@yahoo.com> ☺   View Contact

To: Donna Oeste <donna.oeste@yahoo.com>

Hi Donna,

▼ ◦ ▼

| Applications | ➕ |

- .io Attach Large Files
- oib Automatic Organizer

Ⓒ Click once to display the new message in the Inbox.

Ⓓ Read the message in the preview panel.

Depending on the level of traffic on the Internet and the mail server for your webmail account, it may take just seconds for a message to reach you after it's been sent.

2. Double-click the Welcome to Yahoo! Message in the Inbox (upper-right) panel to view it on the full page rather than just in the preview panel and then read the message.

3. Click once on the scroll bar to scroll down toward the bottom of the message.

4. Click the Continue to Next WebSim button and then continue reading.

Replying to Messages

In a previous exercise, you received a message. There will often be occasions when you want to reply to a message right away. The Reply commands make it easy to respond to a message without having to retype the email address. In addition, Yahoo! Mail automatically adds a prefix to the subject line so your correspondent knows you are replying to a message.

Reply Compared to Reply All

If you look at the buttons above the message, you will see two reply buttons and a forward button. The following table describes the differences among these three commands.

Command	What It Does
Reply	This is usually the best way to respond to a message. This command creates a message addressed only to the sender of the original message.
Reply to All	This command creates a message addressed to sender of the original message and to everyone else who received the original message.
Forward	This command creates a new message with the original message included. You can address this message to anyone you choose.

Including the Previous Message in Replies

Most webmail (and email) programs automatically place a copy of the message you are responding to below your reply. This helps your correspondent know exactly what your reply is about.

 TIP! If you don't want to include the original message in a particular reply, you can select and delete it as you would any part of a normal message, after you click Reply to start the reply message.

Forwarding Messages

Sometimes you may receive a message that really should be handled by someone else. Or you may receive a message that you want to share with another correspondent. You could use Copy and Paste to copy the text of the message and paste it into a new message, but it is much easier to use the Forward command instead. This command makes a copy of the message and attaches it to a new message. The subject line of the new message also indicates that the message is being forwarded (i.e., it originated from someone other than you). You address and compose a forwarding message just like any other message.

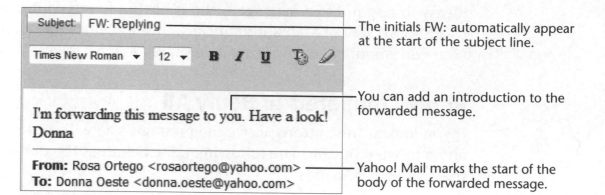

The initials FW: automatically appear at the start of the subject line.

You can add an introduction to the forwarded message.

Yahoo! Mail marks the start of the body of the forwarded message.

⚠ **NOTE!** Skill Builder 7.3 gives you an opportunity to forward a message.

Emoticons :-)

One disadvantage of email over making a telephone call is that you can only communicate with written words. Since English is an inflectional language, some meaning can be lost when something is expressed in writing alone. One way to overcome the lack of inflection is to use emoticons (also called smileys) from time to time in your messages. An emoticon can help convey the attitude or emotion behind a phrase. Following are a few examples of emoticons.

Emoticon	Meaning
:-)	happy, joking
;-)	winking
:-D	Laughing
:-(	Sad

The Insert Emoticon button displays smileys you can insert at the blinking cursor location.

 Emoticon References There are hundreds of emoticons available. The student web page contains links to web pages that list some of the most popular and creative emoticons. In the next exercise, you will use an emoticon.

HANDS-ON 7.4 **Reply to a Message**

WebSim

In this exercise, you will reply to the message you just received with a message that includes an emoticon.

Before You Begin: The Reply to a Message WebSim should be displayed.

1. Choose Breakfast tomorrow in the inbox.

	ⓘ	From	Subject
☐			
☐		**Rosa Ortego**	**Breakfast tomorrow...** ◄──────
☐		Rosa Ortego	Re: New webmail account

2. Click the Reply button on the toolbar.

   A compose message page appears. The email address of the sender is already entered in the To box. The subject line has been filled in for you as well. There is even a copy of the original message in the message body area.

3. Follow these steps to change the subject line for the message:

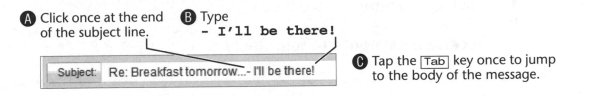

Ⓐ Click once at the end of the subject line.

Ⓑ Type
   `- I'll be there!`

Subject: Re: Breakfast tomorrow...- I'll be there!

Ⓒ Tap the Tab key once to jump to the body of the message.

   You can change the subject of a reply and even the addressee at any time.

4. Click the keyboard icon to simulate starting to type your message.

   The simulation saves you some time typing. Now you will type a winking emoticon to indicate that you are making a joke and not being serious or sarcastic.

Type an Emoticon

5. Click once at the end of the message and then type a semicolon (;).

6. Type a dash (–).

7. While holding down the Shift key, type a close parenthesis [ )].

8. Tap the Enter key and then click the keyboard icon to finish "typing" the rest of the message.

Run a Quick Spell Check

It's often a good idea to perform a spell check before sending a message.

9. Click the Spelling button on the toolbar.

Notice the red squiggly line below the misspelled word *ther* in the last sentence.

10. Click once on the word *ther*.

Yahoo! Mail displays alternative spellings for the word.

11. Click once to choose *there* from the list.

Yahoo! Mail corrects the spelling of the word. Since no other words have a squiggly red underline, the spell check command is complete. (Of course you should still look over the message to make sure there are no misspelled word that spell check could have missed.)

Send Your Message

12. Click the Send button on the toolbar.

Yahoo! Mail displays a confirmation that the message was sent.

13. Click OK to return to the Inbox.

Receive a Response to Your Reply

14. Click the Check Mail button near the top-left corner of the web page.

The reply to your reply appears in the Inbox. Notice that the subject line of this message is in bold type, indicating that this message has not yet been opened.

Notice also that the Breakfast Tomorrow message has a small arrow beside it. This indicates that you have previously replied to this message.

15. Click once on the RE: Breakfast tomorrow message in the Inbox folder and then read the reply in the preview panel.

16. Click the Continue to Next WebSim button and continue reading.

Signing Out

When you are done sending and receiving email, you should make a habit of signing out when you are not using the account at home. This closes your webmail window and makes it impossible for others to access your account by, say, clicking the Back button.

A link signs you out of your webmail account so no one else can view it.

After you sign out, Yahoo! confirms it.

 TIP! It is critical that you sign out of your session whenever you use your webmail account on a public computer such as at a library or an Internet café.

 HANDS-ON 7.5 **Sign Out of Webmail**

WebSim

In this exercise, you will sign out of your Yahoo! Mail account.

Before You Begin: The Sign Out of Webmail WebSim should be displayed.

1. Click the Sign Out link near the top of the web page.

Yahoo! Mail exits you to the Yahoo! homepage. It is critical to sign out if you are using your webmail account on a public computer. Notice the "You are signed out" confirmation on the right side of the web page.

2. Close ⊠ the WebSim's browser window.

The book web page should reappear.

Phishing Scams

Phishing is a technique whereby an unsuspecting victim is duped into giving out personal information to a website that mimics an actual site of a major company. For example, you may receive a message from a bank (possibly your own) that your online account access will be suspended unless you verify your personal information. A link in the message leads to a fake web page that looks just like the actual bank's page. Any information you enter on this page goes directly to the thieves, who can then use this information to access your account.

Account Suspended/Closed   You may receive a message similar to the one below, telling you that your online account services have been suspended, closed, etc., or there may be a claim that the online banking system has been recently updated and you need to confirm your account information to resume access.

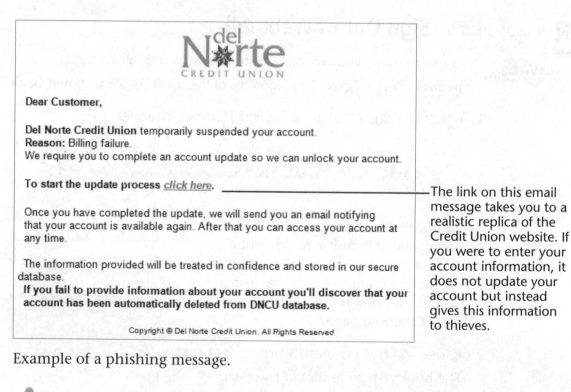

The link on this email message takes you to a realistic replica of the Credit Union website. If you were to enter your account information, it does not update your account but instead gives this information to thieves.

Example of a phishing message.

!TIP!   *No* bank will ever ask you to update account information via an email message.

Modified Account   Another variation is to receive a message that your account has been modified, a purchase made, or some other activity has taken place. The "news" itself is bogus. But some users may feel anxious about their account being modified and try to act on the message to verify this.

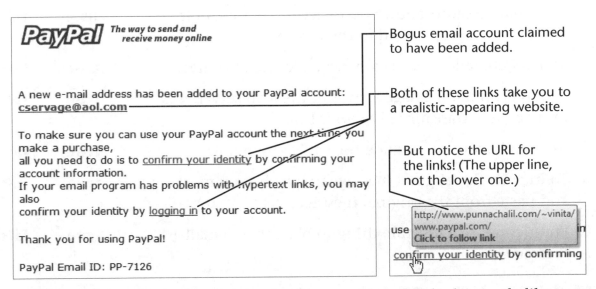

A fictitious "event" asks the victim to log in on a screen that looks exactly like a PayPal web page.

Avoiding Phishing Scams   The following guidelines can ensure that you avoid becoming a victim.

- *Never* give your login information to a web page you arrive at via a link from an email message. Use it only when you go to the page yourself via the address bar or a favorite that you created.

- Look carefully at the URL of any links on email messages asking for *any* kind of personal information.

- Look for basic errors in grammar.

- When in doubt, ignore and delete the message. Any commercial website that does business with you will use messages after you log in to request updates. Such websites will never ask you for personal information or a critical change in your account via an email message.

Concepts Review

All of the Concepts Review quizzes for this book are available on the student web page. Your instructor will let you know how to complete the quizzes (in the book or online).

True/False Questions

Page number

1. Webmail accounts allow you to access your email from any computer connected to the Internet.   **true**   **false**   _____

2. Many webmail accounts are available free of charge.   **true**   **false**   _____

3. When an email message arrives at the mail server, it is immediately transmitted to your Inbox.   **true**   **false**   _____

4. All email addresses include the "at" (@) symbol.   **true**   **false**   _____

5. To include the original message in a reply, you must copy and paste from the original message.   **true**   **false**   _____

6. Emoticons are a juvenile thing to place in an email message.   **true**   **false**   _____

Multiple Choice Questions

7. What should you do if you need to access your webmail account from a public computer?

   Page number: _____

   a. Make sure you log out at the end of your email session.

   b. Don't choose the automatic sign in option.

   c. Check the public computer for spyware first.

   d. Both a and b

8. A mail server program to manage your webmail account is running _____.

   Page number: _____

   a. inside your computer

   b. at the ISP that supports your account

   c. inside the addressee's computer

   d. Both a and c

9. Which of the following is NOT a valid email address?

   Page number: _____

   a. bsmith@ix.netcom.com

   b. bruce@labyrinth-pub.com

   c. www.amazon.com

   d. None of the above

10. What does the AutoComplete feature do?

   Page number: _____

   a. Suggests email addresses you have used before

   b. Completes typing the subject line

   c. Completes typing your signature

   d. Completes sending your message

# Skill Builders

SKILL BUILDER 7.1 Send an Email Message

 In this exercise, you will compose and send an email message.

1. Launch Internet Explorer and then open the book web page at **labpub.com/learn/silver/wtwc4**.

2. Click the Send an Email Message link.

3. Click the Mail button on the left side of the web page.

4. Sign in with the following data and then click the Sign In button:
   - Yahoo! ID: **donna.oeste** `Tab`
   - Password: **4security** `Enter` (not `Tab`)

5. Click the New button on the upper-left side of the page.
   New Email Message form appears.

6. Tap the `t` key on the keyboard (do not hold down `Shift`).
   Yahoo! Mail displays the email addresses that begin with "T."

7. Click once to choose Terry Salcido.
   Yahoo! Mail fills in the email address. This feature can help you avoid typos in email addresses. It also relieves you from having to remember everyone's email address when you send messages to people you've emailed before.

8. Tap the `Tab` key twice and then type **The best film I've seen lately** as the subject of the message.

9. Tap the `Tab` key and then click the keyboard icon to simulate typing the body of the message.
   Let's hope it doesn't give away the ending! :-)

10. Send the message.
    Yahoo! Mail displays a Message Sent confirmation.

11. Click OK.
    Yahoo! Mail displays the What's New tab.

View the Sent Message

12. Click the Sent folder in the folders box on the left side of the window.

13. Click once to display The Best Film I've Seen Lately.

Yahoo! Mail displays your message in the preview panel.

14. Click the Continue to Next WebSim button to continue with the next exercise.

SKILL BUILDER 7.2 ## Check for Mail and Reply to Messages

In this exercise, you will use the Check Mail command to check for incoming email messages and reply to a message.

Before You Begin: The Check for Mail and Reply to Messages WebSim should be displayed.

Check for Incoming Messages

1. Click the `Check Mail` button on the upper-left side of the page.

The Inbox appears and displays any new email messages received since you signed in.

2. Double-click the Most Unusual Film message at the top of the Inbox message list.

The reply to your Most Interesting Film message appears. Notice that a double-click causes the message to fill the entire area once used by the Inbox and preview window.

Reply to a Message

3. Click the `Reply` button on the toolbar above the message.

A new, composed message form appears for your reply. The To box and subject line are already filled in for you.

4. Click the keyboard icon to simulate writing a reply describing the most unusual film you've ever seen.

5. Click the Send button.

A confirmation appears that your message was sent.

6. Click OK to return to the Inbox.

Check for New Messages

7. Use the `Check Mail` button on the toolbar to check for new messages.

8. Click once on the reply to your message in the Inbox. Read over the reply in the preview panel below the message list.

9. Click the Continue to Next WebSim button.

SKILL BUILDER 7.3 **Forward a Message**

In this exercise, you will forward a message to another email address.

Before You Begin: The Forward a Message WebSim should be displayed.

1. Double-click to display the Welcome to Yahoo! Mail message at the bottom of the Inbox.

2. Click the `Forward` button on the toolbar above the message.

The message window you were viewing has transformed from reading an incoming message into an outgoing message. Now the text you were reading appears a few lines into the body of the new (forwarding) message.

3. In the To box, address the forwarded message to yourself:
donna.oeste@yahoo.com

It's OK to send a message to yourself. For example some email users do this to send themselves reminders of appointments.

4. Tap the `Tab` key three times to jump to the body box and then click the keyboard icon to simulate typing the message.

5. Click the `Send` button.

Yahoo! Mail confirms that the message was sent.

6. Click OK to acknowledge the sent message confirmation.

7. Use the `Check Mail` button to check for a reply.

Notice the small arrow (↪) beside the Welcome to Yahoo! Mail message, indicating that the message has been forwarded. This arrow points in the opposite direction to that of the replied message arrow (↩).

8. Close ⊠ the browser window and return to the textbook web page.

LESSON 8

Sending and Receiving Attachments

You can send files along with your email messages. These are called attachments. You can attach any type of computer file to an email message, and you can even attach several files to the same message if you wish. For example, you can attach one or more photos to an email message. The ease of use of email also requires care with security. Some attachments could cause you some inconvenience or actually harm your computer system. Anyone who uses email needs good Internet security software. In this lesson, you will attach files to messages and learn about security issues.

LESSON OBJECTIVES

After studying this lesson, you will be able to:

- Open attachments you receive from others
- Attach files to email messages
- Describe two safeguards against Internet security threats
- Describe email spam

Additional learning resources are available at labpub.com/learn/silver/wtwc4/

Case Study: Sending Photos

Eduardo wants to send some photos to his 14-year-old niece, Rosa. He recently purchased a digital camera, which makes it easy to take photos and store them on his computer. He's been taking pictures of his dog, Shadow, whom his niece adores. Even simple photos Eduardo takes while walking Shadow around the block delight her.

Eduardo attaches some photos to an email message to Rosa. When she receives the message, Rosa stores the photos on the family computer so the entire family can view them. Rosa also forwards some photos via email to her friends.

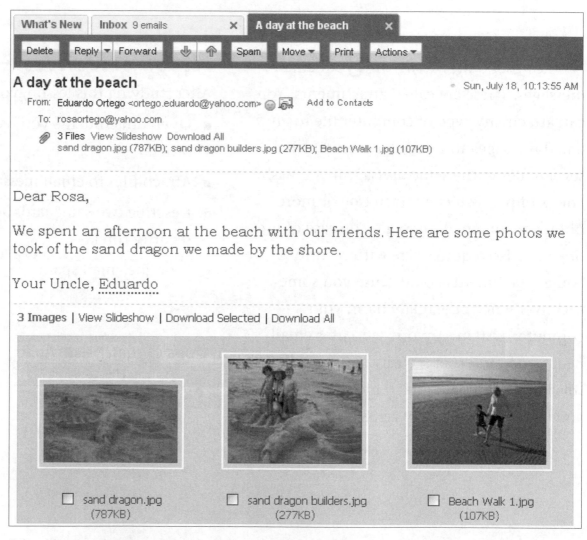

Eduardo attaches new photos to his email message.

Assuring Internet Security

Anyone who uses the Internet needs to take care that the computer is secure. An Internet connection can serve as a two-way communication path that hackers and other unsavory characters can use to install software without your knowledge, track the information you send and receive, or even erase files on your computer's hard drive. Nearly all new computers come with at least a trial version of security software. Many ISPs also provide security software to their customers. This security software is set to run automatically when you first start your computer.

 TIP! If your computer accesses the Internet, it needs to run some form of antivirus software.

Internet Security or Antimalware Software

A special type of application designed to detect and erase potentially harmful programs and intrusions is called *antimalware* software. These programs watch all activities of software on the computer and halt the processing of any suspicious program that might contain a virus. Antimalware programs can detect the unseen activities of most viruses and other malware when they try to invade your system and can usually clean (erase) a virus in an infected file. An antivirus program can even scan a file that you download and warn you before you attempt to open the file.

Malware Defined

Malware is any form of software installed without your consent that can cause harm to your computer or unintended consequences from your use of the computer. The most commonly used term for malware is *computer virus*. However, there are many forms of malware beyond the types of computer virus that are often reported in the media. Your computer may run more than one program to help protect against specific malware threats described in the next topic.

A good Internet security program gives you protection against multiple security threats.

Common Internet Security Risks

There are thousands of computer viruses inhabiting the Internet. Some risks take the form of email messages. Most risks can be grouped into one of the categories below.

- **Virus**—This is any software installed without your knowledge. Most viruses are harmless. However there have been some viruses over the years that have deleted data from hard drives, installed spyware, and inflicted other harmful functions.

- **Spyware**—This is a form of virus that installs itself secretly and then may track and report many of your activities to a remote location. Spyware programs can also sometimes install other programs on the computer or even cause your browser to open web pages you did not intend to open.

- **Adware**—This is a form of software that displays advertising on the user's computer. Some types of adware are installed with the user's knowledge, but others may not. For example, a program may also display ads on its interface.

- **Phishing**—This term refers email messages that lure users into giving out personal information. For example, a message may indicate that your online banking services may be suspended if you do not "confirm" your user ID and password.

Internet Security Protections

Anyone connected to the Internet needs protection from the various risks listed above and the new ones constantly appearing.

- **Windows Update/Critical Updates**—Microsoft tracks various security risks related to its Windows operating system and regularly distributes fixes to negate a newly identified risk. The *Windows Update* feature built into Win 7, Vista, and XP helps you download and automatically install the latest updates.

- **Antimalware Software**—This software is optimized to prevent infections from various types of viruses that travel via the Internet. Norton Antivirus, Macafee VirusScan, Softwin BitDefender are examples of antivirus software. Avast is an open-source Internet security program with a free home antivirus edition.

- **Internet Security Software**—Internet security packages offer all-in-one protection from all major forms of Internet security risk. Popular Internet security programs include Norton Internet Security, MacAfee Internet Security Suite, and Avast Internet Security.

Links to several popular antimalware and Internet security software vendors are available on web page for this book.

- **Virus Definition Updates**—All antivirus programs work by comparing suspicious activity on the computer to *virus definitions* that describe the behaviors of previously observed viruses. As new viruses are introduced and older viruses evolve, these definitions need to be updated in order for the antivirus software to function with peak effectiveness. Most antivirus software can regularly check for new virus definitions and download them automatically.

- **Firewalls**—A *firewall* is software (and sometimes hardware) designed to prevent a remote user from accessing your computer without your permission. Most network hardware (e.g., a router) comes with a hardware firewall. Win 7, Vista, and XP come with a software firewall. Some antivirus programs also feature a software firewall.

The System and Security Action Center displays the current status of various Internet security services.

A Note to Beginners

All this information about Internet security threats you need to safeguard against may seem daunting. Actually, a good Internet security program will protect you against most threats automatically without your needing to do anything special. However, it's good to be generally aware of the threats to your computer and to know something about how security software protects you. The first half of this lesson contains all you need to know for now.

HANDS-ON 8.1 **Check Your Security Settings**

WebSim

In this exercise, you will check the Windows Security Center to see what Internet security settings are in place.

Before You Begin: Many computer labs do not permit access to the Windows Control Panel. In this case, follow the steps below to start a WebSim for this exercise:

- Start Internet Explorer and navigate to the book web page:
  labpub.com/learn/silver/wtwc4
- Click the Check Your Security Settings link.
- You are now ready to start with step 1.

1. Choose Start→Control Panel.

2. Follow these steps to check the security settings:

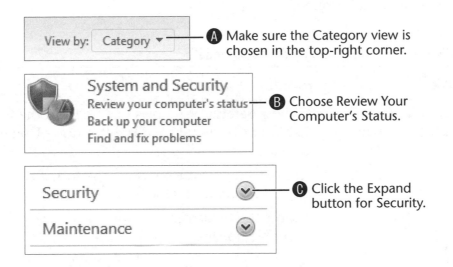

Windows displays the status of the various security settings and programs. A warning of some sort would appear if any setting or security area was not in good order.

3. Click the View Installed Antispyware programs link under Spyware and Unwanted Software Protection item; or, skip to step 5 if this link is not visible.

Windows displays the available programs. Since it would slow down the computer for both to be running at the same time, one of the programs is switched off.

4. Click the Close button for the Action Center.

5. Close ☒ the Control Panel window.

6. Close ☒ the browser window if you were using the WebSim version of this exercise.

Windows Update

Windows Update can routinely contact the Microsoft website to get a list of the latest updates for your Windows operating system and any Microsoft programs you have installed. Depending on your settings, Windows Update can even install critical software updates automatically when your computer is not normally in use.

⊘ Windows is up to date	
Available: 19 optional updates	View available updates
No new important updates are available for your computer.	

Windows Update helps ensure that your computer has the latest security updates installed.

QUICK REFERENCE: Running Windows Update

Task	Procedure
Manually Run Windows Update	• Choose Safety→Windows update from the Internet Explorer command bar. (The Windows Update window appears.) • Choose Check for Updates at the top of the left panel of the Windows Update window. • Follow the on-screen prompts to choose and install available updates
Run System Restore	• Click the Start button. • Type System Restore in the Search Programs and Files box. • Choose System Restore under Programs at the top of the search list. • Follow the on-screen prompts to select a restore point.

HANDS-ON 8.2 Run Windows Update

WebSim In this exercise, you will run a simulation of using Windows Update to install security updates to the computer.

1. If you have not done so already, start Internet Explorer and navigate to the book web page at **labpub.com/learn/silver/wtwc4**.

2. Click the Run Windows Update link.
   The WebSim starts with Internet Explorer already running.

3. If necessary, Maximize ▣ the Internet Explorer window.

4. Choose Safety→Windows Update from the command bar.

5. Click the Check for Updates link at the top of the left panel.
   Win 7 goes online to check for the latest updates. When the scan for updates is completed, it displays the number available.

6. Click the Install Updates button in the right panel.
   Win 7 starts the process of downloading and installing the updates. Depending on the software to be installed, you may be asked to accept an end-user agreement.

7. Close ⊠ the WebSim browser window.

Downloading Files from the Web

The process of exchanging files between computer systems is called *uploading* and *downloading*. When you send and receive email, your computer performs both of these tasks—uploading outgoing messages and downloading incoming messages. A webmail service such as Yahoo! Mail handles these tasks for you automatically, as do POP email programs such as Outlook 2010 and Windows Live Mail. Most of time you will be downloading files to your computer, such as a form from a web page.

Term	Description	Example
Downloading	The act of copying a file from a remote computer to your own computer	You need a tax form. You find it on a website and copy it to your computer.
Uploading	The act of copying a file from your own computer to a remote computer	You send a tax form to the IRS for filing.

Downloading moves attachments from a webmail message to your computer.

Photos attached to a webmail message

Downloading

Photos saved to computer's hard drive

Downloading Files from Web Pages

You can usually download any file linked to a web page. Simply right-click the link in Internet Explorer and choose Save Target As from the pop-up menu. Internet Explorer guides you through the steps of choosing a disk drive and folder destination for the downloaded file then displays the progress of the download.

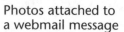

A Photoc	Open
Grand Ca	Open in New Tab
Grand Ca	Open in New Window
Continue	Save Target As...
	Print Target

A right-click on a link displays a pop-up menu you can use to download a file.

Caution! Viruses!

You should be aware that some types of downloaded files (including email attachments) could contain a computer virus. Program files, Word documents, Adobe PDF documents, and zip files all can contain a virus. Although most viruses are harmless, some can damage your system or even erase files. Most antimalware and Internet security programs allow you to scan a single file or an entire folder or drive for viruses.

!TIP! Make sure you can trust the source of any files you download or email attachments you open. When in doubt, use your antivirus program to scan a downloaded file first before you open it.

HANDS-ON 8.3 **Download a File**

WebSim

In this exercise, you will navigate to a web page and then download a digital photo from that page to your exercise diskette.

1. Launch Internet Explorer and navigate to the book web page at **labpub.com/learn/silver/wtwc4**.

2. Click the Download a File link.

A web page appears with links to three photos.

3. Follow these steps to download a photo file:

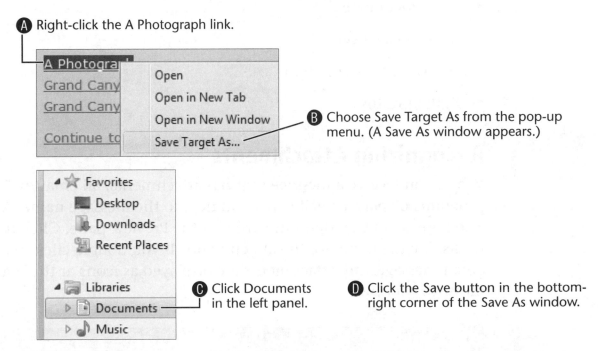

A Right-click the A Photograph link.

B Choose Save Target As from the pop-up menu. (A Save As window appears.)

C Click Documents in the left panel.

D Click the Save button in the bottom-right corner of the Save As window.

Internet Explorer displays the progress of the download as it copies the file over the Internet to your computer's hard drive.

4. Click the Close button if Internet Explorer displays a Download Complete window.

The file is now in the Documents folder on your computer. (This is the same location where you saved Word documents in Lesson 3, Using a Word Processor.)

5. Click the Continue to Next WebSim link.

Continue reading the next topic while the WebSim loads. You will use the WebSim in the next exercise.

Receiving Email Attachments

Some types of information are not as easy to work with in the form of an email message. For example, if you need to submit a multipage report for review by others, you would lose a great deal of formatting (such as pagination) if you converted the report from a word processor file to an email message. It would be much simpler to send the report document as an attachment. An attachment is a file you include with an email message. It can be any type of file.

Here are some examples of attachments:

- Word document

- Excel spreadsheet

- PowerPoint presentation

- Digital photos

Recognizing Attachments

When you receive a message that has attachments, all email/webmail programs display a small paper clip next to the message name. A paper clip also appears in the top-right corner of the Preview pane. Click the paper clip to display the names of the attachments. If you double-click to open an email message, any attachments are displayed as icons at the bottom of the message window.

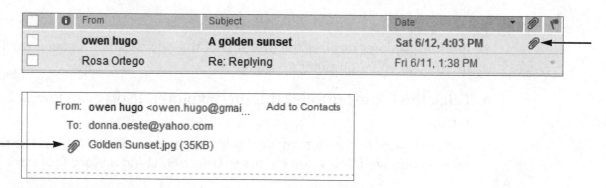

A paper clip shows that this message has an attachment.

Saving Attachments from Webmail

When you receive an attachment, it is embedded *within* the email message. You may wish to store an attachment with related files on a drive on your computer. To work with the attachment apart from the email message it was attached to, you must save the attachment file(s). When you delete a message that has attachments, the attachment files are deleted as well unless you have already saved them.

Internet Explorer asks whether you wish to save or open an attachment.

Example When Rosa gets the email message from Eduardo with the photographs, she saves them into a folder on the hard drive that she set up previously. If she didn't do this, it could be difficult to locate the photos later. Without taking a moment to save the attachments, Rosa would have to go back to the email message that originally contained the attached files.

Attachments and Malware

Some email attachments could possibly contain malware, such as computer viruses. Examples of potentially infected files include program files, documents, and even some types of pictures. Most viruses are harmless but some can damage your system or generate messages from your email account without your knowledge.

Yahoo! Mail will automatically scan any attachment you receive for viruses. But you should be sure you trust the source of any attachment you save or open. However, the best way to avoid a virus in an attachment is not to open it!

!WARNING! *Never* open an attachment from a sender you do not know.

Your Password

"hostmaster@coastalnow.net" <hostmaster@coastal... 📑 Add   To: X-User@yahoo.com

📎 account_info.zip (53KB)

Account and Password Information are attached!

Visit: http://www.coastalnow.net

Virus Scan Results   ✕

The file you attempted to download contains a virus and it cannot be cleaned!

account_info.zip (53KB)

*** Server-AntiVirus: No Virus (Cle

*** "YAHOO" Anti-Virus

*** http://www.yahoo.com

Norton
AntiVirus

[Cancel]

This innocent-looking file contained a virus. Yahoo! Mail's automatic virus scan detected it and will not permit you to download the file.

QUICK REFERENCE: Saving Attachments

Task	Procedure
Save an attachment from a Yahoo! Mail message	• Display or preview the message with the attachment.
	• Click once on the attachment name.
	• Wait for the antivirus scan to complete and then click the Download Attachment button.
	• Click the Save button.
	• Navigate to the destination folder where you wish the attachment to be saved and then click the Save button.
	• Click the Open button if a Download Complete window appears, or click the Open Folder button to open the destination folder.

HANDS-ON 8.4 **Save an Attachment**

In this exercise, you will save three attachments to an email message into a new folder.

Before You Begin: The Save an Attachment WebSim should be visible in Internet Explorer. If it is not, click this link on the book web page.

The WebSim starts by showing the Yahoo.com website, ready for you to sign on to a Yahoo! Mail account.

1. Click the Mail button and then sign in with the following information:
   - User ID: **ortego.eduardo** ⎣Tab⎦
   - Password: **4security** ⎣Enter⎦

   The Yahoo! Mail web page appears. Notice the (1) beside the Inbox, indicating that there is a new message there. When you first log on to webmail, there's no need to click the Check Mail button to see if you have new messages.

2. Click the Inbox on the left side of the Yahoo! Mail page.

   Yahoo! Mail displays the message list. Notice that the What We Made at the Beach message is in bold type, indicating it has not yet been read. There is a paper clip icon at the right side of the row, showing that this message contains one or more attachments.

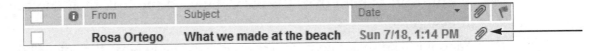

3. Click once to display the What We Made at the Beach message.

   Yahoo! Mail displays the message in the preview panel. Notice that there is file below the name of the sender.

   When you receive a photo, you can usually see it in the body of the message. Yahoo! Mail displays a Show Images button at the top of the preview panel.

4. Click the Show Images button in the center of the window.

5. Click the scroll bar as shown at right to simulate scrolling to the bottom of the message. (Notice that the tip of the pointer arrow is above the scroll button at the bottom of the scroll bar.)

Yahoo! Mail displays a thumbnail version of the photo near the bottom of the message. Let's view a larger version of it.

6. Point (don't click) over the thumbnail photo image until a ScreenTip appears.

Let's try out this feature.

7. Click once on the thumbnail photo.

After a pause, a larger view of the image appears. That's much better. However, the image is still embedded in the email message. Let's download it to the computer.

8. Click Close at the bottom-right corner of the enlarged image.

9. Click the scroll bar on the right side of the message preview to scroll back up to the top of the message.

Download the Photo

10. Point (don't click) over the Sand_Dragon.jpg link near the top of the message.

Yahoo! Mail displays another screen tip telling you what the link will do. That's just what we want.

11. Click once on the SandDragon.jpg link at the top of the message.

Yahoo! Mail immediately begins a virus scan and opens a new window to display the results. Yahoo! Mail scans any attachment file you download for viruses and warns you if a virus is found. (You are not allowed to download a file with a virus.) In this case, there is no virus, so you can proceed to download the file.

12. Click the Download Attachment button.

Internet Explorer displays a dialog box asking what you wish to do with the file. In this case, you want to save the file to your computer.

13. Click the Save button.

Internet Explorer displays the previous location used to save a file. You will save the file to your Pictures folder.

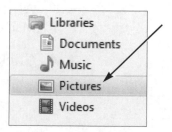

14. Choose Pictures under Libraries in the right panel, as shown at right.

Now that you have chosen the folder location, you are ready to save the attachment in it.

15. Click the Save button.

Internet Explorer displays the progress of saving the attachment. (If the file is small, the download may complete almost immediately.) The speed of a download depends a great deal on the speed of your Internet connection.

16. Click the Open (not the Open Folder) button.

Windows displays a prompt that a website wants to do something on your computer. This is a security measure, in case a web page tries to run malware of some sort. Since you know you've given the command to open the photo, all is well. You can safely allow this action. (If you hadn't tried to do something from the download, then you would not want to allow this action.)

17. Click the Allow button.

Windows displays the newly downloaded photo with the default photo viewer program.

18. Close **X** the photo preview window, but not the WebSim window.

The Internet Explorer window with Yahoo! Mail reappears.

19. Click the Continue to Next WebSim button.

Continue reading the next topic while the next WebSim loads.

Sending Attachments

Attach After you create a new email message, you can attach one or more files to it. The files you select to attach can be anywhere on the computer's hard drive, USB flash drive, or some other location. All email and webmail services have an Attach button you can use to attach one or more files to an email message. These buttons nearly always display a paper clip icon. (The latest version of Yahoo! Mail does not, however, even though attached files always have a paper clip beside the filename.)

Gmail, another popular webmail service, displays the traditional paper clip beside the Attach a file command.

Ensuring File Compatibility

When you send someone an attachment, make sure the recipient uses software that is compatible with your attachment file. For example, if you use Microsoft Word 2010 but the recipient uses Word 2003, you should save the file in a format that Word 2003 can read.

Attaching Multiple Files

It is possible to attach more than one file to an email message. For example, you might wish to send several images or documents with a single email message.

Yahoo! Mail displays the total size of the attachments and the maximum size of all attachments combined.

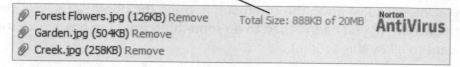

Multiple files are attached to this Yahoo! Mail message.

Attachment Size Limits

Most email and webmail services limit the total size of all files attached to a single message. At the time this book was published, Yahoo! Mail allowed a total size of all attachments of up to 20 megabytes. That's enough to send several high-resolution photos or even a short video clip. The maximum attachment size most email services allow undoubtedly will continue to grow over time.

 TIP! If you need to send a very large file to someone, try a web service that specializes in this. To find such services perform a search such as "sending large files" with your favorite search engine.

QUICK REFERENCE: Attaching Files to an Email Message

Task	Procedure
Attach a file to a message with Yahoo! Mail	• Start to compose the new message as usual. • Click the Attach button. • Navigate to the file you wish to attach and then click the Open button. • Repeat using the Attach button to attach additional files to the message

HANDS-ON 8.5   Attach a File to a Message

WebSim

In this exercise, you will attach a file to an email message.

Before You Begin: The Attach a File to a Message WebSim should be open. As the WebSim begins, you are already logged in to Donna's Yahoo! Mail account.

1. Click the New button on the upper-left side of the page.

2. Start the message with the following information:

   To: **rosaortego@gmail.com**

   Subject: **Puppy takes a bath**

   Body: [Click the keyboard icon to let the WebSim type the message.]

   Now you are ready to attach a photo to the message.

3. Follow these steps to attach a photo to the message:

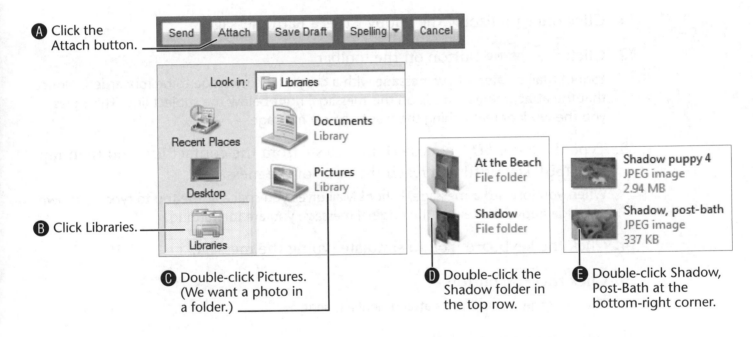

Yahoo! Mail displays a line for the newly attached the photo. You could now attach another photo (or other file). Instead, you will send the message with this one attachment.

4. Click the Send button.

5. Click the Continue to Next WebSim button.

Forwarding Messages with Attachments

You learned about forwarding messages in Lesson 7, Sending and Receiving Email. When you forward a message, any attachments to the original message are sent as well. This is different from sending a reply, which does not include any attachments. For example, if you forward a message with some attached photos, the recipient will receive the photos, too. But if you reply to the message, no photos are sent.

 HANDS-ON 8.6 **Forward a Message with an Attachment**

In this exercise, you will forward a message that has attachments.

Before You Begin: The Forward a Message with an Attachment WebSim should be open.

As the WebSim begins, you are viewing Rosa's Inbox. The message from Eduardo with the attached picture is at the top of the message list.

1. Click once to display the Puppy Takes a Bath message.

2. Click the Forward button on the toolbar.

   Yahoo! Mail creates a new message with a copy of the message to be forwarded. Notice that the attachments are still on this message, right below the subject line. This saves you the work of reattaching the files to a new message.

3. Type the letter "D," choose Donna Oeste from the contact list, and then tap the Tab key until you reach the body of the message.

   When you forward a message, Yahoo! Mail gives you space at the top to type your own message above the text of the original message you are forwarding.

4. Click the keyboard icon to simulate typing the message.

5. Click the Send button.

   The message, including its attachments, is sent.

6. Sign out of Yahoo! Mail.

   It's always a good habit to sign out after you finish a webmail session. This prevents others from being able to view your email.

7. Close ⊠ the WebSim window.

Concepts Review

All of the Concepts Review quizzes for this book are available on the student web page. Your instructor will let you know how to complete the quizzes (in the book or online).

True/False Questions

Page number

1. Attachments are available only from within the email message they are attached to until you save them.   **true**   **false**   _____

2. Downloading is the process of saving a file from a remote location to your computer.   **true**   **false**   _____

3. When you delete a message with attachments, the attachments are automatically saved to your hard drive.   **true**   **false**   _____

4. It is possible for an attachment file to contain a computer virus.   **true**   **false**   _____

5. Windows Update is one form of Internet security that helps protect your computer.   **true**   **false**   _____

6. An antivirus program cannot detect viruses inside email attachments.   **true**   **false**   _____

Multiple Choice Questions

7. Why are attachments useful?

   Page number: _____

   a. They conserve space on the hard drive.

   b. They transmit messages more quickly.

   c. They help you transmit the data in its original form.

   d. None of the above

8. Which types of files might contain a computer virus?

   Page number: _____

   a. Program files

   b. Word processing files

   c. Both a and b

   d. None of the above

9. When you delete an email message with an attachment _____.

   Page number: _____

   a. a copy of the attachment is automatically stored on your hard drive

   b. the attachment opens in the appropriate program

   c. the attachment is deleted as well

   d. You cannot delete a message while it has an attachment.

10. A spyware program _____.

   Page number: _____

   a. can report your computer activities to a remote location

   b. can be installed without your knowledge

   c. might be able to install other programs on your computer

   d. All of the above

Skill Builders

SKILL BUILDER 8.1 Send Attachments

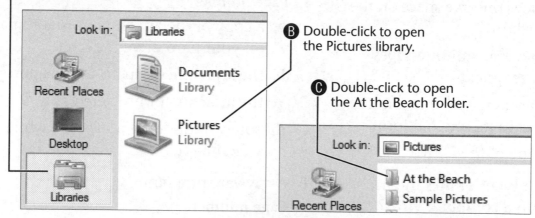

In this exercise, you will attach three pictures to an email message.

1. Launch Internet Explorer and navigate to the book web page at **labpub.com/learn/silver/wtwc4**.

2. Click the Send Attachments link.

   As the WebSim begins, the Login page for Yahoo! Mail appears.

3. Click the Mail button on the left and log in with the following details:

   • Yahoo! ID: **ortego.eduardo** Tab

   • Password: **4security** Enter

4. Click the New button.

   A new message appears. You can add attachments to a message before, during, or when you finish writing the message. In this exercise, you will add the attachments first.

Attach the First Photo

5. Click the Attach button on the message toolbar.

   Yahoo! Mail displays the Choose File dialog box.

6. Follow these steps to display the photos you wish to attach:

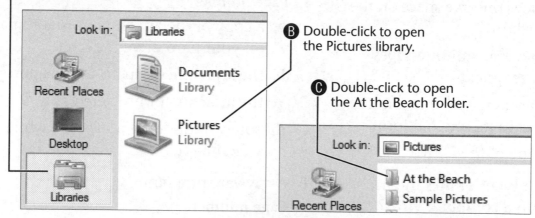

Ⓐ Click once on the libraries button.

Ⓑ Double-click to open the Pictures library.

Ⓒ Double-click to open the At the Beach folder.

The contents of the folder appear. However, it might be useful to adjust the size of the icons as you choose a photo.

7. Follow these steps to set the file icons to a larger size:

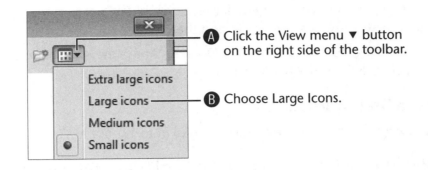

Ⓐ Click the View menu ▼ button on the right side of the toolbar.

Ⓑ Choose Large Icons.

The larger icons make it easier to preview the photos.

8. Click once on the Beach Walk 1 photo then click the Open button.

Attach Another File

9. Click the Attach button again.

10. Click the Libraries button then double-click the Documents library in the right panel.

Windows displays the My Documents and other folders.

11. Double-click the Our Trip to the Beach document file.

Yahoo! Mail adds the document to the attachments. It also shows a total for all the files currently attached. You could continue attaching more files if you wished. For now, these two are enough.

Finish the Message

Now that the attachments are in place, all that remains is to finish writing the message and send it off.

12. Use the following information to compose the message:

- To: **rosaortego@yahoo.com** Tab Tab
- Subject: **A day at the beach** Tab
- Message Body: [Click the Keyboard icon to simulate typing the message.]

13. Click the Send button.

14. Click the Continue to Next WebSim button if you wish to continue to the next Skill Builder exercise.

Receive and Open an Attachment

In this exercise, you will open an email message with an attachment, open the attachment from within the message, and then save it.

Before You Begin: The Receive and Open an Attachment WebSim should be open. If it is not, click its link on the book web page.

Request a Draft Document

As the WebSim begins, you are already logged in to Yahoo! Mail.

1. Click the New button and then use the following information to compose the message:
   - To: **terry.salcido@yahoo.com** `Tab` `Tab`
   - Subject: **Draft Proposal** `Tab`
   - Message Body: [Click the Keyboard icon to simulate typing the message.]

2. Click the Send button.

Open an Attachment from Within a Message

3. Use the Check Mail button to check for a reply.

   A reply from Terry appears. She has attached a Word document to her reply.

4. Click once to display the new message in the preview panel.

   The attachment filename is below the subject line and sender's email address at the top of the preview panel.

5. Click once on the Draft_Expansion_Proposal.docx link to download the attachment.

   Yahoo! Mail runs a virus scan and then tells you the file is safe to download.

6. Click the Download Attachment button.

   Internet Explorer asks what you wish to do with the attachment. Because it's already been scanned for a virus and it comes from a person you know, it should be safe to open.

7. Click the Open button.

   Word 2010 opens the file in a protected view. (Notice that the Ribbon is not visible.) This protects you from a potentially unsafe file. In this case, Eduardo knows the sender, so you can unprotect the file and enable it for editing.

8. Click the Enable Editing button at the top of the document window.

   The Ribbon becomes visible and you can work with the document normally. For the purposes of this exercise, you will finish by saving the document to the Documents folder.

Save the Attachment

9. Chose File→Save As from the Ribbon.

Word opens the Documents library by default. That's a good place for this document.

10. Double-click the Homeless Shelter folder, and then click the Save button to save the document to this folder.

11. Close [⊠] the Word program window.

12. Click the Continue to Next WebSim button.

SKILL BUILDER 8.3 **Forward a Message**

In this exercise, you will forward a message to another email address.

Before You Begin: The Forward a Message WebSim should be displayed. If it is not open, click its link on the book web page.

As the WebSim begins, you are already logged in to Yahoo! Mail.

1. Double-click to display the Welcome to Yahoo! message at the bottom of the Inbox list.

2. Click the [Forward] button near the top of the message.

The message window you were viewing has transformed from reading an incoming message into sending an outgoing message. Now the text you were reading appears a few lines into the body of the new (forwarding) message.

3. In the To box, address the forwarded message to **owen.hugo@gmail.com**.

4. Tap the [Tab] key three times to jump to the body of the message and then click the keyboard icon to simulate typing out the message.

5. Click the Send button.

6. Use the Check Mail button to check for a reply.

Notice the small arrow (↪) beside the RE: Draft Proposal message, indicating that the message has been forwarded. This arrow points in the opposite direction to that of a replied to message arrow (↩).

7. Click the reply from Owen to the forwarded message at the top of the Inbox message list.

8. Close [⊠] the WebSim window.

Creating New Documents

If you did not perform the exercises in Lesson 3, Using a Word Processor or if the documents are not on the computer you use to study Lesson 4, Working with Files, the following exercise will help you create the documents quickly and easily.

HANDS-ON A.1 Create New Documents

In this exercise, you will create two new Word documents.

Before You Begin: The steps in this exercise are only necessary if you did not see the two document files in the My Computer window in step 3 of Hands-On 4.3.

Start Word and Create a New Document

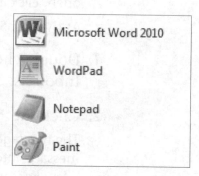

1. Start Microsoft Word from the Start menu.

   ⚠ TIP! Check the list of recently used programs on the left column of the Start menu.

2. If necessary Maximize 🔲 the Word window.

3. Type **Letter to Uncle Charlie** on the first line of the document.

4. Click the Save 💾 button on the Quick Access toolbar as shown at right.

   Word displays the Save As window automatically, since you have not yet saved this document and given it a name. Notice that Word has already begun to fill in a name for the document, taking its cue from the line you typed in step 3.

5. Tap the → cursor key to move the blinking cursor to the end of the filename, and then tap the Backspace key once to delete the "1" at the end of the filename.

6. Type an **e** at the end of the filename.

7. Make sure that the Documents Library is displayed in the Save In box Address bar as shown at right.

8. Click the Save button at the lower-right corner of the Save As window.

Word saves the new document to the hard drive. Notice the name of your new document in the title bar.

9. Follow the step for your version of Word:
   - **Word 2010:** Choose File→Close.
   - **Word 2007:** Choose Office ⬛→Close.

Create a Second Document

Now you will follow a similar sequence of steps to create the second document.

10. Follow the step for your version of Word:
    - **Word 2010:** Choose File→New.
    - **Word 2007:** Choose Office ⬛→New.

    Word displays the New Document window.

11. Double-click Blank Document in the New Document window.

12. Type **Letter to Aunt Carolyn** on the first line of the document.

13. Click the Save ⬛ button on the Quick Access toolbar.

14. Tap the → cursor key to move the blinking cursor to the end of the filename, and then tap the [Backspace] key and fix the end of the filename so it reads **Letter to Aunt Carolyn**.

15. Click the Save button.

16. Close ⬛ the Word window.

    You are now ready to continue with the exercises in Lesson 4, Working with Files.

Glossary

Active Program currently in use

Aero Interface The 3D look of some versions of Win 7

Antivirus program Software designed to stop computer viruses from infecting files on the computer

See also Internet Security or Antimalware Software on page 273

Example: Norton Antivirus

Application program Software designed to help you get work done

See also About Application Programs on page 83

Example: Microsoft Word, Outlook Express

Background Image or color covering your Desktop; also called wallpaper

Byte A single character of data

Example: A, B, C, etc.

Cable modem Device designed to send and receive digital data over television cable system

See also Connecting to the Internet on page 176

Cloud Drive Online storage that resides somewhere on the Internet.

Cursor Blinking indicator where text will appear on the screen when typing; also called an insertion point

See also Computer Displays on page 135

Digital camera Still camera that stores images as computer files rather than on film; most connect to a computer via a USB cable, though some can now connect via wireless signals

See also Organizing Digital Photos on page 159

Example: Nikon Coolpix S7

Domain name The base electronic address of a location on the Internet

See also Internet Domains on page 183

Example: amazon.com, google.com, nps.gov

Dots per inch (DPI) Measure of the sharpness of a printer's output; the higher the dots per inch, the sharper the print will appear on the page

Example: 1,200 DPI (laser printer), 4,800 DPI (scanner)

Drag and drop Method for moving screen objects in Win 7

Drive Permanent storage device

Drive letter Alphabetical designation assigned to storage devices

Example: C:, Removable drive F:

Email Short for electronic mail; email messages travel around the world in seconds via the Internet

Ergonomics Science of creating work environments and furnishings well-tuned to the shape and function of the human body

Example: Natural (split) keyboards

Favorite Bookmark that makes it easy to return to a specific web page

See also Creating Favorites on page 223

File Group of computer data with a common purpose

See also The File Organization Hierarchy on page 139

Example: A letter you have typed, a program

Folder An electronic location in which to store a group of files with some related purpose

Example: My Pictures folder

Gadgets Easy-to-use mini application found in Win 7

Example: Clock, Weathers, Slide Show

Gigabyte Approximately one billion bytes of data

See also Storage Basics on page 94

Example: About 3,000 books

Gigahertz (GHz) One billion pulses of electricity in an electrical circuit in a single second; the speed of most processors sold today is measured in gigahertz

Example: Intel 3.2 GHz Core i5

Hardware Physical components of a computer system

Example: Disk drive, monitor, USB flash drive, processor

Internet The world's largest computer network, used by billions of individuals daily

See also Defining the Internet on page 175

Jump List List of commands on the Start menu or a program button used to quickly launch related files or features

Kilobyte (KB) Approximately one thousand bytes of data

See also Storage Basics on page 94

Example: One single-spaced page of text

LCD panel Monitor that uses liquid crystal display technology to create screen images

See also Computer Displays on page 135

Library A new component of the Windows file storage hierarchy; can contain folders and files from more than one storage drive

Example: The Documents library

Malware Generic term for malicious software viruses that can damage a computer system

Example: love bug

Megabyte (MB) Approximately one million bytes of data

See also Storage Basics on page 94

Example: three average-length novels

Microprocessor *See* Processor

Modem Device that lets a computer communicate digital data to other computers over a non-digital communication line, such as a telephone line

See also Connection Types on page 176

Example: 56K modem, cable modem

Monitor The computer screen

Example: 19" LCD panel

Mouse pointer Indicator that moves on the screen in response to the mouse

MP3 Acronym for Moving Picture Experts Group Layer-3 Audio; first popular format for highly compressed music files

Example: A music file

Operating system Software that manages your system, such as Win 7

Path Shows the location of a fie or folder within the organization of a drive

Peripherals Hardware components outside the system unit box

Example: Monitor, keyboard, printer

Pixel A single dot of light on a computer monitor

See also Computer Displays on page 135

Port A place (usually at the back of the computer) to plug in a cable

See also USB Flash Drive on page 95

Example: USB port

Processor A single silicon chip containing the complete circuitry of a computer; modern processors now can contain 2 (duo) or 4 (quad) processors on a single chip

Example: AMD Athlon 64 ×2 Dual-Core, Intel Core i5

RAM Short for random access memory; computer chip designed to temporarily store data to be processed

See also Random Access Memory on page 10

Example: 4 GB RAM

Resolution Measure of the sharpness of a computer monitor display or a printout

See also Computer Displays on page 135

Example: 1680 × 1050 (monitor), 600 DPI (ink-jet printer)

Ribbon The new interface for some Microsoft Office 2007 and 2010 application programs (e.g. Word, Excel); replaces the menu bar and toolbars with one large toolbar

See also More About the Ribbon on page 84

Scanner Device that turns photographs and other images into computer files; scanners are also increasingly built into popular "all in one" printers

Example: HP Scanjet G3010c

Snap An Aero feature that enables a window to be resized by dragging it to the side or top of the Desktop

Software Logical component of a computer system; composed of digital code stored in the form of files; application software helps you get work done; an operating system (Windows) runs the basic functions of the computer

See also About Application Programs on page 83

Example: Windows 7, Internet Explorer 8, a document file

SSD Short for solid state drive. An SSD stores files using flash technology and has no moving parts.

System unit Main box that contains the primary components of the computer

Tabbed browsing The capability to open multiple web pages within a single browser window in Internet Explorer and many other web browsers

See also Using Tabbed Browsing on page 218

Tablet A small, flat computer that you control primarily with touch gestures on its screen.

Terabyte Approximately one trillion bytes (characters) of data

Example: About 120 hours of HD video

Touch Screen A computer screen you can touch gestures on, similar to those used with a tablet.

Undo Reverses your last action or command

URL   Short for Uniform Resource Locator; the electronic address of a website

See also URLs on page 181

Example: amazon.com, google.com, nps.gov, labpub.com/learn/silver/wtwc4

USB flash drive   A small file storage device that plugs into a computer's USB port; USB flash drives have taken the temporary storage and portability role once played by floppy disks

See also Storage Basics on page 94, USB Flash Drive on page 95, Skill Builder 4.3 on page 165

Example: Flash drive, pen drive, thumb drive

USB port   Short for Universal Serial Bus port; a single USB port can connect several devices simultaneously, including keyboards, scanners, modems, cameras, and more; USB 2.0 ports transfer data about 40 times faster than the original USB 1.0 port; USB 3.0 ports are up to 10 times faster than USB 2.0

See also USB Flash Drive on page 95, Organizing Digital Photos on page 159

Example: Digital camera cable plugged into a USB port, USB flash drive in USB port

Virus   Program that invisibly "infects" files and disrupts operation of a computer in some way; computer viruses are largely spread via the Internet

See also Common Internet Security Risks on page 274, Caution! Viruses! on page 280

Example: Michelangelo, Love Bug

Web   Short for World Wide Web; the collection of billions of pages accessible via the Internet

See also Defining the Internet on page 175

Web browser   An application program optimized for viewing web pages

See also Using Internet Explorer on page 178

Website   A collection of web pages owned by a specific organization or individual

Widescreen   Monitor (or laptop screen) that conforms to the popular 16:9 proportion used for HD (high-definition) video

Index

D

Date/Time on Control Panel, 132, 137
default search provider, 207
Delete key, 69
deleting
    favorites in web browser, 229
    files and folders, 9, 155–158
Desktop, Win 7, 8–9
dial-up modem, 177
disk drives (*see* storage devices)
display, computer screen, 132, 135
Document library window, 139–142, 144
domains, Internet, 183, 251
double-clicking, 13, 134, 136–137
downloading files from web, 279–281
dragging with mouse, 13, 134
drives (*see* storage devices)
drop-down menus, 52–54, 67
DSL (digital subscriber line), 176
dual-core processor, 10

E

editing, text in documents, 115–121
.edu domain, 183
email
    attachments to, 282–290
    definition, 175, 247
    forwarding, 259–260
    and phishing scams, 264–265
    receiving, 256–258
    replying to, 259–262
    sending, 251–254
    service types, 247–248
    signing in/out, 249–250, 263
    transmission process, 255
emoticons, 260, 261
encrypted wireless connections, 177
Enter key, 69, 87–89
Esc key, 114

F

favorites, web browser, 223–229
Favorites Center, Internet Explorer, 228, 229
Feed Headlines Gadget, 17
filenames, 59, 96

files
    as attachments to email, 282–290
    and Control Panel, 131–134, 136–138
    copying, 151–155
    definition, 57, 93
    deleting, 155–158
    downloading from web, 279–281
    folder organization, 145–147
    libraries, 139–142, 144
    moving, 151–155
    and My Documents window, 141–142
    naming, 59, 96, 146
    opening, 112–113, 144–145, 146
    overview, 138–139
    restoring, 155–158
    saving, 150
    sharing on cloud, 160–161
    storage locations, 58, 60–61
    uploading to web, 279
Firefox, Mozilla, 179
firewalls, 276
folders
    comparing to files, 141
    copying, 151–155
    definition, 57
    deleting, 155–158
    email, 256
    moving, 151–155
    organizing, 145–147, 159
    restoring, 155–158
    storage locations, 58
    for web browser favorites, 229
forwarding email messages, 290
full-screen view, web page, 194, 195
full text search engine, 212
function keys, 114
fusion drives, 94

G

Gadgets, 16–19
galleries, 63–65
Google.com, 205
.gov domain, 183
Grammar Check, 109
groups section of Ribbon, 84

N

naming conventions, 59, 96, 146
native resolution, 135
navigation buttons, web browser, 146, 188
Nelson, Ted, 186
networking of computers
    hardware for, 11
    and logging in, 5
new document, starting, 107, 296–297
New Document dialog box, 107
nonprinting text characters, showing/hiding, 89
nonstandard program windows, 46–48
notebook computers, sleep mode, 22
Notepad, 53–54
Notification Area, 9, 49–50
notification of new email messages, 257
Numeric keypad, 114

O

Office, Microsoft, 83
    (*see also* Word, Microsoft)
Office button, 82, 99
online security (*see* security, online)
opening files and folders, 112–113, 144–145, 146
operating systems, 6, 83
    (*see also* Windows 7)
optical drives, 95
order of hits, search engine results, 213
.org domain, 183

P

Paint, 55–57, 63–65
paper clip icon for email attachments, 282, 287
passwords, 5, 250
Paste command (*see* Cut, Copy, and Paste features)
peripheral devices, 108, 132
phishing scams, 264–265, 275
photos, organizing, 159
Photo Viewer Slide Show Gadget, 17
pinning and unpinning programs, 37–39, 50–51
pointer (mouse) (*see* mouse)
POP (Post Office Protocol) email, 247
pop-up menus, 13, 16
power button and shutting down computer, 23
premium webmail services, 248
previous email message, including in reply, 259
Print dialog box, 103
printers, 108, 132

printing
    text documents, 103–105
    web pages, 232–235
    wireless, 109
Print Preview, 104–105, 232
processor, 10
program button on taskbar, 42
programs, application
    (*see also* Internet Explorer (IE); Word, Microsoft)
    closing, 41
    common window elements, 44
    drop-down menus, 52–54, 67
    email, 247
    introduction, 83
    nonstandard windows for, 46
    Paint, 55–57, 63–65
    saving documents, 57–62
    on taskbar, 48
    window controls, 40–46
    window work areas, 63–67
    WordPad, 55, 67–71
proofreading features, 109–111
protection, online (*see* security, online)
protocols, definition, 175
public wireless connection, 177

Q

Quick Access toolbar, 55, 82, 85, 99
quick sizing buttons, 41–43

R

Random Access Memory (RAM), 10, 93
receiving email messages, 256–258
Recent Documents list, 112–113
recently used programs list, Start menu, 37
Recent Pages button, web browser, 184
Recycle Bin, 9, 155–158
Refresh button, 181
relevance ratings, search engines, 213
replying to email messages, 259–262
Reply vs. Reply All options for email, 259
resizing windows, 44–46
resolution, video display, 135
restart mode, 22
restoring
    files and folders, 155–158
    windows (size), 42
Ribbon, 55–56, 67–68, 82, 84–86
right-clicking, 13, 16, 134, 218